'YOUR CHURC

This study is dedicated to Fenning Parke 1801–1872: schoolmaster, parish clerk and chronicler of Minchinhampton, who did so much to preserve the history of Holy Trinity.

'Your Church Newly Built…'

a History of the Church of the Holy Trinity, Minchinhampton, Gloucestershire

Chiz Harward

with
†Jon Cannon, Dan Humphries, Gaynor Western
and James Wright

HOBNOB PRESS
for the
COTTESWOLD NATURALISTS' FIELD CLUB

First published in the United Kingdom in 2025

for the Cotteswold Naturalists' Field Club
by The Hobnob Press,
8 Lock Warehouse, Severn Road, Gloucester GL1 2GA
www.hobnobpress.co.uk

© Chiz Harward and contributors 2025

The Authors hereby assert their moral rights to be identified as the Authors of the Work.

All rights reserved. No part of this publication may be reproduced, stored in a retrieval system, or transmitted in any form or by any means, electronic, mechanical, photocopying, recording or otherwise, without the prior permission of the publisher and copyright holder.

British Library Cataloguing in Publication Data
A catalogue record for this book is available from the British Library

ISBN 978-1-914407-87-1

Typeset in Adobe Garamond Pro, 11/14 pt
Typesetting and origination by John Chandler

Front cover: Holy Trinity church and its graveyard viewed from the southeast; photograph by Jonathan MacKechnie Jarvis

Rear cover: Oil painting of Holy Trinity seen from the Market Place, by W Brigad, dated 1890; from the collections of Museum in the Park, Stroud

CONTENTS

Foreword	*vii*
Acknowledgements	*ix*
Cotteswold Naturalists' Field Club	*xi*
Introduction	1
The Evolution of the Church	6
The Norman church (1066 to late 12th century)	6
Holy Cross, Avening	9
Early English (late 12th to late 13th century)	12
Decorated Gothic (late 13th to late 14th century)	14
Minchinhampton: Decorated architecture in context	27
Perpendicular, the mid fifteenth century	46
The Sixteenth century: Reformation and Counter-Reformation	49
The Seventeenth century	71
Queen Anne and the Georgians	77
Minchinhampton in 1842	92
Foster's church	108
1868–9 Oldfield, Burges and the new chancel	123
The Twentieth century	132
The 2016 re-ordering	139
Death, Burial and Memorial	146
The burials	167
Discussion	177
Appendix 1: Shepstone's 'Builder's Report' of 1845	184
Appendix 2: William Burges' Letter of 1869	188
Appendix 3: The Pews in 1841	194
Appendix 4: The Rectors of Holy Trinity, Minchinhampton	212
Endnotes	214
Bibliography	229
Index	236

Picture Acknowledgements
All illustrations and photographs are by Chiz Harward, Urban Archaeology, with the exception of the front cover (Jonathan MacKechnie Jarvis), Figs 4 and 69 (Nick Hurst), Fig. 23 (David Goldsmith), Fig. 38 (Laurence Keen), Figs 49 and 50 (Chapter of Gloucester Cathedral), Fig 55 (Evelyn Simak), Fig 79 (John Chandler), Figs 106-108 (Dan Humphries), Figs 103, 112 and 149 are courtesy of Howard Beard, and the rear cover illustration and Figs 70, 80, 109, 110, 147, 150 are from the collections of the Museum in the Park, Stroud.

About the author
Following an initial career excavating sites in Sussex and then the City of London, Chiz Harward now specialises in ecclesiastical and monastic archaeology. He has worked at Gloucester cathedral and at many of Gloucestershire's parish churches. Chiz has generously agreed to make a contribution from sales to the upkeep of the church.

FOREWORD

The story of Holy Trinity Church is not simply a record of bricks and stones; it is the living narrative of a sacred space that has been shaped by centuries of faith, transformation, and the hand of God moving through the lives of His people. As told through the meticulous research and archaeological insight of Chiz Harward, this history invites us to glimpse the divine threads woven through each phase of the church's existence, a history that is still unfolding today.

From Norman beginnings through the 14th-century rebuilding, and subsequent works, Holy Trinity has borne witness to profound social, cultural, and liturgical changes. Each layer of its architecture echoes the aspirations of those who have worshiped here. These transformations are more than just physical alterations—they are the ongoing reflection of a living, breathing community of faith. The church has always been at the heart of Minchinhampton, not only as a physical landmark but as a spiritual hub, a place where the light of Christ shines through history and into our present lives.

The most recent chapter in this story—the reordering of 2016-2022—marks a bold step forward into a new season of community and hospitality. What was once a traditional and rather austere space has been transformed into a vibrant, welcoming environment. The light-filled, uncluttered interior invites all who enter to experience a deeper sense of the sacred. Visitors, whether members, parishioners or tourists, often exclaim "Wow!" as they encounter the warm, open beauty of the church, with its stunning limestone floor, flexible seating, and underfloor heating—a place where tradition and innovation harmonize to offer comfort, beauty, and a profound sense of the holy.

This recent transformation would not have been possible without Chiz Harward's invaluable archaeological investigation, which uncovered the church's rich and often complex history. While much of the original Norman structure has been lost to time, we are fortunate to still have precious remnants of the 14th-century rebuild, including the striking Lady Chapel with its magnificent Rose window, the North transept, and the crossing. These architectural treasures serve as spiritual landmarks for me, anchoring us in a long tradition of faith that stretches back more than 900 years.

The church has not only witnessed the passage of time but has been shaped by it. From the upheaval of the Reformation in the 16th century to the rebuilding of the nave, chancel, and aisles in the mid-19th century, each phase has been marked by deep change, reflecting the evolving needs of both church and town. The surviving Churchwardens' Accounts offer a fascinating glimpse into the lively, sometimes turbulent, history of this place, including the purchase of pews and private access to the balcony—a testament to the complex relationship between wealth, worship, and society in the 18th and 19th centuries.

Indeed, it was a local voice of passionate opposition that ensured the survival of key medieval elements, such as the crossing and Lady Chapel, during the 19th-century restoration. The renowned architect William Burges then added his own touch, designing the chancel and the double East window—a rare and beautiful feature that continues to inspire awe today.

Through it all, Holy Trinity has remained steadfast—a sanctuary where God's presence has been felt through the ages. The reordering of the past decade, while marking a significant milestone, is part of a continuous thread of renewal and growth. Holy Trinity is more than a place of worship; it has become a vibrant centre for community life, offering a space where people gather not only for prayer but for fellowship, celebration, and support.

As we look to the future, we embrace the church's ongoing journey. Chiz Harward's book provides us with a fascinating record of the past, a reminder of God's faithfulness through every season, and a guide to the rich, layered history we continue to write together.

May this history inspire us to live out our own part in the ongoing story of Holy Trinity Church, a place where the sacred and the everyday meet, and where God's light continues to shine brightly in the heart of Minchinhampton.

Rev. Canon Howard Gilbert
Rector of Holy Trinity Minchinhampton
(2019–present)

ACKNOWLEDGEMENTS

The writing of this book was prompted by the reordering of 2016–22, a process that arose partly out of issues with damp caused by the previous reordering of 1842 that had torn down so much of the medieval church. I was commissioned to carry out the necessary archaeological research and fieldwork, and this sparked a deep interest in Holy Trinity and the town of Minchinhampton.

The reordering process took several years to complete, and the church is now dry, warm and welcoming - testimony to the hard work of the PCC especially Howard Browning, David Goldsmith, Mandy Jutsum, John Jutsum and Caroline Thackray, the Revd Canon Howard Gilbert, verger Darren Clements, the architect Antony Feltham-King (St Ann's Gate Architects) and the wider project team.

Nearly every stage of work required archaeological input and I would like to thank Nick Miles, Charlotte Baker and the team at Nick Miles Building Contractors Ltd, Mark Hancock and his masons at Centreline Architectural Sculpture, and all at Terrascapes for their assistance and good humour throughout the works. Urban Archaeology site staff consisted of Chiz Harward (Urban Archaeology) with assistance from Thomas Wellicome (Archaeological Landscape Investigation) and Annette Fuller. The site survey was by Thomas Wellicome and Chiz Harward.

The archaeological works were monitored by the Diocesan team at Church House, Gloucester; Adam Klups, Senior Church Buildings Officer, and Dr David Thackray, Diocesan Archaeological Advisor, are to be thanked for all their advice, help and support during the project. Dr Thackray was instrumental in the production of this book and the Cotteswold Naturalist Field Club are also to be thanked for their support.

Many archaeologists and historians have provided advice and feedback on the findings, in particular James Willoughby, Stuart Blaylock, Paul Dryburgh, Evan Jones, Maureen Jurkowski, John Reeks and Laura Sangha for advice on the Black Letter text, Sir George White Bt. FSA on clocks and Nick Hurst for discussions of Minchinhampton local history; Laurence

Keen provided encouragement and sound advice on myriad queries, as well as diversionary rabbit holes. Any errors in the text however remain those of the author. Urban Archaeology would like to thank Gloucestershire Archives for access to the Minchinhampton church archive and Angie Ayling, David Goldsmith, Michael Gwilliam, Hilary Kemmett and Margaret Sheather for transcribing documents.

Jon Cannon penned the section on the architecture of the glorious and under-rated south transept, placing it in the regional context he knew so well. Sadly Jon died before the publication of this book: he is much missed. James Wright (Triskele Heritage) contributed to the sections on the architectural fragments and the mason's setting out slab, Dan Humphries (Dan Humphries Stained Glass Ltd) on the stained glass, and Gaynor Western (Ossafreelance) wrote the section on the burials and their osteology. All these contributions have been edited by Chiz Harward who bears responsibility for all errors and omissions. Steven Blake, Paul Butler, Caroline Thackray, David Thackray and Laurence Keen all kindly read drafts and made many useful suggestions.

Traditionally the archaeological work for such a project would have resulted in a technical 'grey literature' archive report seen by a handful, or an academic paper in the county journal seen by a few more. However as the site works continued we felt that we could take this opportunity to combine the archaeological findings and the documentary history to produce a history of the church. A church is at the heart of a community and its history should be accessible to all so, with the support of the PCC, Church House and the Cotteswold Naturalists' Field Club, we plotted a third option that could bring together the archaeology and history of Holy Trinity and set it out for a wider readership. This book is the result, and it is hoped that it does that job for parishioners and townsfolk, visitors, and students of church history and archaeology.

Chiz Harward BA MCIfA,
Urban Archaeology,
Stroud

COTTESWOLD NATURALISTS' FIELD CLUB

THE COTTESWOLD NATURALISTS' Field Club, founded in 1846, is one of the oldest of its kind in England. It was established and continues to promote interest in the natural history, environment, archaeology, geology and local history of the Cotswolds, Gloucestershire and more widely. Its activities also provide the facilities for its members to study, appreciate and enjoy those activities. The Field Club has a distinguished history, firstly for its contributions to scientific study in Gloucestershire and the publication, through its annual Proceedings, of its research, an invaluable source of information. It has also maintained a long programme of monthly lectures, visits and excursions, promoting and enjoying the range of interests set out in the Club's Purposes. For more information see the Club's website: https://www.cotsnatsfield.club/p/home.html

In 1868 the Club visited Holy Trinity when members toured the church and met with local historian and schoolmaster Fenning Parke; following the excursion local member GF Playne wrote a paper on the cross-slabs discovered during the 1842 rebuilding, which was published in the Club Proceedings.[*] 150 years later the club is delighted to support the publication of this study of Holy Trinity Minchinhampton.

---

[*] Playne, GF 1868 'On the Incised Grave-Stones and Stone Coffins of Minchinhampton Church', *Proceedings of the Cotteswold Naturalists' Field Club*, V, 39–46

INTRODUCTION

The small market town of Minchinhampton lies near the western edge of the Gloucestershire Cotswolds, a few miles from the Stroud valleys (Fig. 1). The Grade I listed parish church[1] sits within a walled graveyard that lies both above the town's market square, yet also on the edge of Minchinhampton Common (Fig. 2). A church has stood on the site since at least Norman times and as with most English parish churches it has been altered and developed

Fig. 1 Map showing the location of Minchinhampton and places mentioned in the text.; inset location relative to Bristol and Gloucester. Contains Ordnance Survey data © Crown copyright and database right 2024

over the centuries; its evolution reflecting to some extent the fortunes of the town and its people, but also the development of the church in England, and in more recent centuries the Church of England.

Fig. 2 Minchinhampton as shown on the First Edition Ordnance Survey map of 1882. Holy Trinity is shown top centre with its churchyard outlined in red

Cruciform in plan, the current church comprises chancel, central tower, north and south transepts and an aisled and clerestoried nave, with a modern porch room to the west. The present church is an amalgam of three main periods: the 14th-century tower and transepts are all that remains of the medieval church structure, the nave and aisles date from the comprehensive 1842 rebuild designed by Thomas Foster of Bristol, and the chancel was rebuilt in 1869 to a design by Gothic Revival architect and designer William Burges of London (Fig. 3).[2]

By the early 21st-century the church was facing long term and severe issues from damp and following lengthy deliberation, consultation and fundraising a major reordering of the church was carried out between 2016 and 2018. The design, by Antony Feltham-King of St Ann's Gate Architects,[3] addressed the damp and heating and set out to improve the church's internal space to provide for more flexible worship; archaeological implications were considered from the outset and accompanied the work. Comprehensive internal works were required with new underfloor heating in the nave, Lady Chapel and aisles, where the floor level was raised to match the chancel, and with internal reordering to allow the church to better serve the current congregation. The 1842 pews were replaced by chairs, and the 1919 rood screen by FC Eden was moved to the arch between the Lady Chapel (south transept) and the crossing.

Design work was accompanied by the research on the known history of Holy Trinity and a detailed consideration of the significance of the building and its individual features. The biggest archaeological impact of the project was clearly the taking up of the floor in the nave, aisles and transepts to allow for the installation of underfloor heating; documentary research, recording work, and a series of archaeological test pits established that due to the Victorian rebuilding, archaeological survival inside the church was relatively low and the design strove to minimise the impact of the reordering on any surviving archaeological remains[4].

Fig. 3 Phase plan of the present church showing areas of archaeological work 2016–21

Following extensive consultation and comment a Faculty was granted by the Diocese on the 28th July 2017 allowing the works to go ahead; a programme of archaeological mitigation and fieldwork was approved and works started in September 2017.[5] A comprehensive archaeological watching brief by Urban Archaeology[6] accompanied the reordering work, the archaeologists working hand-in-hand with the teams from Nick Miles Building Contractors Ltd[7] and Centreline Architectural Sculpture Ltd (Fig. 3).[8] Following the main reordering, further archaeological work attended construction of a new soakaway north of the chancel in 2020 and 2021.[9]

The work uncovered many new details of the medieval, post-Reformation and Victorian church and triggered a programme of research and analysis that has culminated in this publication. Combining documentary and archaeological evidence, this account describes the development of the church from its earliest records to the present church.

The research has combined the archaeological evidence from the watching brief, the standing fabric of the church, and a range of documentary records many of which provide fascinating details of the life of the church. Documents include the Domesday Book, Churchwardens' Accounts and the Vestry Minutes, as well as papers relating to the Victorian rebuilding. Dates in the Julian calendar have not been converted to the Gregorian calendar which was implemented in 1752.

Only the tower and transepts survive from the medieval church, the chancel, nave and aisles being demolished in 1842, but we are very fortunate to have an account of the 'Old Church' in a report by builder William Shepstone in 1845[10] and plans of both the 'Old Church' and the proposed building designed by Thomas Foster.[11] In addition there is a detailed letter of 1869 written by the celebrated Victorian architect William Burges in which he refers

Fig. 4 Painting of Holy Trinity dating to before the 1842 rebuilding

to the report and gives his own valuable contemporary opinion on the quality and significance of the remaining medieval parts of the church -and on Foster's 1842 work.[12] A small number of 18th- and early 19th-century illustrations and plans provide valuable information on the appearance, form and internal layout of the church before 1842 (e.g. Fig. 4). From all these sources a history and archaeology of the church has been built up that hopefully sheds light on the development and use of a building that lies at the heart of its town.

THE EVOLUTION OF THE CHURCH

The Norman church (1066 to late 12th century)

THE EARLIEST MENTION of a church at Minchinhampton comes, as with so many English parish churches, with an oblique rather than explicit mention in the Domesday Book: the recording of a priest at *Hantone* in the survey implies that a church had probably been founded by 1086.[13] An earlier Saxon church, quite possibly built in timber, may perhaps be presumed, but as yet there is no direct evidence and no trace was found during the recent archaeological works. Before the Conquest Minchinhampton had been held by Countess Goda, sister of Edward the Confessor; in 1082 the manors of Hampton and nearby Avening were given by King William and Queen Matilda to their new foundation of Benedictine nuns at the *Abbaye de la Sainte-Trinité* [14] at Caen, France, and the name Minchinhampton is derived from *Mynece Hampton* -the nun's Hampton.[15]

In the Domesday survey Minchinhampton was valued at £28 a year; its population included 32 *villeins* or small tenant farmers, 10 *bordarii* who held less land than villeins, and 10 *serfs* who lived in bonded servitude -as well as the priest. The manor covered some 4940 acres, with 3,480 under cultivation, 20 acres of meadow and 1,440 of woodland; there were eight mills in the wooded valleys around the edge of the parish.[16]

The parish included several outlying settlements which would have been served by the rector of Holy Trinity. Initially all parishioners would have attended services at Holy Trinity including all baptisms, weddings and funerals, with burial in the graveyard. The north aisle was later known as the 'Rodborough Aisle' and was set aside for that community.[17]

Excavation at Holy Trinity has shown that little if anything survives of the Norman church, with little in the way of diagnostic structural or architectural remains and a single sherd of Saxo-Norman Oolitic Limestone pottery found in the churchyard excavations. The evidence for this period is very largely limited to Shepstone's report (Burges' description is directly based

THE NORMAN CHURCH

on Shepstone's) which contains the only detailed description of those Norman parts of the church that survived at the 1842 demolition including the north arcade.

According to Shepstone, the Norman north arcade consisted of 'rather massive' columns with '…the capitals slightly ornamented, the arches plain with a drip stone terminating with a Shark's head'. Above these '…widely carved on the quarters of two of these arches we discovered two small Norman windows walled up six inches in width splaying inwardly towards the Nave having small shafts at the angles with ornamented capitals …and a moulded arch over, in taking down this wall we found several pieces of net work zigzag [chevron] and other ornaments belonging to this order of which I made sketches.'[18]

Sadly Shepstone's sketches have not survived, nor have the fragments of Norman carving that he apparently salvaged from the old church, but there are tantalising clues to the form and appearance of the Norman church. The 'Old Plan' of the 1841 church clearly shows the north aisle with an arcade of four arches resting upon three round Norman columns.[19] Rough foundations for the north arcade were recorded during the recent excavation and given their poor construction, and their repair in 1842, these are probably Norman in date. Most importantly they confirm that the dimensions of the Norman north arcade, and probably nave, were followed by the 1842 rebuild. Two blocks from round columns[20] recovered during the excavation are probably from these Norman columns and indicate that the columns were made up of many small, tapered blocks, dressed with axes, rather than larger column drums (Fig. 5). The excavated fragments suggest a column diameter of between 0.78m and 1.2m, the foundations suggesting a size at the lower end of this range. The plan of the Old Church shows that the columns fitted within a standard 3-foot box pew and were therefore less than 0.91m in diameter (Fig. 6).

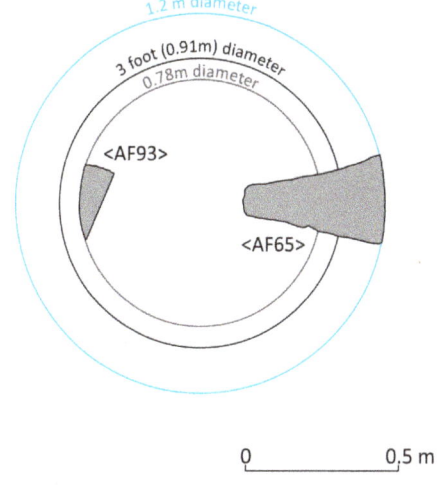

Fig. 5 Norman column fragments <AF65> and <AF93>

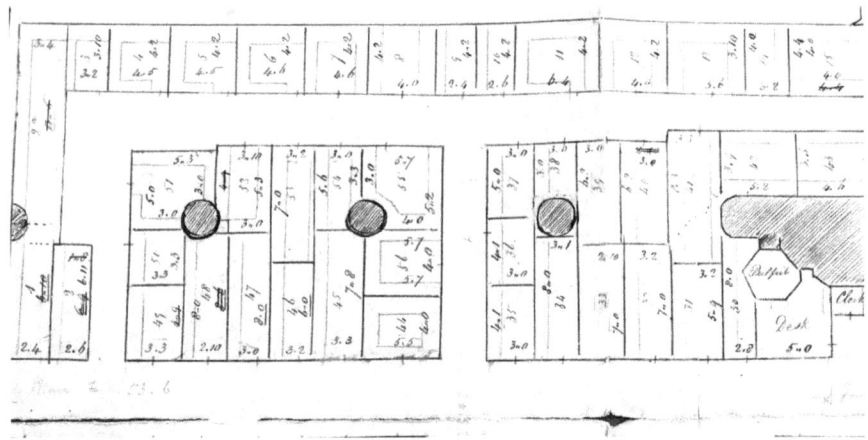

Fig. 6 Detail of plan of Old Church showing Norman arcade with columns within the 3-foot box pews[21]

Shepstone's description of Norman chevron mouldings reused apparently in the upper clerestory wall suggests there was an earlier Norman phase, or more likely re-use of Norman stone in a later remodelling.[22]

Local resident and historian AT Playne suggested that when the plaster was stripped from the east end of the nave in the 19th century, that the original pitch of the Norman roof was visible. Since this would be on the side of the 14th-century tower it seems rather unlikely. The original roof was most likely at a pitch of approximately 45 degrees if Cotswold stone slates were used, or steeper if thatched.[23]

Shepstone finally notes '...on cleaning out the foundations of the old chancel the basement of an oblong projecting five feet beyond the line of wall and nine feet in length' of Norman date.[24] It remains unclear what this foundation was -perhaps a tomb, although Shepstone would surely have recognised one, however it does suggest that there were Norman foundations well to the east of the nave.

Holy Trinity fits a common pattern of Early Norman parish churches in the Gloucestershire Cotswolds: a 'two cell' plan with nave -often with opposed north and south doors- and a chancel with a small east window, sometimes varied by the addition of a massively built central tower between the two; arcades and aisles become more common later in the 12th century as appears to be the case here (Fig. 7).[25] The survival of the Norman north arcade strongly suggests that any Norman tower was of the same dimensions as the later tower; there could have been one or more 12th-century transepts but these may not have projected as far as the later versions. The east end of the chancel is

THE NORMAN CHURCH

unlikely to have been apsidal, a more common feature in Norman churches on the Continent but rare in the Gloucestershire Cotswolds where there is a lone example at Temple Guiting.[26]

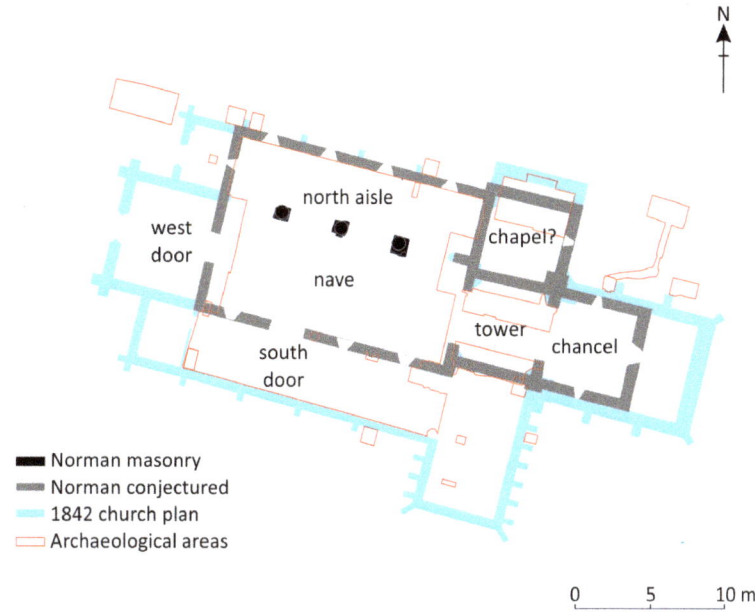

Fig. 7 Plan of the Norman church of Holy Trinity

Setting aside its form, the detail of Holy Trinity's finer appearance must be extrapolated from Shepstone's description and conjectured from the wealth of surviving Norman architecture in the locality. The round-headed windows would have been fairly small with shafts of light illuminating an interior that was probably at least partially painted. The floors are likely to have been of beaten earth or plain mortar, and there would have been no seats or pews for the congregation standing in the nave, separate from the clergy in the chancel.

Holy Cross, Avening

THE NEARBY CHURCH of the Holy Cross at Avening was also held by the Abbess of Caen and its surviving Norman fabric may provide some close parallels for the form, appearance and development of the church at Minchinhampton. The two Norman churches were of a similar size: the nave at Avening measures approximately 13m by 7m, compared to 15.7m by 6.67m at

Holy Trinity, and Avening had a central tower between nave and chancel. The tower at Avening measured approximately 5.5m by 5m internally, compared to 4.2m by 4.2m for the 14th-century tower at Holy Trinity; the columns of the north arcade at Avening are *c.*0.65m in diameter.[27]

Holy Cross is first mentioned in 1105[28] and the chancel arch and original nave walls may date from the late 11th or early 12th century.[29] The tower, western bay of the chancel, and north aisle were all 12th-century additions; the decoration on the north doorway dates it to *c.*1160.[30] Avening therefore underwent at least two major phases of Norman building (Fig. 8) and it likely that Minchinhampton saw similar investment and development by the Abbess of Caen.

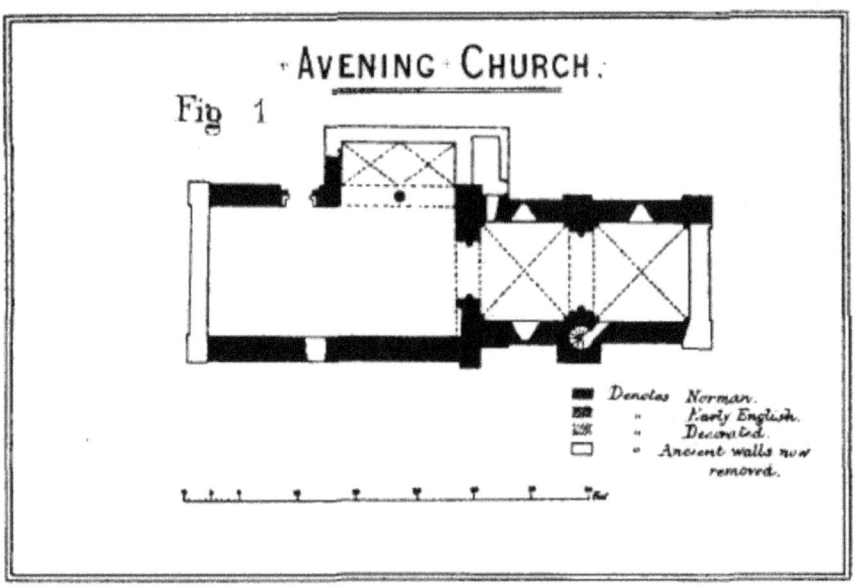

Fig. 8 Plan of Avening church in the Norman period (Carpenter and Ingelow, 1889–90 fig 1)[31]

The surviving Norman fabric at Holy Cross also hints at the type of architectural decoration and detail that would have originally been seen at Holy Trinity, and which is referred to by Shepstone. Compared with later Gothic architectural styles the church would have appeared simple and massive, round columns with squat simply decorated capitals carrying simple round-headed arches. Windows would have been relatively small and round-headed, with inward splays to spread light into the interior, but there would have been decoration in places, with the walls whitewashed and often brightly painted.

The north door at Holy Cross is decorated with twisted jambs, chevron decoration and figurative sculpture (Fig. 9) and Holy Trinity would have had at least one of its doorways carved in a similar style, whilst the chancel arch may have also been elaborately decorated. Surviving fragments of a rectangular stone font at Holy Cross are carved with an arcade, each bay populated by pairs of now-mutilated figures, probably the Apostles;[32] it seems probable that Minchinhampton would also have had a stone font, perhaps similarly decorated.

Fig. 9 The north door of Holy Cross, Avening

Early English (late 12th to late 13th century)

From the later 12th century, the Norman or Romanesque style of architecture gave way to the Gothic 'Early English' style, with its taller pointed lancet windows that originated in Caen, the home of Holy Trinity's mother church. The first alterations to the Norman church noted by Shepstone were in Early English style with two small windows added to the north wall of the chancel and '…the wall below the East Window [of the chancel] and the rubble work of the wall for a few feet in height on the East side of the North Transept' was also of this date.[33] From this it can be assumed that much of the

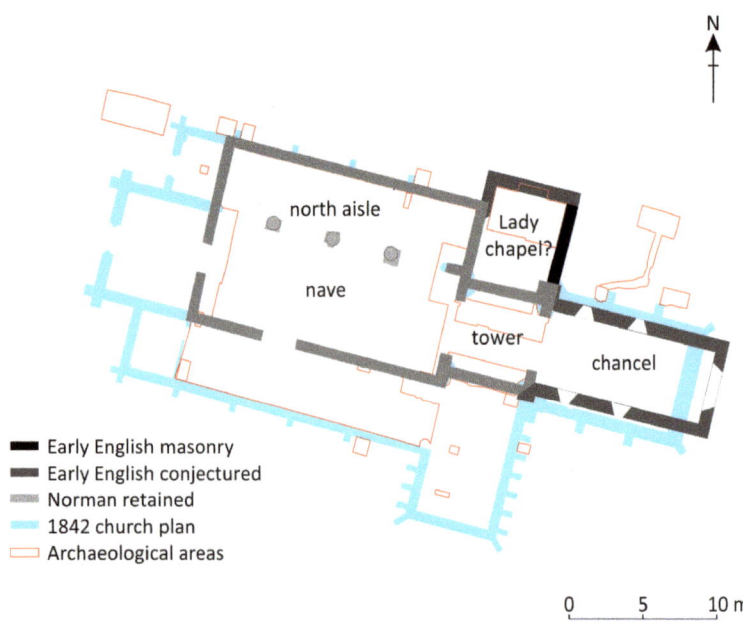

Fig. 10 Plan of the church c.1250

chancel was rebuilt and probably extended, a fairly common alteration at this time which reflected an increased distinction between the laity in the nave and the clergy in the chancel, mass being a 'a clerical undertaking at which the laity were essentially observers'.[34] The rector from 1260, Roger Salange, was absent for much of his tenure with a chaplain, Laurance, mentioned in 1273.[35]

A new east window would likely have been of three lancet lights and, given the addition of new lancets to the north wall, the south wall may have been similarly provided. A tomb recess, probably in the north wall, could date from this period.[36] The north transept had clearly been built by this time, although it may have been modest compared to its Decorated replacement; there is no evidence for a south transept at this date (Fig. 10).

There is only one excavated architectural fragment with features that may date to this period, a piece of potentially early-13th-century moulding featuring a roll and quirk[37] similar to column capitals from Much Marcle in Herefordshire,[38] however the Minchinhampton design is far smaller in scale and may relate to an altogether different function and, potentially, date (Fig. 11).

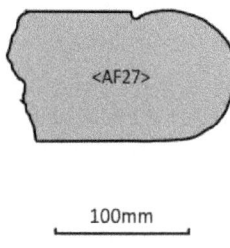

Fig. 11 Profile of early-13th-century moulding <AF27>

Decorated Gothic (late 13th to late 14th century)

B Y THE 14TH century Minchinhampton had a market and annual fair and was a nascent urban centre. Sheep farming had possibly overtaken the three-field arable rotation as the principal type of agriculture in Minchinhampton as early as the later 12th century, with the manufacture of cloth also well established by this date. By the early 14th century the manor's flock was over 1000 sheep and in common with many monastic holdings in the Cotswolds these were its largest source of income.[39] In 1269 the Abbess had acquired the rights to a weekly Tuesday market and to a six-day fair at Trinity[40] bringing trade and a prosperity to the new town that derived largely from the wool and cloth trade.[41] By the early 14th century Minchinhampton's strategic position for these trades meant that the town was becoming well

Fig. 12 'Drawn on the spot and on zinc': engraving of the church from the south shortly before the rebuilding of 1842, by HE Relton

established with several other merchants setting up shops, including butchers and shoemakers, and with a number of mills sited on the town's streams providing employment processing and fulling the wool.[42]

This burgeoning prosperity and status in the first half of the 14th century was reflected in a comprehensive building programme at Holy Trinity with the church very largely rebuilt in the Decorated Gothic, an architectural style involving, as its name suggests, more architectural decoration with developed tracery and more ornamentation than the previous Early English style. The work was both a massive and a radical undertaking, a remaking going far beyond the earlier modifications and additions of new windows to the Norman church. From Shepstone's report we can see that the tower was rebuilt completely, and that the west and south wall of the nave, any south aisle and its arcade, parts of the north transept, any south transept, and the south wall and upper parts of the east wall of the chancel were all rebuilt and reroofed. There was a new south transept and a new south aisle was provided with a small porch (Fig. 12).

The retention of some elements of the old church may help suggest its form immediately prior to the rebuilding. Shepstone's report tells us that much of the Norman nave and north aisle survived, with parts of a north transept, and the north and lower part of the east wall of the chancel.[43] This might suggest that there was not yet a south aisle or transept, although the design of the south transept was novel enough that any precursor would have required a complete new build.

The design of the new tower and spire, with its four crossing arches, meant that the Norman tower had to be completely taken down, and new foundations were laid on the limestone bedrock. The upper part of the chancel east wall was presumably taken down to allow insertion of a new and larger Decorated window, but it is not clear why its south wall was demolished. The north wall may have been retained due to the presence of a wall tomb; one Early English window here was blocked up.

According to Shepstone the north aisle was the only area of the church to remain largely intact during the 14th-century remodelling, but changes were still made. A pre-1842 watercolour of the north side of the church shows a pair of small two-light windows and the shallow pitched roof is depicted as surrounded by a low, plain parapet (Fig. 15). The painting appears to show the edge of a larger window at the eastern end. The north aisle was set aside for the inhabitants of Rodborough which was part of Minchinhampton parish. They paid an annual fee towards its upkeep in 1651[44] and this may have been the case as far back as the 14th century. If so, then work to this 'Rodborough aisle' would have been raised from the Rodborough congregation and individual benefactors who also had their own chapel-of-ease -St Mary Magdalene- to keep in repair. The first indirect mention of St Mary Magdalene was in 1316–17 when a graveyard is mentioned in a dispute.[45]

At Holy Trinity, most of the major rebuilding was carried out during the term of William of Prestbury, rector from 1318 until his death (probably of the Black Death) in 1349, and who endowed a Lady Chapel in 1338.[46] In normal times the Abbess of the Abbaye aux Dames, far away in Caen, would have had the ultimate say on such a comprehensive rebuild of the church, which was a significant investment in the religious infrastructure of the prosperous town. The role of the Abbess was complicated as war with France, culminating in the Hundred Years' War (1337–1453), meant the manor was often forfeited to the Crown, and it seems unlikely that one of the interim custodians would have invested so significantly in the church. The Abbey regained possession of the manor in 1324 on payment of a fine of £200,[47] but by 1341, with the war with France under way, the manor was held by Maud de Burgh, countess of Ulster, and then came the Black Death.[48] Potential benefactors must be sought more locally.

The lack of uniformity in the tracery of the windows may suggest multiple patrons, and potentially several teams of masons worked on the church. Although it had to work as part of the whole, the design of each element would have evolved through a complex series of conversations between the benefactors, incumbent and the masons. Alongside the rector it is likely that local gentry and wool merchants provided the bulk of the funds; the two transepts with their chantry chapels would have been built in part as their memorials and the names of the benefactors of the south transept have been established as John and Lucy Ansley, or Ansloe (see below). The wider parish would have been pressed to contribute, either into the general building fund or for specific items (such as the new font), all of which would have stood the souls of the benefactors in good stead.

Work on this scale would have taken several months if not longer and was both a very significant financial and logistical undertaking. It would have caused massive disruption, not least to worship, and the work would have been carried out in stages over a number of years with no work outside in the winter season. Of the dated elements, it appears that the chancel was completed first in 1315 and logically the tower would also have been one of the earliest phases, followed by the south transept in 1330 and the north transept in 1338. The impact on the community cannot be underestimated, with an almost entirely new church rising, with its new spire, from the site of the old Norman church.

DECORATED GOTHIC

Decorated work on this scale is rare in the Gloucestershire Cotswolds, there is only one church entirely of this style -at Todenham near Moreton-in-Marsh; more usual is the embellishment of the chancel, the addition of transepts and spires, and insertion of fenestration in the new style.[49] Minchinhampton's rebuilding is therefore not part of a more widespread pattern such as the later widespread Perpendicular wool churches for which the Cotswolds are renowned. Quite why Holy Trinity was rebuilt remains unclear, but it must surely have been linked with confidence in the town's economy.

Stone from the old church would have been reused, and wherever possible any new stone would have been brought in from quarries on the church's lands. Local limestone would have been used for the rubble work walls, local Minchinhampton Weatherstone used on quoins and hood mouldings, and fine-grained Painswick Freestone brought in for tracery, ashlar and detailed work. The church may have required a complete re-roofing, although the old timbers may have been reused, and the roof would have been clad in Cotswold stone slates[50] or lead sheet over timber boards.

Chancel

The chancel, originally Norman and already remodelled in the Early English style, was not completely rebuilt; at least some of the north wall was retained.

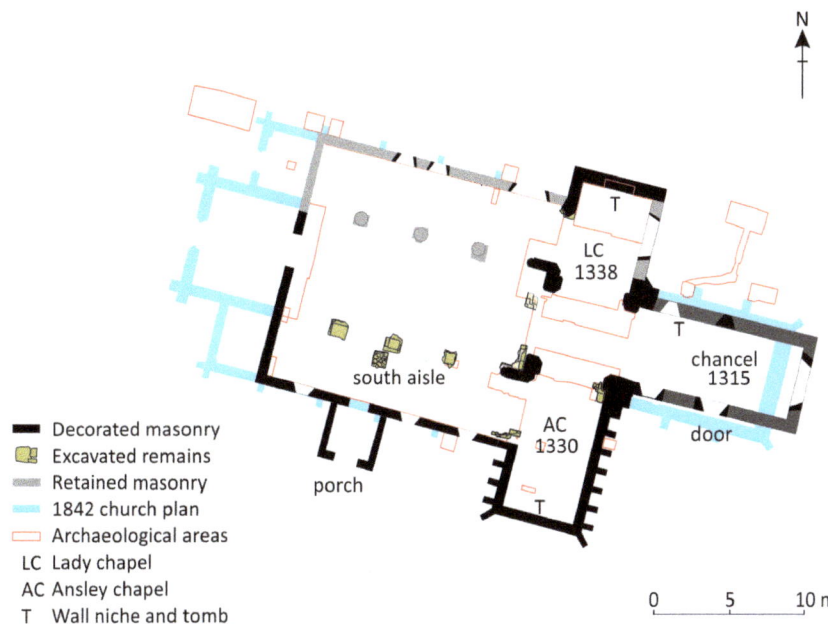

Fig. 13 Plan of the Decorated church c.1340

In 1842 the chancel contained a tomb recess, if this was on the north wall it may have been this feature that had saved the wall from demolition.[51]

A reference in Thomas's 'A Survey of Worcester' refers to the *great altar* dedicated by the bishop of Worcester in July 1315,[52] this may have been following alterations to the chancel; it is probable therefore that the chancel was the first part of the church to be updated, followed by the tower and transepts, nave and aisles (Fig. 13).

Illustrations of the church from before 1842 show the chancel from both the south and the north; three bays long, it had three windows on the south side, the central one immediately above and contiguous with a Priest's

Fig. 14 South window of the chancel with retained 14th century tracery; reset and restored in 1842

Fig. 15 Watercolour painted before the 1842 reordering, looking to the southwest

Door, and one window survives in part to this day (Fig. 14). The windows have two trefoil-headed lights, surmounted by a quatrefoil, and with a heavy-hood mould; the mouchettes in the surviving window are echoed in the wheel window of the south transept. A view from the north shows a single small window high on the retained north wall (is this wall largely blank due to a wall tomb on the interior?), while a tantalisingly oblique glimpse of the Decorated east window suggests it had five lights with a sexpartite wheel or sexfoil above (Fig. 15); a 13th-century cross-slab was reused as its sill.[53] A strong projecting corbel table runs around the chancel with a steep roof of stone slates capped by stone ridge pieces.

Nave and aisles

The Norman windows of the north aisle were replaced, although the north arcade and north wall appear to have survived the rebuilding largely unscathed. The west wall of the nave is not mentioned by Shepstone so was probably rebuilt, as was the nave roof was also rebuilt; a photograph of 1901[54] shows a steeper roof line on the west wall of the 14th-century tower demonstrating the contemporary nave roof was of steeply pitched Cotswold stone tiles.

Fig. 16 Medieval foundations at the junction of the south aisle and transept, looking south-east; scale 0.3m

It is not clear whether there was a south aisle before the 14th-century rebuild; if so it was completely rebuilt with many 13th-century cross-slabs built into the foundations[55] and excavation has showed these foundations were contiguous with the new south transept (Fig. 16). The south aisle appears to have had rather meagre fenestration with HE Relton's engraving showing only one medieval window: two slender trefoil-headed lights under a square head with 'dropped ear' stops. It is not clear if this window is entirely original, or whether the windows were altered later; certainly there are later window insertions that would have removed original openings although Shepstone does not mention any blocked windows here. The new nave followed the earlier footprint with a new south arcade of pointed arches carried on octagonal pillars whilst the Norman north arcade was retained. The 14th-century font survives, it is plain and octagonal, with a cylindrical shaft on a square base.

North transept
The north transept retained at least some of its earlier fabric but was fitted with two new three-light Reticulated windows on the north and east walls (Fig. 17, Fig. 18).

Fig. 17 East elevation of the north transept

In 1842 the base of an altar and two niches were discovered under the east window '…one had been partly destroyed by the fixing of a monument the other was walled up with pieces of its beautifully carved shafts and canopy the pedestals are (for there are still those) in the form of a cross rudely worked

DECORATED GOTHIC

Fig. 18 North window of the north transept, with rebuilt gable and inserted oculus

and fixed level with the face of the wall, on these stood figures about one half the full size this was quite clear as evidenced in light and shade on the plastering at the back of the niche but we saw no fragments of the figures their destruction was undoubtedly was the work of the reformation they have been guarded by an iron fence attached to the wall as we found the holes in which it had been inserted'.[56]

These ornately carved and decorated niches would have contained statues of the saints to whom this chapel was dedicated, set either side of the altar at which mass would have been sung for the soul of the benefactor. The north wall contains an ogee-arched tomb recess (Fig. 19) and GF Playne reports that it contained a stone coffin set above floor

Fig. 19 The early-14th-century wall niche in the north transept formerly contained a stone coffin, possibly that of William of Prestbury, who founded and endowed a Lady Chapel in 1338

level, its lid bearing a 14th-century *cross florette* in relief. The coffin 'contained a skeleton of an adult, together with traces of habiliments and clouted shoes' and was destroyed in 1842; the central part of the lid was retained by Fenning Parke.[57] The coffin is most likely to have been the last resting place of the benefactor of the chantry, it is possible that the skeleton was that of William of Prestbury, who founded and endowed the Lady Chapel in 1338. It is likely that the Hampton family were also buried in the chapel, with Rudder and Bigland reporting their memorial brass was here.[58]

South transept

Thankfully, despite an original plan to demolish it, the south transept survived the 1842 rebuilding and is the jewel of the church (Fig. 20); Shepstone tells us that '…(I have heard from good authority that) there is scarcely another roof of the kind in the kingdom, this applies to its plain simplicity as there are stone roofs almost innumerable belonging to this date and afford specimens of architectural skill (it is considered) that would compete with anything of the kind the world has ever witnessed'[59] whilst the renowned Victorian architect William Burges describes it as '…one of the most perfect and curious specimens of the Architecture of the middle of the 14th Century'.[60] David Verey holds the 'remarkable' south transept as 'the outstanding example' of Decorated Gothic in the Gloucestershire Cotswolds.[61]

Fig. 20 The south transept with its rose window

The transept is of six narrow bays; externally the east and west walls have diagonal corner buttresses, the side walls have slender pointed two-light windows set between deep and close-set buttresses. There is a curious and unexplained masonry structure, possibly structural, filling between buttresses on the east side.

DECORATED GOTHIC

Fig. 21 *The vault and transverse arches of the south transept looking south to the rose window*

Inside '[o]ne suspects stone vaulting; the interior none the less is a surprise, as it is not really vaulted. The pitched roof of stone slabs is visible, supported by close-set single-chamfered transverse arches, crossing below the top scissor-wise, exactly as if they were of timber, not stone. In the top above the scissor crossing a mandorla shape (Fig. 21). The only English parallel, apart from several porches in (for example) Northamptonshire, seems to be the chapels of St Mary, Scarborough, in North Yorkshire. A more likely influence at Minchinhampton may be the transverse arches in the choir aisles at Bristol Cathedral, probably completed *c*.1320'.[62] The stone slabs of the ceiling include a re-used 12th–13th-century cross-slab. The roof is steeply pitched and tiled with Cotswold slates.

The south wall is mostly occupied by the large five light window, rose tracery forming its upper section. The rose has eight radiating arms, enclosing sixteen equilateral compartments (Fig. 23). The window was altered after 1842 with the alteration of the horizontal transom beneath the rose, however the original form is shown on HE Relton's etching of the church and in two engravings of the transept that appeared in The Builder (Fig. 22).[63]

Fig. 22 *The south window and stone roof of the south transept, published in* **The Builder** *in January 1858*

Fig. 23 View of the south transept wall niche and effigies

Effigies

The date, attribution and history of the south transept has often been confused, largely due to difficulties establishing the identities of the two recumbent stone effigies within the pair of ogee-arched tomb recesses set into the south wall

DECORATED GOTHIC

beneath the window. The arches have ogee foils and floral cusps, below crocketed ogee arches (Fig. 22, Fig. 23, Fig. 24.). The tomb chests have quatrefoils in relief, with simple effigies on their lids; the eastern effigy is of a Lady in a wimple (Fig. 25), the western a knight in bascinet and surcoat with a heater shield, legs crossed, and with his feet resting on a lion. His armour dates to the 1340s (Fig. 26).[64]

Identification of the individuals, presumed to be benefactors of the south transept, has varied over the years and was hampered by a lack of precise architectural dating (see below), and several confusions over names and heraldry. Atkyns claims the knight as 'Ainsloe', but Bigland

Fig. 24 The effigies of Lucy and John Ansley in the south transept wall niches

Fig. 25 Lucy Ansley's effigy, her feet resting on a dog

Fig. 26 John Ansley's effigy, his shield bearing an eagle displayed and his feet rest on a diminutive lion

states that the transept was built in 1382 by John and Maud de la Mere.[65] GF Playne settles on Robert and Matilda de la Mare,[66] whilst AT Playne -noting that the coat of arms of the de la Mares include an 'eagle displayed' which appears on the shield of the knight effigy- decided that the monument was to Peter de la Mare and his wife Matilda, set up by his son Robert between 1292 and 1308 and that the south transept therefore dates from this point.

AT Playne also suggests that the 'Ainsloe' of the south transept is a corruption of 'St Loe', the home of the de la Mares.[67] The churchwardens' accounts refer to an unlocated Ansleyes/Anslowes chapel in 1578[68] although Bruce believed this to be in the north transept.[69]

Originally *The Buildings of England* volume agreed that the effigies were of Sir Peter de la Mare and his wife Matilda,[70] however VCH deduced 'that there seems little reason to doubt the tradition that [the south transept] was built as a memorial to John of Ansley, who held de la Mare's manor in the 1330s, or that the two effigies lying in integral recesses beneath the south window represent John and his wife Lucy.' The conclusions of the VCH are followed in the latest edition of *The Buildings of England*, and fit the architectural dating. [71] The confusion is compounded as the eagle displayed was in fact also the arms of John of Ansley and, at some point before 1330, he married Peter de la Mare's widow! The couple may have resided at the la Mare's property (known as Delameres, Lamers and later The Lammas). Watson mentions an entry in the reeve's accounts which suggests that the chapel was completed in 1330 (although the effigies may have been added on the death of the benefactors).[72] The transept was built to contain a chantry altar at which prayers would be said for the souls of John and Lucy Ansley who were buried in the south wall, and by whose name it was known for several centuries before being named the Lady Chapel in the early 20th century.

Tile pavement

Whilst much of the church interior may still have been floored with beaten earth or mortar, by the later 13th-century tile pavements might have been laid in key areas such as the chancel, and the new chantry chapels in the transepts are likely to have been fitted with richly decorated pavements decorated with heraldic and foliate decoration.

According to GF Playne a pavement of encaustic (*sic*) tiles was found under the stone flags of the south transept in 1842; the tiles were decorated alternately with lion *passant* and eagle displayed[73]. The floor was all taken up, but four tiles -two lion *rampant*[74] and two eagle displayed- were

Fig. 27 Medieval floor tile of an 'eagle displayed' now set on the south transept wall, probably originally from the tile pavement of the south transept

retained and set in a wall tablet, now sadly lost. A single tile decorated with an eagle displayed is set into the west wall of the transept and presumably comes from the pavement[75] (Fig. 27).

The eagle displayed is a fairly common motif on medieval tiles and there may be no heraldic significance, however along with the lion *passant* it is an emblem of the De La Mares, and an eagle displayed appears on the shield of the knight's effigy in the south wall.

Fragments of medieval floor tiles found in the excavations may also date from this period and could derive from the south transept pavement, or the other areas of the church which may have been tiled.

Minchinhampton: Decorated architecture in context
†Jon Cannon

NOTE: JON'S TEXT, written in 2021, has been left unaltered, although further research since his untimely death suggests that the medieval Lady Chapel was sited in the north, rather than the south, transept. He wrote that: the south transept of Minchinhampton church is a premier work from one of the great periods of architectural creativity in England. This period, which dominates the first half of the 14th century, saw the appearance of a sophisticated, inventive and sometimes experimental phase of Decorated gothic; a phase in which the west country played a central role – and of which Minchinhampton is an overlooked gem.

Defining works in the region -major projects that might particularly have influenced the anonymous designer- include the new east end of St Augustine's abbey, Bristol (now the cathedral), attributed to an important designer known only as the Bristol Master: works began in 1298, though the design may not have been fixed until 1307;[76] the continuation of the rebuilding of Exeter cathedral, underway under Thomas of Witney and William Joy (Witney first appears as a consultant on the existing project in 1313, Joy about 20 years later);[77] the new east end at Wells cathedral, also attributed to Witney and Joy, where the main fixed date is the completion of Lady chapel in 1326;[78] the rebuilding of the collegiate church at Ottery St Mary, probably under William Joy, from 1337;[79] and the re-casing of the east end of St Peter's abbey, Gloucester (now Gloucester cathedral), possibly with Royal patronage and designed by one of the 'of Canterbury' dynasty of masons, from 1331.[80]

Minchinhampton's south transept was clearly designed to be an eye-catching and impressive part of the building, and this in turn implies the presence of a single, powerful local patron, such as John and Lucy Ansley, put forward here as the most likely occupants of its double tomb recesses. It is striking, for example, that it outshines the east end -- in theory the more significant part of the church– in both size and architectural elaboration.

Indeed the scale of the building in itself supports that proposal that it was here that the new Lady chapel recorded in 1338 was located, for Lady chapels were the only space in a church which might appropriately compete with or even outshine the east end.[81] It may also be that the extra expense and grandeur given the south transept was perhaps also designed to make it a 'show feature' when approaching from the town: the elaborate 13th-century south transept façade at York Minster and the massive 15th-century transept at St Werburgh's abbey Chester, now Chester cathedral, are comparisons here.

It is also a work that shows awareness of the latest architectural developments. This is interesting in itself as, though the 14th century detailing of other parts of the church is poorly recorded, there is little sign of such boldness in what evidence we have; though Relton's engraving of 1842 (Fig. 12) shows the sides of one chancel window being extended downwards to enclose a Priest's Door below, the kind of motif that is typical of an era that wants to occlude evidence for structural divisions. Thinking like this, from 1331, would lead to the coining of a new architectural style in the south transept at Gloucester.

Fig. 28 The south transept: 'the tight rhythm of two-light windows and buttresses'

The transept is traditional in form if exceptional in scale. It is a single, un-aisled space, with a colossal south window, and a row of attenuated bays in which externally in particular, great play is made of the tight rhythm of two-light windows and buttresses (Fig. 28). The heavy use of buttressing may partly be designed to support the heavy stone roof, but goes far beyond the requirement of a roof that was (for example), significantly lighter than a true rib-vault would have been. The intention is thus clearly more than practical, though it may have started with the perception that the stone roof would need more buttressing than a timber one. The designer wants to give the impression of an ambitious building and encourages us to enjoy the intense light and shade (which must block light into the windows), and the staccato rhythm created by the buttresses.

This kind of thinking, in which a practical/engineering requirement becomes the springboard for an artistic exercise, is one sign that the designer is aware of some of the bolder thinking going on in the architecture of the region. The famous aisle vaults at St Augustine's, Bristol probably began with a perception that a hall church vaulted in stone would still need flying buttresses; William Joy's scissor arches at Wells are designed to shore up an unstable central tower; yet both become an exercise in a kind of architectural sculpture.[82] Such structures are relevant to understanding the vault itself, as we will see. The tightly spaced buttresses, in turn, are almost unique to Minchinhampton, though the chancel at Urchfont church in Wiltshire (after 1302), possibly an early work of William Joy, also has as a major feature of its design the alternation of buttresses and two-light windows.[83]

Inside the building, the double tomb recesses in the south wall are a pretty plain indicator that burial and commemoration were a major intended function of the space. It is more than reasonable to assume that its occupants were the major patrons of the transept as a whole, and that it is intended as both a Lady chapel and a space where commemorative events of some kind, such as a chantry masses, were to be carried out. The creation of a Lady chapel which is also a chantry chapel has local precedents, for example in the Elder Lady Chapel at Bristol, which I have suggested was repurposed as a chantry chapel by Thomas III Lord Berkeley (†1361) following the death of his wife Lady Margaret Mortimer in 1337.[84] The Mortimers and the Berkeleys are two of the major families in the region.

The proposed combination of 'Marian' and 'commemorative' space is just one aspect of the ways in which, at this time, a search is being made to find ways of expressing the establishment of chantry masses architecturally. Transepts, two-bay aisles and other spaces had often been associated with

Fig. 29 The rose window

chantry foundations, but the desire to create a specific space as a setting for these masses seems particularly intense at this time, and the solution of making it a transept with very prominent recesses is not unusual: we see it at Witney, Oxfordshire and Great Bedwyn, Wiltshire for example.[85] The matter would be resolved from the 1360s with the invention at Winchester of the Perpendicular 'cage chantry'.

It is this combination, the desire to draw visual attention to the patronage of the incumbents of the tomb in the hope that their works would encourage prayer for their souls, combined with the extra level of architectural elaboration appropriate to a Lady chapel, and perhaps a desire to display the rebuilt parish church to best advantage when approached from the town, which probably explains both the scale of the building -- and its most spectacular feature: the window tracery.

Displays of elaborate and inventive window tracery – presumably settings for equally spectacular displays of stained glass (for contemporary survivals of the latter, the east window at Wells and the apse at Tewkesbury are exquisite and contemporary examples in the region) are a major theme of the era. In terms of window tracery, Exeter features two different large and elaborate window designs in each bay of the building, requiring a level of inventiveness in design unmatched at any other church. The east window at St Augustine's, Bristol was one of the most spectacular anywhere.[86] The tracery of the window installed in St Anselm's chapel, Canterbury cathedral in 1336

DECORATED GOTHIC 31

was more expensive than its glass,[87] a remarkable indicator of the priority being given to this aspect of a church's design at this period.

left: Fig. 30 Interior view of the east window of Old St Paul's Choir drawn by Wenceslaus Hollar in 1656[88]

below: Fig. 31 The east end of Old St Paul's drawn by Wenceslaus Hollar in 1656[89]

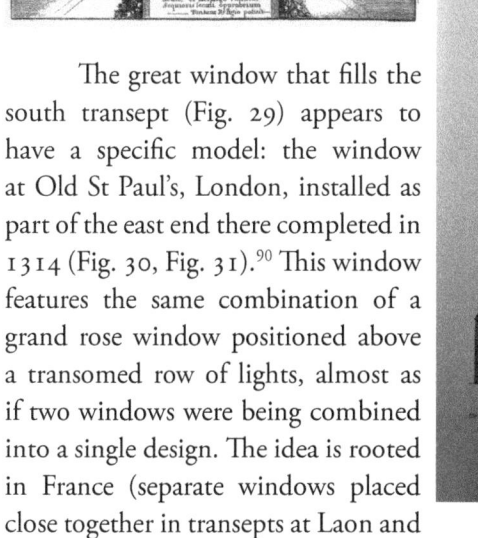

The great window that fills the south transept (Fig. 29) appears to have a specific model: the window at Old St Paul's, London, installed as part of the east end there completed in 1314 (Fig. 30, Fig. 31).[90] This window features the same combination of a grand rose window positioned above a transomed row of lights, almost as if two windows were being combined into a single design. The idea is rooted in France (separate windows placed close together in transepts at Laon and Chartres from c. 1205–15 and 1212; integrated into tracery at St-Denis from c. 1231)[91] but the scale of the lower lights here was much more emphatic: it reflects the direction French *Rayonnant* design was taking generally. In c. 1290 Strasbourg too had made great play of the potential for integrating the whole concept into a single spectacular display. However rose windows are rare in England and almost unknown in the 14th century, and the St Paul's example had a particularly emphatic transom, seen in HE Relton's engraving of Minchinhampton, and the very comparable motif of reversed ogees in the outer lights; so the connection is clear. The possibility that this window made a particularly great impression on people is suggested by Chaucer, who has a clerk's shoes decorated with 'Poule's window'.[92]

Indeed it seems possible that the window is the work of a local team of masons specialising in elaborate tracery designs. St Mary's Cheltenham was much rebuilt in perhaps the 1330s (its east window shows knowledge of the work at Gloucester) and features a very comparable display of window tracery, again clearly designed to be the most spectacular aspect of the building as a whole, and including another rare Decorated gothic rose window, complete with an outer row of inwardly-turned ogees, in the south transept.[93]

Tracery aside, architecture of that church is rather plain, and this may be itself a result of another tendency seen in the architecture of this era: a desire to create aesthetic contrasts, changes of 'mode' as Christopher Wilson puts it;[94] and these are often used to draw attention to the windows at the expense of other aspects of the interior. Stanford-on-Avon, Leicestershire (glazed *c.* 1324),[95] has spectacular glazing and high-quality tracery in a building whose other architectural details, such as arcades, are almost brusquely plain; and St Mary's, Scarborough (1380-97),[96] where the row of chapels in the outer south aisle have simple, heavily ribbed tunnel vaults, standing in contrast to the enormous windows that fill their ends.

It is with this borne in mind that we should turn to the other most interesting aspect of the Minchinhampton, transept, the vault. Burges was right to make comparisons with timber ceilings, for such cross-media quotation is another major theme of architecture at this time; and again, comparisons with Bristol are relevant because the aisle vaults there have been understood as replications in stone of the elaborate timber roofs of castle great halls.[97] Likewise the decision to make the stone flagging of the roof visible on the inside is typical of an era that liked to make displays of structural elements that would usually be hidden, almost as a kind of architecture in-joke: the 'skeletal vaults' at Bristol, St David's, Lincoln and Southwell are an example.[98]

Fig. 32 The vaulted sacristy at Willingham, Cambridgeshire, drawn and engraved by Samuel Lysons[99]

The geographical footprint of this motif – the south west and the East Midlands – may be relevant to an intriguing aspect of the Minchinhampton vault: that it has a virtual doppelganger in the vaulted sacristy/vestry at Willingham church, Cambridgeshire.[100] Here, too, thin, cross-ribs pierced with quatrefoils appear to imitate timber or metal, while revealing the stone-flagging behind (Fig. 32). The motif could be an example of the kinds of coincidences that occur when many designers are thinking on comparable lines; but there are plenty of signs that East Anglian and West Country designers are closely aware of each other at this period. The vault of the 1330s in the choir at Wells is replicated in the easter sepulchre at Irnham church, Lincolnshire (before c. 1340–5);[101] the quatrefoils which enclose the windows in the south transept at St Mary Redcliffe, Bristol (probably 1330s) crop up at Mildenhall church, Suffolk and Prior Crauden's chapel at Ely cathedral (1324–5).[102] So it is just possible that these two buildings are aware of each other, or are imitating a common, lost, model.

All in all, the transept at Minchinhampton is indeed, as Verey and Brooks call it, 'most extraordinary and beautiful';[103] it is a work by a local team of masons aware of the major developments in contemporary architecture, perhaps particularly those at Bristol, translating these often rather self-consciously innovative motifs into a powerful, but more traditional, design for a locally significant patron and a parish church context.

~~~~

Chantries and the Lady Chapel

IN THE MEDIEVAL church saints could be enrolled to intercede on behalf of the living, reducing time to be spent in Purgatory. After one's death the process could continue through prayers and masses for the deceased, often funded by an endowment. A 'chantry' was the prayers and services, including mass, said or sung for the atonement of the souls of the dead, specifically the founder and their families.

The first mention of a chantry at Holy Trinity is in the Minchinhampton Customal, a document dating from c. 1300, when Adam Spileman 'provides a lighted lamp every year in the chapel of the Blessed Mary the Virgin [to burn] night by night.'[104] This chapel, quite possibly in the north transept, would have been rebuilt in the years following his benefaction, but the dedication and its location probably remained.

On 1st July 1331 Walter Schire Senior granted the rector William of Prestbury a messuage worth 12 shillings a year and 16 acres of land 'on condition that they celebrate masses for the well-being…of…King Edward III and his successors and for the souls of his progenitors, kings of England, and for the souls of Walter and his heirs.'[105] Schire's grant stipulated that mass would be held on Sundays, Wednesday and Friday and on every double feast. The location of Schire's chantry is not known, it may have been in the Lady Chapel or at another altar in the church.

Seven years later in 1338 Prestbury endowed his own chantry dedicated to the Virgin Mary at Holy Trinity 'a priest maintained singing daily at the altar of our Lady in a chapel situated within the parish Church yard and every holy day to help sing the divine service in the Same Church and to pray for the founder's soul and all expired souls'.[106] As well as a priest, an acolyte named Philip Arome was mentioned in 1349 at the chantry of the 'Blessed Mary.[107] To fund the chantry Prestbury donated a considerable endowment to fund the chantry: two messuages (dwellings with their outbuildings and plots of land), a watermill, 2 1/2 yardlands (approximately 75 acres of ploughland) and 20 shillings in rent.[108] An estate known as Forwood was added to the endowments by a John Croft c.1400, whose name would have been added to the prayers. The chantry priest was chosen and presented by Holy Trinity's rector with Prestbury presenting a local man Thomas of Chalford in 1341, Peter of Avening in 1348, and Peter de Ashwell in 1349.[109] Philip Arena was presented by the new rector John de Middleton in 1349, perhaps reflecting the impact of the Black Death.[110]

Income from each chantry's assets would have paid for the chapel upkeep and for the chantry 'singing' priest to sing Mass and prayers for the dead at the altar and assist the rector; chantry priests could also assist in education in the parish. Schire's and Prestbury's are the only chantries recorded at Holy Trinity. However it is likely that several other chantries had been endowed but were for less expensive fixed-terms of one to ten years. Whilst Prestbury's, endowment was sufficient to fund a perpetual chantry, where his soul would be prayed for forever, other chantries could expire or fail for some reason, and Schire's chantry is not mentioned again.

Each chantry did not require its own altar and several could be performed at the same altar, including at the high altar, however chantry chapels were often established within the church. Chantry chapels could be elaborately decorated as highly visible expressions of wealth and as physical memorials to the founders, as is demonstrated by the building of many architecturally distinguished chapels in major churches and cathedrals.

The location of the two chantries is not recorded other than Prestbury's being in a chapel in the churchyard[111] which does not have to mean a

DECORATED GOTHIC

*Fig. 33 The south transept, with altar, from Playne's 1915 book **Minchinhampton and Avening**, probably taken after 1911*

separate building apart from the church but can mean one extending *over* the churchyard. Prestbury's endowment was dedicated to the Virgin Mary. The Marian cult was increasingly popular in western Europe from the 12th century onwards and Lady Chapels were endowed in cathedrals, monastic and parish churches alike. These are most frequently found at the east end of the church, however in parish churches they could be in a side chapel, an aisle or a transept. At Avening the Lady Chapel was on the north side of the chancel.[112] It seems almost certain that Prestbury's Lady Chapel would have occupied one of the transepts and although the evidence is not conclusive, it seems more likely that it was in fact in the north transept. Although now known as the Lady Chapel the south transept does not appear to have been referred to by this name in the medieval period and was the chapel known as Ansleys, Anderlays or Ansloes chapel in 1578. It is unclear when the name Lady Chapel became attached to the south transept and it is not called that by the Victorians, but a drawing of 1916 is labelled 'south trancept [sic] now Lady Chapel'.[113] It seems likely that the name was given when the old altar was moved there in 1911, creating a new chapel in the south transept probably for the first time since the 16th century (Fig. 33).

There are no known references to a chantry for the Ansleys, however the Schire chantry only came to light during the finalising of this book, with the publication of the Escheator's Inquisitions in 2022.[114] The physical evidence of an altar and two statue niches indicates that the north transept was also dedicated as a side or chantry chapel, and it may be either Schire or Prestbury that was buried in the stone tomb in the north wall.

Many, perhaps most, chantries are not recorded and several chantries could share the same altar. Several chantries would have been located in the north and south transepts and depending on the bequest these might have been for prayers and mass for shorter terms such as five or ten years. It is highly likely that Dame Alys Hampton, who gave a bell to the church in 1516 just before her death, would have founded a chantry at Holy Trinity.

The establishment of two major chantries within seven years, at the same time as the rebuilding of the church further highlights issues around patronage raised by Jon Cannon above. Whilst the church and manor were held by the Abbaye des Dames in Caen, local benefactors would have contributed to works, and chapels would have been an appealing cause. The donation of money or endowment of lands and property supported both the building work and the ongoing maintenance of the fabric and provision of a chantry priest, the physical fabric and decoration honouring and celebrating both a Saint and the benefactors. The patrons would have been heavily involved in the design

Decorated Gothic

and construction of the new chapels, with detailed discussions with masons, carpenters, painters and tilers; the chapels were an opportunity to show off and leave a lasting physical as well as spiritual legacy.

Tower and crossing

The Norman tower was taken down and replaced with a new tower in the same position, and probably of the same footprint (Fig. 34). The square crossing tower is supported on four massive piers, the shafts terminating at foliate capitals with a tiercon-star vault crossing adorned with carved heads and bosses (Fig. 35). The upper tower is built externally in ashlar; the bell chamber openings are deeply recessed, with decorated tracery and pierced quatrefoil baffles. The tower carries an octagonal truncated broach spire -whether this was ever finished is discussed below.

Fig. 34 The south-east corner of the crossing showing the foundations; scale 0.5m

When the church was rebuilt in 1842 it was noted that the 'walls of the Tower (inside) had been covered with painting',[115] evidence for the internal decoration of surfaces survives in the remains of red painted foliate scroll decoration on the chancel arch, as well as the 'M' surmounted by a crown for Mary, and IHS (Iesus Hominum Salvator) Christograms painted in black on the aisle arch leading to the south transept (Fig. 36, Fig. 37). Such monograms were perhaps more frequent than these survivals may suggest: too many

Fig. 35 The tiercon star-vault of the crossing beneath the tower

removed when interior plaster was taken off in the 19th century. They survive in other media, for instance a graffito with entwined HIS at Framlingham, Suffolk[116] and both a crowned IHS and a crowned M on tiles made in 1455 for Abbot Sebroke in St Peter's abbey, Gloucester, now the cathedral (Fig. 38).[117]

The spiral tower-stair is accessed by a door in the external angle of the chancel and north transept, the rood loft was accessed by a door –now blocked up- from the tower stair, it was revealed when the plaster was stripped from the internal walls of the tower in the late 19th century.[118] The presence of the rood loft door indicates that by the 14th century at the latest there was a rood screen separating the chancel from the nave. The rood formed a physical barrier between the sacred and lay spaces of the church and was often highly decorated. Above it was the Rood Cross, with figures of the Virgin

Fig. 36 Medieval painted 'IHS' and Marian monograms on the arch between the south aisle and the south transept

Fig. 37 Medieval painted 'IHS' and 'M' surmounted by a crown, from the arch between the south aisle and south transept.

Fig. 38 'IHS' and 'M' surmounted by crown, on tiles in the Sebrok pavement in Gloucester Cathedral

Mary and St John, and the screen and cross would have hindered access and visibility between the nave and chancel; those in the aisles would have had a very limited view through the crossing to the chancel.

Architectural fragments

Several excavated architectural fragments can be dated to this period, including five fragments of a slab bearing the inscribed design of a Decorated window tracery design (pages 42-4). This, and the remaining Decorated fragments, date from the early–mid 14th century and are probably from the extensive rebuilding works of this time. Much contemporary fabric (parts of the chancel, south aisle, porch, windows of the north aisle and east end) was lost during the Victorian restoration works and so these fragments are likely to relate to features demolished in the nineteenth century, principally the chancel, nave, clerestory and aisles.[119] A sunken chamfer moulding <AF19> dates to *c.*1320–40 and scroll moulding <AF96> dates to *c.*1280–1340 (Figs. 39-41).

<AF66> is a fragment of late medieval window tracery featuring a glazing channel, simple hollow chamfer mouldings and chamfer cusps which seem to indicate a date after *c.*1310; the tracery does not match any of the surviving drawings of the church, however it does align broadly with the geometry of the mason's setting out slab and may represent a survival of that scheme.

<AF67> is the crown of an ogee arch with attached base of a pilaster shaft or finial; this is the sort of feature that might be found at the apex of an arch surmounting a wall tomb, arcade, window or doorway. The moulding is highly diagnostic as it features a scroll (*c.*1280–1340, wave (*c.*1310–1350) and ¾ circle (*c.*1270–1330) which seems to indicate a date of *c.*1310–1330. Could this be from the wall tomb noted on the north side of the chancel? Based on the consecration of its altar, the chancel was rebuilt by 1315,[120] and the tomb that could be of the benefactor.

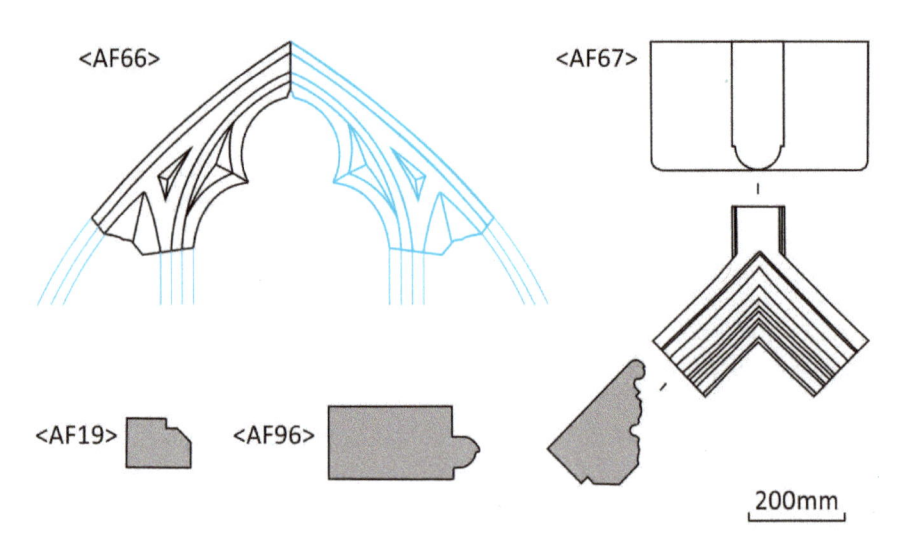

Figs. 39-41 'Decorated' architectural fragments from the excavations <AF19>, <AF96>, <AF66> and <AF67>

The appearance of the church

Whilst the external appearance of the church can be surmised from the surviving pre-1842 drawings, and we have surviving architectural detail inside the church, there is less evidence for much of the finer detail of the interior. Some evidence has been provided by the excavation, but other areas must be inferred from what we know from other churches and excavations.

The tracery in the new windows would have been filled with glass quarries set in lead cames and supported by horizontal iron window bars. If a benefactor had been generous then this might be pictorial stained glass, such bequests to the church fabric would have been linked to prayers and intercessions for them and their family.

The floors in the nave and aisles may largely have still been of rammed earth or mortar, but areas like the chancel and chantries were almost certainly at least partially tiled. The church would have been physically subdivided: a large carved and brightly painted wooden rood screen, surmounted by the life-size rood statue of the crucifixion with flanking statues, would have physically separated the chancel from the choir emphasising the clear division between laity and clergy. Other wooden *parclose* screens may have demarcated areas such as the chantry chapels and possibly around the altars.

The chancel and south transept arches have surviving painted decoration hinting at the detail of decoration that would have covered all the surfaces of the church. The walls would have been plastered and whitewashed, probably with complex wall paintings depicting scenes from the Bible and St Christopher opposite the south door for the worshippers to contemplate during services. A bench may have run around the walls of the nave and aisles, later more benches would be added, the forerunners of pews.

Stonework was elaborately carved and painted, often with micro-architectural detail like the crocketed pinnacle <AF23> found in the excavation (Fig. 42) or exemplified by the wall tombs of the south aisle. Painted statues of the Virgin Mary and saints would have stood in elaborately carved niches, or on moulded socles around the church. The stone altars, topped by the *mensa* slabs, in the chancel and chantries would have stood against the eastern walls, each would have had a carved piscina for washing the chalice and patten used in Mass, and an aumbrey for their storage. The altars themselves would have been covered with white linen altar cloths and a waxed cere cloth and frontal, with the crucifix, candles and perhaps devotional objects on the altar top. Behind might be a wooden or stone reredos, and to the side might be silken banners used in the processions around the church. The visual impact of the often-sumptuous decoration under flickering candlelight and stained glass would have been accompanied by the smell of incense and the sound of the chanting of the mass, creating an environment for worship very different to that familiar in our post-Reformation Anglican churches today.

Mass was celebrated regularly, but Communion was rarely given to the whole congregation, often just at Easter. The church however would have been inextricably linked to the life of the town and the parishioners whose year would have been marked by services and processions at Easter and Christmas, Saint's days and other Holy days, and the ceremonies marking individual births and baptisms, marriages -conducted in the porch, and death and burials. Memorial and intercession for the dead were key parts of the church, with the very fabric of the church designed to expedite this through the chantries.

Fig. 42 Fragment of a crocketed pinnacle HTC<AF23> from the excavations

---

The completion of the 14th-century rebuilding marked the highpoint in the development of the medieval church of Holy Trinity, and the church must have been newly completed at the moment the plague now known as the Black Death hit Minchinhampton. The death of William of Prestbury in 1349 may well have been from the plague; the number of plague deaths in the town is not known, but its impact can be suggested by the deaths of three successive rectors over the spring and summer of 1349, with Stephen Mauleon only surviving in post for a month.

The Black Death is estimated to have killed 25 million people across Europe over 5 years. Arriving in the new town of Melcombe Regis (now Weymouth) in early summer of 1348 and spreading rapidly, it killed between 40% and 60% of the population and by 1400 the population was still only at half its pre-plague level. The plague has been linked to changes in religious outlook and to an increased piety linked to the fear of death and a consequent changing relationship with God. The plague caused radical changes across every part of society triggered largely by the deaths of so many bonded farm labourers and the upward pressure on wages which was strongly resisted by the Crown and landowners. Eventually, following unrest culminating in the Peasants' Revolt of 1381, feudal labour was ended, with cash wages increased. The depressive effect of the plague on much of medieval agriculture is linked to the reduced market for grain, and a switch to sheep farming, although Minchinhampton had already largely moved over to wool production as its principle agricultural activity by the later 12th century.

Mason's setting out slab

Five fragments of finely dressed Painswick Stone slab were found reused in the Victorian pew bases and bear the incised lines of an architectural design sketch. The fragments fit together into two separate parts, but it is likely that they were originally part of the same slab, used by the mason to work out a 1:1 scale drawing of window tracery. The mason's design kit would have included a masons' square, dividers and parallel rule; a scriber or chisel corner would have been used to incise the lines. With these simple tools and a knowledge of geometry and proportion the mason would work up his design: the slab shows the initial laying out of Decorated tracery, with ogee curves, and the hint of cusps and quatrefoils (Fig. 43, Fig. 44).

First a 'grid' was established: a horizontal primary baseline formed the basis for a grid of straight lines: a parallel horizontal was set out 140mm above the baseline and again at 347mm. Perpendiculars were then added 350mm apart, and a series of diagonal lines were laid out at approximately 60° to the primary baseline.

Near-equilateral triangles created by intersecting diagonals set out

DECORATED GOTHIC 43

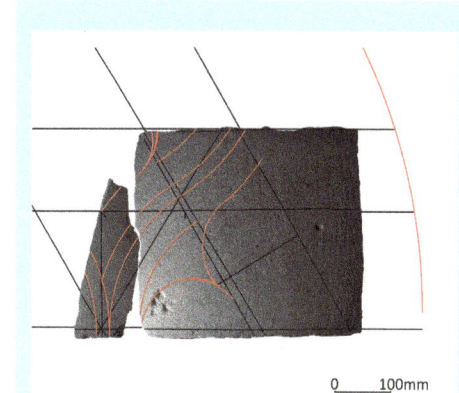

left: Fig. 43 Two of the stone slabs with the incised design. The underlying grid is in black, the design in red

below: Fig. 44 Fragments of Painswick Stone slab with inscribed architectural design: the black lines are the inscribed baselines and grid. The red lines are the incised curves of the tracery, and the blue are the wider extrapolated design; the lack of precision of the laying out is clearly shown.

both the apex of the overall window and of the two lights, a method of design known as *ad triangulum*[121]. The curve of the window arch is set by arcs centring on the ends of the horizontal baseline, each having a radius equivalent to the width of the window.

Superimposed upon this grid are a series of smaller arcs, some joining to form sinuous ogee curves which switch from concave to convex at the intersections between the diagonal gridlines; the centres of some compass-scribed arcs survive although these are not all aligned to the incised grid; further arcs radiate from centres aligned with, but not marked by, the grid. The design appears to show the basis of tracery for a window with at least two window lights, with the suggestion of a quatrefoil above. Each light has a trefoil head with semi-circular cusps; further arcs suggest a cusped quatrefoil between the two lights. Assuming a scale of 1:1, each light would have a width of c.350mm between mullion centres, giving a window width of c.750mm for two lights, with an arch height of c.590mm.

Despite its clear geometric setting-out, the execution of the design is not without fault, one diagonal has been marked out twice on slightly different angles and several of the lines are inconsistent and 'sketchy'; extrapolation of the design serves to highlight the errors. Although the orthogonal grid and diagonals may have been constructed geometrically using dividers, no constructional arcs are visible although at least two 'tickmarks' were made marking intersections. Many of the arcs and centres of the tracery design are not aligned to the grid suggesting a lack of care in execution. Extrapolation of the arcs clearly shows that the incised grid is only a small part of an *implied* base grid suggesting the use of parallel rules. Much of the design appears to have been laid out on-the-fly without the use of incised lines and leaving no clear compass centres in a series of freeform geometric actions that have left no trace.

The mason at Minchinhampton appears to have employed one of the most conventional medieval proportional values in the design: one to the square root of two (1:1.41)[122] which could be constructed using just a straight edge and a pair of compasses. To do so a mason would bisect a square diagonally, draw an arc by opening the compasses across the diagonal and then enclose the area above the square and arc in a rectangle. Vestiges of this process appear to be contained within the scribes of the Minchinhampton incisions – in particular the presence of three parallel horizontal lines which are spaced according to the ratio 1:1.41.

The design in the church
The design does not exactly match any surviving tracery at the church so cannot be unequivocally linked to a surviving window, although it is certainly similar in some respects to the side windows of the south transept. The author may well be the same mason who created the south transept with its glorious wheel window and remarkable scissor roof, a transept described by the renowned Victorian architect William Burges as '…one of the most perfect and curious specimens of the Architecture of the middle of the 14th Century'.[123] If this is the case then the lack of geometric precision may be not due to a lack of care or ability, rather a surety of purpose and a rightly held confidence to carry the design from base grid through to final curves.

Perpendicular, the mid fifteenth century

IN 1415 THE manors of Minchinhampton and Avening, as property of a foreign abbey, were like so many others throughout England confiscated by Henry V, ending the 333 year connection with the Abbaye-aux-Dames in Caen. The manors were passed to the newly founded Syon Abbey in 1424, confirmed in 1444, after a lifetime grant to the earl of Suffolk.[124] A survey of the Syon estates in 1492 gives the annual value of Minchinhampton manor at £91.1s.2 1/2d.[125]

In the 15th century a clerestory was added above the nave, and included reused Norman stonework. AT Playne records that it had 'late square-headed windows of two lights, and the brackets, which supported the beams of the roof, rested on large bold corbel heads'.[126] HE Relton's engraving shows three of these clerestory windows on the south side, each light cusped with trefoil heads under a square hood, a fourth window at the eastern end is clearly a later alteration or insertion. Two two-light windows with square heads are shown on the north side of the clerestory in the pre-1842 watercolour (Fig. 15).

The addition of the clerestory necessitated the lowering of the angle of the nave roof, which was covered with lead sheet; when the plaster was stripped from the church interior in the late 19th century, an earlier roof line was visible on the west wall of the tower and AT Playne suggested this was the Norman roof line, but this seems improbable given that the tower is 14th century. It is more likely that the earlier roof line was from the 14th-century nave.

There were also late medieval alterations to the windows of nave and to the chancel, where Perpendicular lancet windows were added. A new chancel east window may have been added at this time: Burges notes that it was small and with four lights, but otherwise there is little evidence for significant physical change to the church in this period.

Excavated architectural fragments that may derive from these alterations largely date between *c.*1370 and 1550 with two roll, fillet and cavetto mouldings, <AF29, AF61>, which are relatively similar to examples from the small shafts of the Lady Chapel at Gloucester Cathedral dating *c.*1500[127] (Fig. 45).

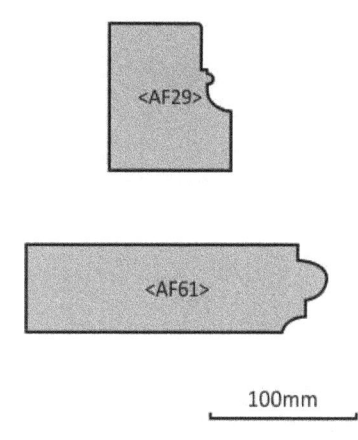

Fig. 45 Perpendicular Gothic profiles

Decorated tile pavements

Part of a decorated inlaid tile[128] found during the excavations suggests that a new tile pavement was laid in the church sometime in the mid-15th to early 16th centuries, most likely in the chancel or one of the chantry chapels. Only a small fragment survived, but it is from a 16-tile design of which a number of slight variants are known that were in use for some decades (Fig. 46). The general design crops up across the region from the mid-15th century onwards, with examples at Canynges House (Bristol), the Deanery chapel at Gloucester Cathedral, Acton Court (just north of Bristol), Heytesbury House (Wiltshire), St Mary's Glanville's Wootton (Dorset) and Halesowen Abbey (Worcestershire) whilst there is a further cluster in south-west Wales including at St David's Cathedral, Pembrokeshire where it is laid in a very similar pavement as at Canynges.[129] The Gloucestershire examples would have been made at Malvern.[130]

The Canynges pavement suggests how it might have appeared if such a pavement existed here. Laid after 1500 in the former dwelling of William Canynges (c.1399–1474, a wealthy merchant, MP and five times mayor of Bristol) the pavement has a series of 16-tile patterns laid as a continuous diaper, set diagonally corner to corner, with the 16-tile pattern alternating with four tile designs surrounded by 12 plain, dark glazed tiles, all set within a border

Fig. 46 The late medieval tile fragment from Holy Trinity alongside a similar design from Canynges House, Bristol

of two rows of plain glazed tiles set square to the walls.

The pavement may have been laid as part of a refurbishment of part of the church, probably paid for by a wealthy benefactor, perhaps associated with endowment of a chantry. Although only a small fragment, the tile gives a further glimpse of the sometimes-sumptuous medieval flooring of parts of the church, and to links in fashion and style that match those used in the houses of the mercantile and ruling elites, and in important monastic churches and cathedrals.

The Sixteenth century: Reformation and counter-Reformation

THE EARLY 16TH century saw the start of a Europe-wide movement that questioned the supremacy of the Pope and the legitimacy of the authority, practices and beliefs of the Church of Rome. Sparked in 1517 by the monk Martin Luther's 95 theses, the Reformation gathered pace and influence across western Europe, spreading with the new printing presses. In England Henry VIII was initially opposed to the new Protestants, awarded the title 'Defender of the Faith' by Pope Leo X in 1521, however political expediency over the need for a male heir combined with the temptation of confiscating monastic wealth and land led to the Act of Supremacy in 1534, the establishment of the Church of England, use of English as the language of the church, and the Dissolution of the monasteries by Thomas Cromwell.

As a holding of Syon Abbey, the Dissolution directly affected Minchinhampton. Syon was surrendered to the Crown in 1539 and Minchinhampton passed in 1543 to Andrew, 1st baron of Windsor, in whose family it stayed until 1642. From 1538 to 1551 the rector was Thomas Powell, he was presented by Agnes, the abbess of Syon, in one of her last appointments. Powell would have arrived in Minchinhampton at a moment of great turmoil; the medieval Catholic church was to be dismantled through a series of reforms whose practical implementation he would have had to oversee, with changes affecting every element of belief and liturgy.

The medieval church had been physically adorned and beautified with decoration and ornaments imbued with symbolism; the walls had painted plaster and stone expressing theological messages, altars, statues and chapels were lit by candles and the censor smoked from frankincense. The unmarried priest carried out the Latin Mass in his vestments, separated by the Rood screen from his congregation who were reduced to mere observers.[131] The remembrance of the dead, with the masses and prayers for their souls to speed their passage through purgatory, was key to later medieval belief as seen in the chantries and tolling of bells. As well as the theatre of mass, there was more participatory events too: as well as the major services of the Christian calendar additional celebrations for saints' feast days for saints and church ales brought the church and community together.

All would be swept away in a fitful series of edicts under Henry VIII, his son Edward VI and later Elizabeth I. As will be seen, the physical expression of the changing beliefs and liturgy would be seen in the internal arrangements of the church, in the division between secular and holy space, in the provision of seating, of the rise of preaching and pulpits, and the frequency of Communion.

From the 1530s onwards the impacts of the Reformation ebbed and flowed, with short-lived reversions to Catholicism under Mary (1553–1558) before Protestantism was reaffirmed under Elizabeth I. Gloucestershire was not exempt from the decrees which were enforced by the bishops, the radical protestant Hooper's visitation of his new diocese in 1551 painted a poor picture of the priesthood -nearly half could not repeat the Ten Commandments,[132] leading to enforcement of the learning of the Decalogue, the Creed and the Lord's Prayer –all in English rather than Latin (Hooper's life and fate was tied intimately to the religious turmoil, he was burnt at the stake in Gloucester in 1555).

Hooper's visitation came to Minchinhampton: Gilbert Bourne, rector to Holy Trinity's 500 communicants, was not examined as he was non-resident however the minister John Edwards answered satisfactorily enough. Edwards could recite the Ten Commandments and Lord's Prayer, and he could repeat, but not confirm the scripture and the Articles of the Faith.[133]

Hooper's visitation is one example of the type of enforcement visitations that were frequent occurrences for the 16th-century parish church, these checks were disliked intrusions requiring preparation and changes, expensive acquisitions of new books or disposal of valued religious artefacts, as well as numerous trips to Gloucester to give evidence to the Diocesan Consistory Court. New books like the Great Bible in English or the Book of Common Prayer, would all need to be acquired, as well as new records of Births, Marriages and Deaths to be kept weekly from 1538, and secured in double-locked coffer chests.

One of the key changes at Holy Trinity was the dissolution of the chantries that were a key physical and spiritual component of the medieval church but, as they both went against the new Protestant teaching, and were endowed with land and property, they were a clear target for the King. Henry VIII confiscated all chantries by Act of Parliament in 1545, with a county by county survey of chantries the following year, but Henry died before many could be transferred. His son Edward VI instigated surveys of the surviving chantries and they were dissolved from 1548.

The endowments of the Lady Chapel at Holy Trinity were valued at £8.17s.3½d, with no ornament, plate or jewels recorded at this time.[134] The last chantry priest at the Lady Chapel was Richard Gravener, who had been the chantry priest for 40 years and received a £6 annual stipend and had no other living. Gravener was granted a pension by the Crown after the dissolution.[135] The assets were granted by the Crown to John Thynne and Laurence Hyde.[136] There is no mention of Schire's, or any other chantries, suggesting that these had lapsed in the intervening centuries.

The suppression of the chantries marked the end of purgatory and intercessionary prayer for the quick and the dead, marking a major change in the liturgical and practical underpinnings of the church -as well as the livelihood of chantry priests- and one which cut to the heart of the medieval belief in the salvation of the soul. Edward VI re-introduced changes first implemented by his father that would compound the changes and mark the start of a distinctly Protestant church. Processions were banned, there would be no rosary, shrines, statues or glass images, and candles were banned, with only two allowed on the altar; tolling the bells –the death knell- for the deceased was also stopped. Each church also had to provide a triple locked coffer for the poor man's box.

The rood screen was to be torn down, removing the barrier between clergy and laity, and communion became a more frequent celebration by the priest, although it was still very infrequently shared by parishioners; the single altar was renamed the communion table. Of lesser theological, if not social and financial, importance was the banning of the church ale -that occasion of great communal festivity and important income stream. The rites, paraphernalia and rhythm of medieval church community had been almost completely stripped away.

Whilst the new Protestantism would have been embraced by some it was also resisted by many, and the tides of reform and counter reform ebbed and flowed throughout the sixteenth century in what would have been a confusing and worrying time for the general population who had no say in the matters. These tides can be seen in the purchases and expenses listed in the churchwarden's accounts (below), but also on an individual level in the fluctuating fortunes of Gilbert Bourne who was Minchinhampton's rector from 1551–3. Bourne was a staunch Catholic, being sent to the Tower of London by Edward VI, before reversing his fortunes under Mary as the bishop of Bath and Wells, only to be exiled to Somerset by Elizabeth I for denying her supremacy.[137]

Bourne was replaced in 1553 by Thomas Taylor, who was already parson at North Cerney and had probably been ordained under Henry VIII.

Throughout his tenure Taylor was frequently called to the Consistory Court at Gloucester, sometimes to defend complaints against his actions, and sometimes to sue for tithes and defamation. He was frequently called before the court for the decay of the church, especially the chancel.[138] In 1563 a complaint was made that he 'dothe not the custome that hathe bene usid on Christmas daye, that ys he dothe not refreshe the poore people'[139] and he kept being called to answer complaints 'probably more frequently than any other cleric in the diocese.'[140]

Taylor's religious knowledge was questionable and during Hooper's visitation in 1551 Taylor had not been able to prove the Creed, but had managed to retain his benefice at South Cerney. In 1573 he was excommunicated for failing to appear at the Consistory Court, his proctor claiming it was due to his advanced years, Taylor continued to fail to comply with its orders.[141] Finally in 1575 Taylor was charged with failure to subscribe to Elizabeth I's Articles of Religion, after 25 years of evading sanction of the ecclesiastical courts Taylor was removed from office in 1575–6 by the High Commissioners, he died in 1583.[142]

Taylor appears to have been a divisive and disputatious figure, although the frequent legal cases may reflect underlying divisions and disputes within the parish. Whether these are based on religious differences -or simply his personality- is unclear. It is also not clear whether, like Bourne, Taylor was a staunch catholic, yet he was clearly out of step with the Elizabethan courts. Presented by the lord of the manor, how far a rector's views were in line with the majority of his Gloucestershire parishioners is hard to say, and there may have been vocal adherents in both camps, with others trying to keep their heads down. The incumbents' influence may be inferred from the (later) churchwardens' accounts which show that the parish appear to have re-embraced Catholicism under Mary with an enthusiasm slightly lacking from the early Elizabethan years.

Minchinhampton in the mid-16th century appears to have suffered a dip in its fortunes and in 1565 the town was said to have been 'much decayed'; the key to the town's wealth was the market, and keen to reverse the decline Edward Windsor secured the Tuesday market and the two fairs on Trinity Monday and on the 18th (later 29th) October.[143] There were about 500 communicants in the parish in 1551,[144] with 134 households counted in 1563.[145]

As well as religion, many parish churches had a major role in the education of children, a role that sometimes started with the chantry priests, and which had to be recast after the Reformation. At Holy Trinity a schoolmaster was recorded in 1572[146] and in 1594 the curate was also the schoolmaster.[147] In 1651 pupils were still being taught in the chancel,[148] a situation that would have lasted until a schoolhouse was built.

Surviving from 1555, the churchwardens' accounts[149] detail not only the income of the church, but also the many outgoings -large and small- that illuminate our knowledge of the mundane and spiritual life of the parish church. It is in these small items that the internal life of the church can be partially understood, with the ebb and flow of religious beliefs marked by the purchase of wax and frankincense, payments for services and items. The start of the accounts sadly comes after the reign of the protestant Edward VI (1547–1553) so we do not have an account of the start of the Reformation and its impact on the church, but it does cover the reign of Mary (1553–1558), who reintroduced Catholicism and reversed most of the Henrican and Edwardian reforms. Mary was shortly followed in 1558 by the accession of the protestant Elizabeth 1 (1558–1603). These pendulum swings would have been very difficult for the parish to navigate, being injuncted one way and then the other, and would have caused both spiritual distress and financial hardship, with much of the spiritual, social and financial fabric of the church being radically altered or even stripped away.

The accounts were partially transcribed, at the instigation of Minchinhampton's Vestry clerk and Schoolmaster Fenning Parke, by John Bruce who lived at Hyde House and who published a discussion and extensive extracts from the accounts in 1853 and from whose transcriptions the following is taken (Fig. 47).[150]

'When I was appointed Vestry Clerk in 1825 I received this Book from my predecessor Mr Samuel Keene, it was coverless and in a very tattered condition. Finding the Entries curious and locally interesting I showed it to Mr H J Thistlethwayte who was Churchwarden he had the injured leaves repaired and the Book bound at his

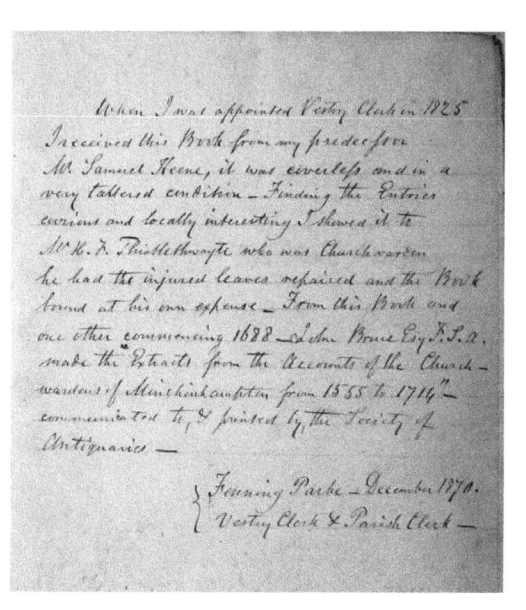

Fig. 47 Fenning Parke's foreword to the Churchwarden's accounts

own expense. From this Book and one other commencing 1688 John Bruce Esq FSA made the "Extracts from the Accounts of the Church-wardens of Minchinhampton from 1555 to 1714" communicated to, & printed by, the Socety of Antiquaries– Fenning Park-December 1870 Vestry Clerk & Parish Clerk'

In the 16th century, following the Reformation, the church's income was based on a number of different sources, whilst some were customary dues like the annual payment of 20 shillings from the churchwardens at Rodborough for the maintenance of the church,[151] or rental income from various church properties, including land, there were others which were inextricably tied in with the social life and structure of the community, events which tied church and parish together.

A major income, until its final demise in 1589, was the Church Ale held at Whitsun. This event was a great social occasion and celebration and a cause of social cohesion, as well as providing a good income for the church whose loss would surely be keenly felt. The ale was brewed by the churchwardens and sold at a feast in the church-house with entertainments and much revelry.[152] Until 1595 another source of church income was from *Hogling money*,[153] which does not refer to a one to two-year old sheep, but to the activity of *hogling*, carried out by menfolk, who went around the town carrying out forfeits and entertainments in exchange for food and money for the church; *hogling* appears to have developed into a male counterpart to *Hock-tide*, where forfeits were demanded by the women including tying up men, who were released on payment of a ransom to the church.[154]

The last income was Paschal money, the annual customary payment when the parishioners received communion at Easter, although after 1604 the Offertory was increasingly collected at each communion. There was an annual collection of money or goods in kind, collected from each property in the parish, after 1634 this was replaced by an annual Rate.

These changes to the income streams, which would have caused a significant impact on the communal life of the church and town, perhaps as great a change as the liturgical changes.

Queen Mary 1553–1558

In 1555 the accounts show that, having presumably followed the protestant reforms of the previous decades, the parish was still catching up with the impact of the Marian reversion: it was only just purchasing two books (2*s*. 6*d*.) from *Sir Roger* (were these catholic texts, hidden by Sir Roger through the protestant years?) and an Antiphonary, or book of liturgical chants required for the catholic services (16s. 4d.) with a leather cover for the same (12d.). Perhaps these purchases were inspired by a visitation (cost 2s.4d.) from the diocese which would have been intended to establish and enforce compliance in the parish? A trip to Gloucester to discuss the church's debts had itself cost 16d., and 10d. had to be found to pay the *smoke farthing* tax to the bishop.

As well as the services and Latin, other long held Catholic traditions had returned and the list of payments evokes their ceremony, liturgy and practice through many small but evocative purchases, but also through the direct recording of ritual: an Easter Sepulchre was constructed by Spennel (12d.) and watched by Rych. Rysley (12d.) and John Long (6d.). Drink on Good Friday cost 4d. Candles were a common outlay: payments were made for making the Paschal candle and the font candles using seven pounds of wax (7s.3d.), with 5s.6d. for the altar candle and 2d. for candles and paints; 5d. was spent on yet more candles, a pennyworth of frankincense for the censer, and a pyx for storing the sacrament cost 3s.10d.. Mending of the *cloke*, probably the priest's cope, cost 3s.[155] As Bruce puts it so well, 'so far as could be expected in a distant country parish, the restoration of the old service was complete'.[156]

Structural changes were made too: in 1556 the major purchase was of a new rood at 20 shillings and two shillings was paid for '*a womyne*', possibly an image of the Virgin Mary (Fig. 48). A new surplace was purchased for 3s.4d. and four girdles for the vestments at fourpence. A cope was mended (12d.). The liturgical practices can be visualised through purchases: payments were made for wax for a Paschal and font candle (6s.), making altar candles (3d.), and 8d. for further candles. The Easter Sepulchre was made (12d.) and watched (12d.), and the organ was repaired (12d.) indicating the return of musical accompaniment. Frankincense was again bought (6d.). A copy of the Articles was purchased for 6d., and 4d. for paper, possibly for recording christenings, marriages and deaths. The parish was again called for a visitation, this time at Painswick (2s.) and again had to go to Gloucester, perhaps about its debts (cost 12d.).

There are no entries for 1557, but in 1558 the parish again spent 12d. on the Easter Sepulchre and a further 2d. on pins and nails for it. Candle expenses were more frequent: 2lb of candles (7d.), 8lb of wax (8s.), 12d. for making the Easter candle, the font candle and two altar candles; Walter Barber was paid 2d. for making two altar candles, another tuppence went on altar candles and 2d. on frankincense. A '*little pillow*' cost 1d, mending the best surplice 2d. and making a small surplice 3d..

A carver at Gloucester was commissioned to make an image of the Trinity, to whom the church is of course dedicated, and was paid 12d. in

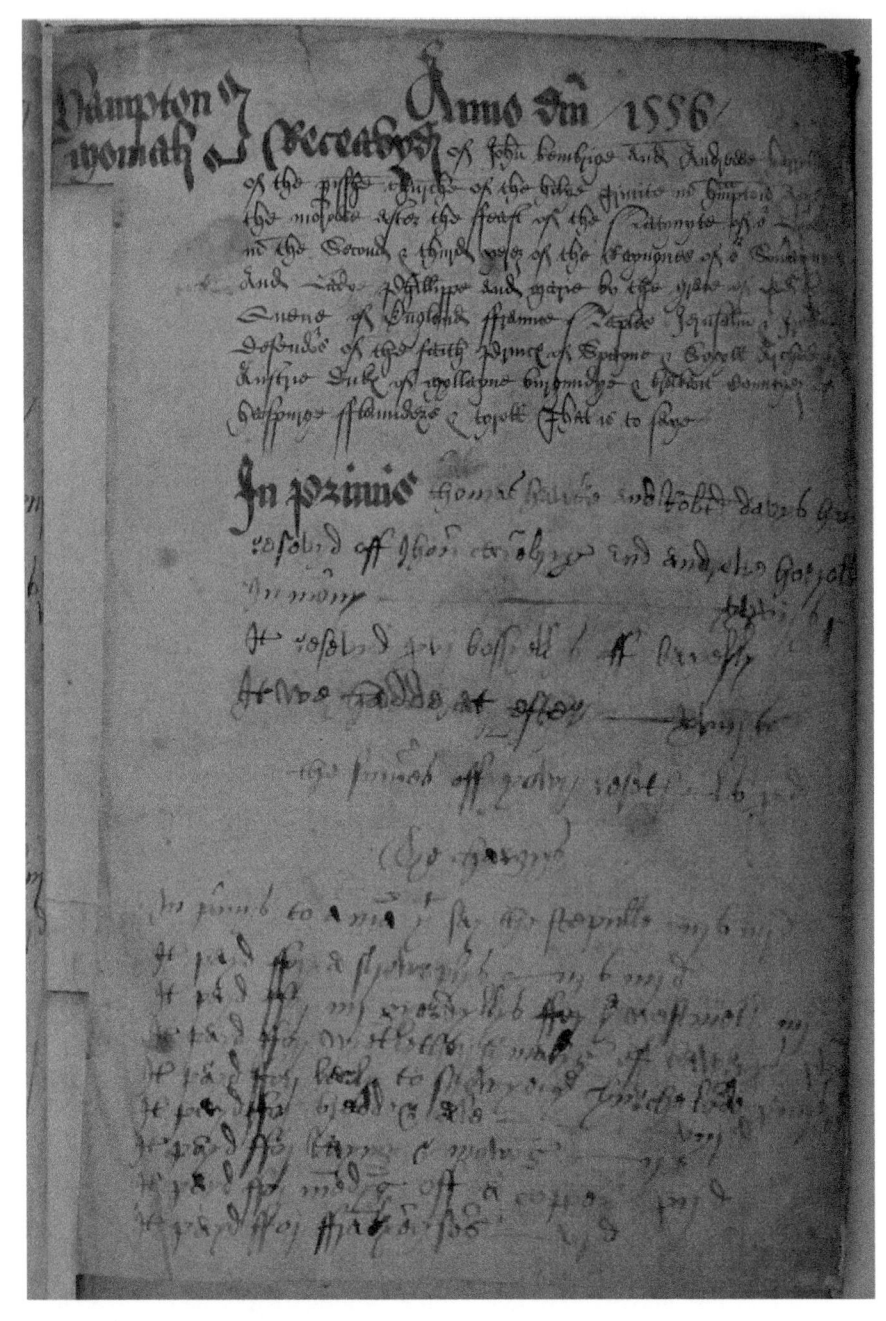

Fig. 48 Churchwardens' Accounts, entry for 1556

Earnest money in advance of the work being completed. A tabernacle cost 12*s*.. A further book was acquired at 2*s*. from a man named Pokmore.

The effect of new requirements on the church are also evident in the accounts: Edward Spenner was paid 16*d.* for keeping the new weekly *crystnyng boke* of christenings, marriages and deaths, written on paper. This had been a requirement since 1538, although not always done, and was confirmed by Elizabeth I in 1558. The book had to be kept in a chest with two locks, certainly the church coffer kept by Alys Coke (cost 2*s.*). An inventory was made of the *church goods*, during which 5*d.* of bread and drink were consumed.

Elizabeth 1

With the death of Mary in November 1558, Elizabeth, daughter of Henry VIII and Anne Boleyn, took the throne and brought a return to Protestantism which was embraced immediately by its more zealous adherents and the English service resumed. At Holy Trinity, however, Easter with all its services, ceremony and the annual Communion, was still celebrated in the Catholic rite: the Easter Sepulchre was made, and watched, costing 2*s.* 8*d.* with 2*d.* for 'poyntes, pynnes, and packe thredde for the sepulture'. Eight pounds of wax was bought at a cost of 7*s.* 4*d.*, with 12*d.* for making and fetching the Easter candle.

From midsummer of 1559 Holy Trinity, with all of its recently and expensively restocked Catholic purchases, was suddenly forced to perform an about face and go through the expense of a further set of purchases. Whether the carved image of the Trinity ordered from the Gloucester carver was ever completed is not known, but it would have been no use in the new protestant times, and the new rood, paid for in 1556, would likely be shortly removed and the doorway blocked up.

The parish appears to have been less than speedy in its return to protestantism; the churchwardens, accompanied by six parishioners, were called to Gloucester for the Queen's 'General Visitation', a check on compliance of all parishes who were expected to attend with full inventories of the church goods including items that might relate to Catholic rite. Holy Trinity failed to provide an inventory and had to return again to Gloucester once it had been completed. The visitation appears to have had some effect and a new book of the Injunctions was purchased, largely based on those of Edward VI this cost 4*d.*, and a new 'service book and administration of the sacraments' -the Book of Common Prayer (Fig. 49) was acquired at a cost of 5*s.* 4*d.*; at last the English rite could again be practised.

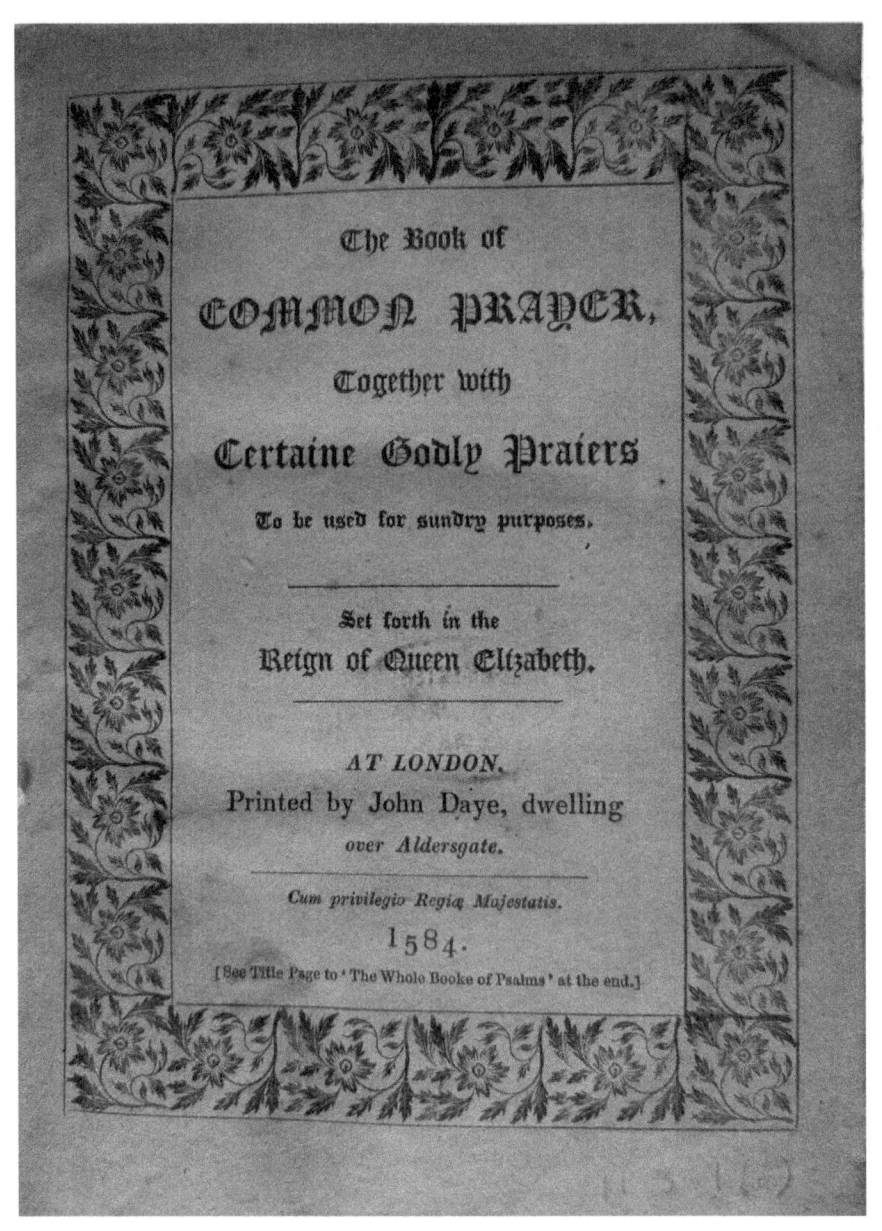

Fig. 49 Title page from a 1584 edition of the Book of Common Prayer

In 1559 the fee was 2s. 'for makynge of the inventory and the bookes of chrystenynge, bureynge, and weddynge' whilst Edward Spynner received his 16d. for keeping the record. This year the church chest was kept by William Foster (2s.).

By 1560 further expenses from the return to Protestantism under Queen Elizabeth I were being recorded. The about-turn in religion meant a new Bible had to be begrudgingly bought at the cost of 12s., the old bible from Edward's reign had not been kept safe through Mary's reign. The Easter Sepulchre was no more, and tellingly there are no payments for candles, although there is a payment of 3s.9d. for bread and wine.

Pest control was the responsibility of the churchwardens by statute of 1532/3, each parish providing itself with a net to catch them.[157] A payment in 1560 of 4d. for 'a paire of bates legges' is the first entry listing payment for control of animals considered vermin, such as bats, foxes and crows. Minor items included further repair to the surplices (2d.) and sixpence for buckles, and the purchase of a mattock, perhaps for digging graves through the limestone brash of the churchyard.

The standard fee of 16d. was paid for keeping the registers, and 12d. for keeping the church chest. This was 'removed' at a cost of 2d., a later mention of carriage of the chest (6d.) suggests it may have been repaired. The church still had issues to deal with the Diocese, charges at the Archdeacon's Court cost

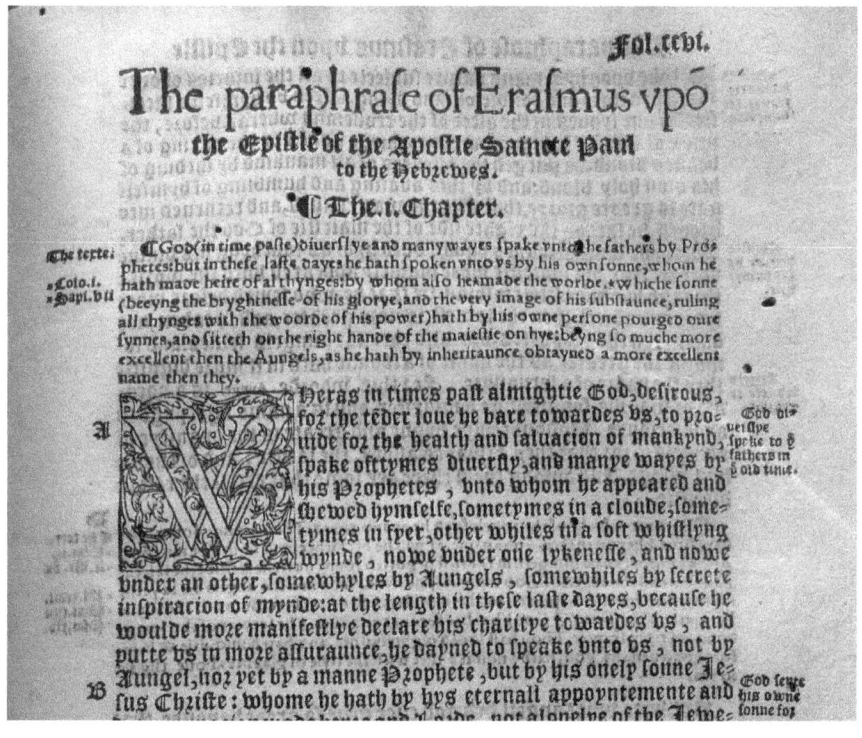

Fig. 50 Erasmus's Paraphrases: Hebrews. Printed in 1548/9 in a Black Letter font

2s.8d.. The church's *bill* was made up for the year and sent to Dursley at a cost of 18d..

1561 saw two entries for bread and wine – 6 shillings fourpence at Easter, and a separate entry of only 11d. for the rest of the year; the main parish Mass was still celebrated at Easter, with only infrequent sacraments throughout the rest of the year.

A copy of Erasmus's 'paraphrase' was bought for eight shillings; 'The First tome or volume of the Paraphrase of Erasmus upon the new testament' had been published in 1548 and was an English language translation Erasmus's key commentary on the New Testament (Fig. 50). In 1547 Edward VI had ordered a copy to be kept in every parish church, clearly the copy –if ever bought- had been lost or destroyed during the Marian Reversion and a new copy had to be acquired within 12 months of the Queen's visitation.

Keeping the church chest cost 2 shillings. In 1562 there were again separate entries for bread and wine for Easter (6s.3d.) and 'the whole year' (2s.8d.). Keeping the chest again cost 2 shillings. A new rope was bought for the well (2d.) and lime (for plastering, limewash or mortar) and wood was acquired (16d.).

A clerk is recorded in 1563 and was paid 10 shillings 'in money'; a quire of paper (24 sheets, or 1/20th of a ream) was bought to make up pages for the register book; paper, and less often ink, was a regular purchase down the years until 1598 when the last paper was bought. That same year, following the 1597 decree that the register book should no longer be on paper, 11s.2d. of parchment was purchased, with a further 'skin' of parchment bought the next year for sixpence.

Both volumes of the newly published *Book of Homilies* had to be acquired anew (15d. and 3s.6d.); 'Certain Sermons or Homilies Appointed to Be Read in Churches' was a collection of officially sanctioned sermons published in 1547 that every parish was required to have with a homily read out each week in lieu of preaching. Another unspecified book was bought for 4d. Bread and wine was bought, for Easter (7s.) and the rest of the year 2s. A chain was bought for 'the book' in 1566 (8d.), presumably the Bible. There was a change from the church being divided by a screen between the lay and the clergy, to it being a division between one part for the laity and one for sacrament; altars were moved against the east wall in the high church, or to the choir.[158]

A new *Book of Common Prayer* was purchased for 8d in 1568, with a copy of the 'omilye' acquired for 8d. in 1570. This may be a further copy of the Homily, a new edition in 1571 was promptly acquired along with a new copy of the Bible for 45s and 'books for our parte' for 6d.

The accounts suggest that the parish was slow to cast off the catholic faith, no doubt due to the affiliation of Lord Windsor and his rector Gilbert Bourne. The parish therefore may have followed its Lord and priest and stayed loyal to the Catholic faith.

Bread and wine is first listed in 1561, most years from then to 1567 there are payments for bread and wine at Easter, with a separate far smaller payment covering the rest of the year. This follows the medieval practice of annual confession, absolution and communion, whereas in the Protestant rite communion became more frequent. In 1568 there is the usual entry for 'wine at Easter', but the second entry is for 'wine for communicants at several times in the year' a clear indication that communion was now being taken more often, although Easter was still the main celebration of communion for the parish. This split continues to be recorded however the amount spent outside Easter increases dramatically from in the 1570s as communion was celebrated more frequently. The change appears to occur with the death of Lord Windsor and appointment of the new rector Thomas Freeman in 1575.

Although Elizabeth had been on the throne several years, it was not until Freeman's appointment in 1575 that 6s.8d. was paid 'to John Mayo and John Lyth for for pullynge downe, dystroyenge, and throwynge out of the churche sundrye superstycyous thinges tendinge to the maynetenaunce of idolatrye'. This may have included the 1556 rood, but also the statues of saints in the north transept niches, as well as clearing out banners, streamers and other catholic paraphernalia. Protestant feeling seems high this year as the accounts list the 10d due for the payment of Peter Pence or smoke farthing previously payable to 'the Antichrist of Rome' and this new rhetoric may be linked to the new rector. Allegiance to the Protestant Queen is indicated by the entry 'For ringing, the day of the Queen's majesty's entering into the Crown, whom God long time we seek to preserve' and a corner appears to have been turned.

Visitations and inquiries continued and were a constant expense and annoyance for the parish. The churchwardens were called to give evidence at various towns, but also were visited by the sumner or paritor, an episcopal official who would attend, read the summons and exhort the parish to buy various new ecclesiastical tracts. A new Book of Common Prayer was purchased in 1576 (5s.). In 1581 the parish acquired a 'book of co-sanguinities' (3d.), which was the 'Table of Kindred and Affinity' that set out which relations could, and could not marry. In 1582 4d. was spent on clasps for the Bible, and in 1584 the Homily was bound (10d.), and a new Communion book bought for 6s.8d. The Book of Common Prayer was bound in 1586 (8d).

In 1594 William Coldruppe was paid 12*d*. for crosses, and in a final act of iconoclastic fervour payment of 6*d*. was made to 'remove the woman out of the churche porche' probably a statue of the Virgin Mary. At the same time the well-named Adam Painter received 4.*s* for painting the Ten Commandments and 'other charges' on the church walls. The Decalogue, a key text in Protestant faith and morality, was required to be displayed in the church and was either painted on the wall or on timber boards erected behind the altar, as was the case at Holy Trinity in 1606. Preaching, other than readings from the Homilies, was only allowed by licensed preachers who could be trusted to keep to the established church line, and these are recorded at Holy Trinity from 1596.

> **Black letter text: the Ten Commandments?**
> The discovery in the nave of fragments of wall plaster painted with *Black Letter* text sheds light on the appearance and decoration of Holy Trinity, but also on the changing nature of the church in the 16th century. Excavation of the backfill of a secondary grave within a masonry tomb[159] uncovered part of a dump of painted wall plaster; only the top of the grave backfill was excavated so not all the plaster was excavated, but enough was excavated to tell us much about the painted inscription.
>
> The assemblage is dominated by fragments painted with text in a finely executed Black Letter *textura quadrata* script (Fig. 51). The painted wall plaster appears to be from a discrete deposit with several conjoining sherds. The script is neatly and precisely painted in black on a whitewashed background. A few fragments contain blurred, faded or smudged script, but on the whole the text survives in crisp, if fragmentary, condition.
>
> The letters are all set out on horizontal scribe lines, with all the letter fragments appearing to be set out on a base and mid line; some letter fragments also appear to have horizontal scribe lines for the descenders, but not for ascenders or capital heights. Some fragments have closely set parallel scribe lines, presumably from consecutive lines of text. There are relatively few blank pieces although many of these do have scribe lines.
>
> None of the fragments are large enough to contain complete letters, and no complete letters could be reconstructed. As the Black Letter script is made up of letters sharing many similar elements such as the vertical downstrokes known as *minims* it is hard to deduce letters from most of the fragments, however two conjoining fragments include the descender and tail of the letter *y*, and the lower part of a letter *z*. The top of a letter *thorn* is also present, a letter still in use (with a superscript *e*), in the 1611 King James Bible, and which indicates the text is in English rather than Latin,

Fig. 51 Selection of the fragments of the Black Letter text painted on wall plaster

giving a post-Reformation date for the text. One group of four conjoining fragments shows that there were at least two lines of text and contains part of a capital which is positioned underneath a lower-case letter s; there appear to be two different sizes of letter. The presence of a comma places the script post c.1520[160] and the text is most likely to be of 16th-century date.[161]

The Reformation saw a series of waves of destruction of medieval wall-paintings;[162] the painted monograms and scrollwork are the only survivals at Holy Trinity. Wall painting did not stop at the Reformation however, and framed blocks of English text in Black Letter script were frequently added during the reigns of Edward VI or Elizabeth I -although the practice continued into the Puritan Revolution, post-Restoration period and indeed the 18th century. Texts were typically of the Ten Commandments (The Decalogue), the Creed, or scriptural extracts. The text was often painted on the whitewashed walls but may also be on cloth hangings (as at Chichester cathedral)[163] or on wooden boards.

In 1594 the churchwardens' accounts lists a payment of 4s to the well-named Adam Painter, 'for paintinge the ten Commandementes, and other charges'; could this be the payment for the Black Letter text painted on the plaster? There is no letter z in the Decalogue, but the 'other charges' could refer to a further Scriptural text. By 1606 the Ten Commandments and 'the degrees of marriage' were repainted with the table of consanguinity, this time on new timber boards with 'a ring to hang them from'. A new table of consanguinities and frame was made in 1632, and again in 1662.

The plaster is in good condition with clean breaks, suggesting that it was stripped from the wall and dumped fairly quickly in the tomb. It is possible that the plaster was stripped off the wall as part of a wider programme of refurbishment, or deliberate destruction of the text, but it is also possible that this was a discrete area hacked off to allow, for example, a new monument or memorial to be mounted to the wall. The date of the deposition cannot be dated precisely due to a lack of other finds, although it was clearly deposited before 1842, and is likely to have been deposited before box pews were constructed above the tomb, probably in the 17th century.

In 1595 the parish bought a new Communion book and a 'booke of prayers for the queenes maiestie' for 7s. 8d., and a new prayer book was bought in 1597 (4d). The communion *table* -not altar- was mended in 1599 (4d).
Maintenance and the spire

Structurally, the years following the 15th-century appear to have been concerned with ongoing and frequent maintenance rather than new building campaigns and from 1555 the expenditure is listed in the churchwardens' accounts. The greatest impact on the physical structure of the church was the taking down of the upper part of the spire, other than this, externally the church would remain largely the same until the rebuilding of 1842, although what happened inside was another matter.

Work on the spire figures heavily in the years after 1555, with both maintenance and survey work featuring —clearly something was wrong. It is not always clear which payments are for the steeple, rather than numerous other issues with roofing and leadwork. Church roofs have long been a continual expense. The steeple door needed repair and a new key in 1555, costing 8*d*.,[164] and in 1556 a man was paid 3.*s* 4*d.* to survey the steeple. There was work on the bells in 1558 and in 1559 several 'dream holes' in the steeple were repaired, along with the porch, the north side of the church and the first payment to a John Ingeram for work on the church. The next year, 1560, John Ingeram, John Newman and Henry Pole did 2s of work on the steeple 'lettynge down the stanes', whilst three men (possibly the same three) were separately paid 8*d.* for 'lokyng on the steeple for ther chargis', presumably making a survey of work that might be required.

Fig. 52 The truncated spire and coronet

The plumber or leadworker first appears in the accounts in 1555 with a payment of 3*s*. 3*d.* 'for soder and mendynge the churche ledde', and again in 1560, when there is payment for 'ridding the lead', stripping part of the roof. A possibly related payment is for stone roofing tiles and their delivery. The leadworker returned in 1561, and there was also tiling done on the roof. In 1563 there was significant leadworking to the value of 21*s*. 4*d.*, the mason Slye was paid 6*s*.4*d.* and there was a payment of 'their dinner' for the carriage of stone, while 10s. was spent on 'meat and drink when the stones were carried', this appears the most likely date for the reduction of the spire. Lime was purchased in 1561, 1562 and 1563. In 1564 there is payment for stonework. More leadwork in 1565 of 6*s*.8*d.*, the same payment again made in 1567.

At Holy Trinity the newly reduced spire was topped by a weather-vane; in 1577 2*s* was paid to the man that took the vane off the steeple. It is possible that all was not well with the new truncated spire as in 1582 the mason Slye was called back to inspect the 'steeple' (2*s*.6*d*.) but the parish had to send one John Poore to Slye at Painswick to 'wille hym not to come accordinge to promyse, because the paryshe was not at leasure'. A second mason was called in from Malmesbury to inspect the 'tower', charging 16*d.* for his visit. It seems Slye kept the contract as the next year he was paid 6*s*. 8*d.* for his 'reward' and the carriage of his tumbrel or cart.

In 1588 it seems there was another phase of significant work on the steeple with the men working on it paid £8.16s. Lord Windsor donated 20s. and a further 10s.6d. was given by John a Deane. A wooden scaffold was erected of poles, probably of lime wood, and the men paid and given meat and drink and stone carried to the church. The following year the lead worker spent three days on the tower (3s.) using thirty pounds of lead. Ockepool was paid 12d. for 'laying of the restes upon the towar'. Could this be when the embattled masonry coronet and crocketted pinnacles were added?

Holy Trinity is not alone in Gloucestershire churches with a truncated spire, at St Nicholas Westgate, Gloucester the 200-foot spire was apparently built with its coronet in the 15th century, the spire was hit by canon fire during the Siege of Gloucester but was only reduced down to the coronet in 1783 by John Bryan.[165] Also in Gloucester, the mid-15th-century spire of St John the Baptist survived the church's rebuilding of 1732 but the top three metres was removed in 1910 and rebuilt in the former graveyard.[166] Much of the spire of St Mary Radcliffe in Bristol fell after it was struck by lightning in 1446, with it being capped off and only rebuilt in 1872.[167]

The current roof of the spire has a stone vault supported by eight stone ribs. The embattled coronet has four crocketed pinnacles, with a larger central pinnacle currently surmounted by a gilded cockerel weathervane (Fig. 53).

The reasons for the truncated state of the spire have been long discussed, there is a local legend that there was a race between the masons at Bisley and Minchinhampton to see who could finish first, won by the Minchinhampton masons changing the design. The spire was certainly in its current state by 1712 when it was illustrated by Kip (Fig. 58). Some antiquaries held that the spire was never finished, whilst others suggested that it was truncated in the 17th century. Bigland wrote in 1792 that 'the Tower, which is placed in the centre, had originally a spire, which was blown down in 1602, when it was finished with an embattled parapet' (Bigland 1792), however he is apparently misquoting earlier documents that suggest that the spire was lowered, rather than blown down. The numerous references in the accounts to inspections, survey, masonry and leadwork on the steeple leading up to 1563 when the payment of large sums to Thomas Slye, master mason of Painswick, and the *'Plommer'* or leadworker suggests that the top was removed because of its instability, although the coronet as we know it now may not have been completed until 1588 when there was a further spate of work.

But why did the spire need reducing? Shepstone reports that having stripped off the plaster from the tower, there were '…Sets on all of [the piers] what (but for the walls of the Church surrounding the Tower on all sides)

Fig. 53 The current weathercock, atop the central crocketed pinnacle of the coronet

must have been considered sufficient to endanger its stability. These were not in consequence of the foundations having given way, it assumed altogether the character of a crush occasioned by the weight or pressure from above, as in all cases commenced at the Springing of the Arches and extending downwards, very few cracks reaching the floor line; this circumstance led to the questioning of the authenticity of the opinion entertained by the inhabitants of the town and which has been currently reported in this history of your county that the Tower when built terminated with a Spire'.[168]

Shepstone could find no evidence for any alterations to the tower and firmly believed that the cracks occurred during building, and the spire had always been in its current form in order to prevent collapse. The informed view of a builder needs to be respected, however the accounts clearly indicate monitoring of developing structural problems and subsequent substantial works on the spire; it seems most likely that following worsening structural problems the upper part was been taken down, probably in *c.*1563.

Work was also needed on the rest of the church, especially the south transept, known as Androse or Ansleyes chapel; in 1558 a glazier was hired in to repair the holes in 'Androse chappelle' using the old glass, but also 42 square foot of new glass; iron glazing bars were made by Phylyp Chamber for the window. The glazier returned in 1559 to repair more windows, and in 1560 he had to be fetched twice to make more repairs, and more iron bars were bought for *feramenta*.

Still in 1560 keys were bought for the steeple, the parlour, the cellar door and locks were mended. In 1561 a key was made for Thomas Barne. In 1562 the church house locks were mended, and Roger Cosbourne, later the church clerk, mended windows, and there was a further payment to glaziers, and for four iron window bars, with a further payment of 3*d.* in 1563. In 1578 a tiler was paid 20*s.* for 30 days work tiling the roof of Ansleyes chapel (a tiled pavement would have been fitted by a pavier), and 16*s.*4*d.* to a mason for the 'water tablinge of Anslowes chapel'.[169] Cosbourne was a useful man about the church, helping the plumber and obtaining sand -presumably casting sand for lead sheet- in 1578, and being paid 'for his daye's worke' in 1579.

Another part of the church, intriguingly still called a chapel in 1567, was also refurbished. This, by a process of elimination, must be the north transept. The chapel was plastered —there are entries for nails, lathes, hair and lime, but also timber and stone, and possibly work on the windows by a glazier. One of the former chapels —still referred to as such in 1589- was tiled and mended by William Webb at a cost of 4*s.*2*d.*. Webb was clearly a roofer as the next year he did further roof work on the church house.

Work on the porch in 1577 included payment of 2s.4d. to the quarrier for stone, the mason received 10*s.* for the battlements and there was work on the porch bench.

A reading desk was built at the pulpit, costing 10*d.* in 1574. This would have been the desk from which the week's Homily and readings would be read out, previously readings would have been from the altar in the Catholic manner. Materials for a new pulpit in 1579 cost 16*d.*, with a further 16*d.* for its construction. In both 1577 and 1579 the font received new cord or rope for suspending its wooden cover. In 1597 a mat was purchased for 'the parson's seat' (6*d.*).

There was also maintenance to be done in the churchyard; in 1567 a stile was made in the graveyard (20*d*), work on the dry stone wall costing 11*s.*4*d.* in 1577. In 1581 the wall was built from 'Mr Windsor's garden' to the stile (16*s.*6*d.*), the 'Mr Windsor' being the Lord Windsor, lord of the Manor. The wall was then continued from the stile to the Parsonage Close, with 26*s.* paid for the digging and carting of the stone. The church gate was mended in 1594, a pillory and cursed stool were set up (4*s.*). The 'stock house' was made in 1573 at a cost of 10*s.*, the 'feet' of the stocks cost 8*d.*, whilst mending the iron parts cost a further sixpence.

The church clock

Although water clocks (*clepsydra*) and sand hourglasses were known from antiquity, the earliest references to mechanical church clocks in England are from monastic and cathedral sites in the 1280s, and it is likely that these were amongst the first escapement controlled clocks in Europe;[170] clocks could chime the hour from the 14th century.[171] Early clocks were housed inside the building at ground level, only later being placed in the tower,[172] the dial itself was originally internal, many external dials being an 18th or 19th century addition and originally clock dials had only the hour hand.[173]

For centuries the church clock would have been the most complex mechanical device in the town and required regular winding, careful upkeep and ongoing maintenance. The date the first clock was installed at Holy Trinity is not known, and it is likely that for several centuries a simple sundial known as a 'scratch' or 'mass' dial, inscribed on a south facing wall, would have been used to tell the time for services. There must have been a clock before 1555 when it is first mentioned as being 'kept' by Richard Rysley for what appears to be an annual payment of 4s (4s. in 1556 but 3s. in 1558) whilst repairs cost an additional 3s. In 1559 Roger Callesborne was keeping the clock, which required a new 'greate rope' for the weights, and the clock needed further repair by 'a stranger' presumably a specialist clockmaker, and again in 1561 when it needed attention twice.

Roger Cosbourne (presumably the same as Callesborne) kept the clock in 1562 when he also mended glass windows in the church. Once more the clock needed repair in 1562, and again in 1567 when it needed a new rope for the weights and the 'clapper' was mended using sixpence of wire. The presence of the clapper, strictly a hammer, indicates the clock chimed the hours at least. Further rope was bought in 1568 and 1581. The clock received further attention in 1582, and was 'kept' by Colsburne, now the clerk, in 1586 and 1587, but by 1599 it was kept by John Flowar.

In 1606 an iron part needed mending, in 1614 the clock needed repairs and new rope, and it was again repaired in 1634; between 1639 and 1646 new cogs were made. The dial was painted in 1662, that entry probably refers to the clockdial but the 'mending of the dyall over the church porch, 6 d' in 1692 may refer to a sundial, whilst in the same year a 'one hour glass' would have been used to time the sermons.

In 1672 'Edward Filder', almost certainly Edward Feilder of Tetbury, was paid £3.6s. for 'for making the clock' –the striking mechanism- with seven shillings spent on the associated timber and carpentry, possibly a stand or

Fig. 54 The clock dial at Holy Trinity with 'VR' and '1897' around the dial; many clocks were built or renovated to mark the occasion of 60 years of Queen Victoria's reign, the north face is marked by ER 2002 for Queen Elizabeth II's Golden Jubilee

cupboard to contain the mechanism. Feilder had been mending Tetbury's clocks since at least 1649; in his will of 1674 he described himself as a 'blacksmith' and left all his working tools to one of his sons, Francis who presumably continued his father's trade.[174]

In 1692 the church installed 'a new clock and watch, and all things belonging to it, £14.18.s.8d'. 'The Watch-part of a Movement is that which serveth to the measuring the hours.... the last part which I shall speak of, is the Clock, which is that part which serveth to strike the Hours...'[175] It is very likely that the new clock was regulated by a pendulum, which had been patented by Christian Hugyens in 1656; pendulums started to be fitted to church clocks around 1670.[176]

Kip's engraving of 1712 shows a diagonally set square dial, with hour and minute hands and the hours marked, the same dial appears to be shown by Relton just before 1842.

The current clock was reconstructed by John Smith and Sons, of the Midland Steam Clock Works, Derby in 1963 and was donated by Alfred Simmons. The current dial is painted black with gold hands and numerals (including the common use of the Roman numeral IIII instead of IV so as to balance the numerals) and with the initials VR and date 1897, for Queen Victoria's Diamond Jubilee set about the quarters of the dial (Fig. 54), with ER 2002 on the north dial commemorating Queen Elizabeth II's Golden Jubilee.

The Seventeenth century

EPISCOPAL VISITATIONS INCREASED under James I and then Charles I and would have been a constant annoyance, inconvenience and expense for the parish, and the churchwardens and sidesmen in particular. The parish was excommunicated in 1606 after failing to appear at court when they had been warned already. The churchwardens had already been warned to appear at Gloucester to answer 'for that our cushion for the pulpit was not prepared' where they were fined; they had previously been called to Cirencester and Stroud. As well as being called to appear at diverse towns including Stonehouse, Painswick, Tetbury, Cirencester and Stroud which of course incurred expenses and fees. The paritor or visiting episcopal official came directly to Holy Trinity to read the summons, check on the parish for recusants -and also press them to acquire the latest ecclesiastical tracts. There was of course a fee, and his expenses to cover.

The 17th-century church was, essentially, an auditorium dominated by the 'triple decker' of the pulpit, reading desk and clerk's desk (Fig. 55) Despite the increasing celebration of the Eucharist, in the later 17th century and onwards through the 18th century it was the sermon, timed by the hourglass, that was the main event of the service. To emphasise the division between preaching and the sacrament, the pulpit was usually placed at the east end of the nave.[177] The interior space was

Fig. 55 The Jacobean 'triple decker' of pulpit, reading desk and clerk's desk at All Saints Wilby, Norfolk. Photo ©Evelyn Simak (cc-by-sa/2.0)

subdivided into the private spaces of box pews and later first-floor galleries; social divisions and class physically manifested in the seating and furniture.

The accounts continue to mark purchases of approved books, a Book of Statutes (2s.2d.) in 1602, and a Communion book, a book of the constitutions and a copy of the newly approved book of Canon Law in 1604. A new bible was acquired in 1613, and its carriage to Minchinhampton paid, the same year a new copy of the *Book of Common Prayer* was bought. The church had a visitation or inspection by the diocese and had to write up its 'presentament' at a cost of 1s.10d. in 1614. A book of constitution was bought in 1622, and a new communion book in 1623. After a long gap, candles were bought in 1624. A book 'to be read in the church in the fast time' was acquired in 1625. In 1630 two 'prayer books for the Queen's safety' were added to the church library, and in 1634 the book of *Canon Law* and constitutions was bought.

In 1634 a book of liberties was bought for 4d. The next year a copy of the book of Homilies and book of Canons were acquired, and a new *Book of Common Prayer* and another book of Canons bought in 1636.

From 1600 wine and bread again appears in the accounts, wine was purchased from Goode Wife Halle in 1600 and 1602, with a further 24 quarts of wine from Cirencester at 20s. in 1600. The bread was bought from George Hill (14d.) in 1600. A specific entry notes wine bought for Christ-tide (a Puritan term for Christmas) for the first time in 1603, the year of James I's accession. In 1606 wine for Easter cost 16s.3d., with 7s.6d. for the rest of the year: communion was clearly taking place more often.

The Ten Commandments painted by Adam Painter in 1594 were superseded in 1606 by new timber boards 'and a ring to hang them from' with the Ten Commandments and 'the degrees of marriage' table of consanguinity. There is mention of pine end tables being mended in 1600. The new layout of the church is reflected in the construction of a pulpit and canopy and a new 'dixit' or reading desk in 1611. The pulpit received a cushion in 1606, again in 1621 and a new mat in 1629. A pulpit cloth was bought in 1635 for £1.17s.1d., suggesting it was an ornately decorated item. The pulpit was mended in 1636, and again in 1648–9.

Laundry and mending of the surplice, clothes and cloth appears in 1606, 1614 and 1615. Richard Deane paid 5s. for the old surplice and a new surplice was made, at the cost of 35s.10d., from 'Holland cloth' linen in 1620. This surplice, and the church cloth, understandably was in need of mending in 1634.

A new 'communion table' was acquired in 1620 and needed repair in 1625. In 1635 a 'flagon' was purchased for the communion table for 12d. A rail was constructed across the chancel in 1635, the price of £1.7s.8d. again suggesting a level of quality of work.

Alterations to the masonry fabric appear to have been limited, and the excavated fragments probably derive from monuments and memorials which would have started to appear more commonly within the church (Fig. 56).

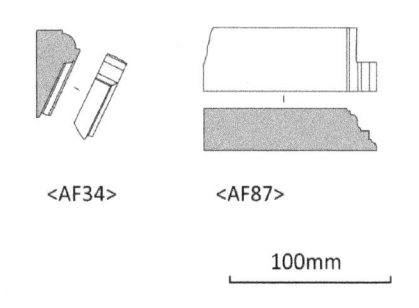

Fig. 56 Renaissance and Neo-Classical mouldings from the excavations

Maintenance

Maintenance on the church roofs was still a major expense and must have been a major pre-occupation for the parish. In 1600 there was work in the roof 'for making one rafter and a stone crest' (12d.), whilst 4 bushels of lime were bought (2s.). In 1603 work on the roof required timber boards, timber, nails and stone. Nineteen pounds of lead was bought, probably for the nave or aisle roofs, and old lead exchanged for new. More new lead was carted from Gloucester in 1606 and taken up to the roof, and the cross taken down. Spare lead was sold to the glazier of Stroud in 1610. In 1608–09 William Rimar mended the weather cock but £1 was spent on a weathercock in 1613, and two iron window bars were fixed in the chapel window.

Work in the tower continued: a loft was made in 1612 for 'bird nestes' and for a new ladder. The surveyor of the church was paid in 1614, and the Lord Bishop's man surveyed the church in 1617, but it is not clear whether the latter was a structural survey, or a visitation and inspection.

In 1618 there was substantial work on the tiled roofs, these included the transepts and chancel, with 3s. for 'gathering of moss' off the roof, £1.6s.2d. paid for tiling, and 2s. for carrying two loads of tiles. Further extensive work was done in 1624, this time on the lead roofs, probably of the nave or aisles, with payment to 'Moses Beaten, for newe casting of six sheets of lead, and for three hundred of new leade, [£]61.14s.8d.; for wine, [£]21.12s.6d.; for carrying the lead to Cissiter [Cirencester], and bringing of it againe, 7s.6d.; to William Rimer, for a days worke, 1s.; to Nicholas Dorbye, for a days worke, 8d.; for healping the lead downe, and drawing of it up againe, 1s.4d.; for our denners at Cissiter, 1s.6d.; for a boord to laye under the lead, 6d'.

In 1628 it was the turn of the tower, with a mason paid £16 for mending the tower, corbel stones were set (14s.) and the plumber was paid £7.10s. for new lead and recasting the old lead from the roof so it could be reused. The tower door received a new lock in 1634, and the church windows were repaired in the same year. The purchase of four bushels of lime suggests the interior of the church may have been whitewashed in 1634, it was washed and painted in 1635 at a cost of £5.17s.3d.

The porch was next. In 1636 Richard Helder was paid £2.5s.8d. for 'buildinge and mendinge and stone for the porch', with a labourer to help him over 9 1/2 days. Another payment of £1.9d. is for 'pulling down the porch and for lead', and £30. 10s. went to the leadworker, with further payments for 'divers workmen, who wrought with the plomer att all tymes' and one William Barnfield who helped for only a day. This appears to be a comprehensive rebuild of the church porch, with associated work to the roof; the sums involve suggest it may have also involved work to the nave or aisles. The new porch partially obscures a large square headed window on the south wall, perhaps intended to illuminate the pulpit and desk, it seems unlikely that the window post-dates the 1634 porch, and it may be that this window, the moulded parapet shown atop the south aisle, and a square headed clerestory window all shown in 19th-century illustrations are all of early 17th century date.

The church stile and wall were fixed in 1604 (4s.), the church-hay wall mended in 1606. The wall about the churchyard and stile were mended in 1617. The southern churchyard wall is partly 16th century in date, with a Tudor arch gate. In 1635 the church path was mended (8d.).

The religious turmoil of the 17th century is reflected in the curious to-ing and fro-ing of two rectors; in 1611 Henry Fowler was due to be rector, but was shortly after replaced by the Puritan Anthony Lapthorne, chaplain to King James, and who had once confronted the King for swearing during a game of bowls 'The King sweares, and the Nobles will sweare, and if the Nobles sweare, the Commons they will sweare, and what a swearing Kingdom we shall have.'[178] Lapthorne was rector from 1613, but the Royalist Fowler returned in 1618, with Lapthorne back in 1622. Fowler was rector yet again from 1636 until 1643 and was targeted by the local Roundhead Captain Jeremy Buck. Fowler died in 1644 shortly after being set upon and attacked in his home by parliamentary soldiers led by Buck, whose memorial is in the south transept.[179]

Commonwealth 1649–60

The churchwarden's accounts continued to be kept during the Commonwealth, listing purchases and payments for maintenance work. Religious matters were not completely ignored - the bible was mended in 1650 at a cost of 12s.8d. and in 1657 an 'Act for the better observation of the Lord's Day' cost the church 1s. In 1650 a survey of church livings lists the rector

Samuel Hiron MA as a 'constant preacher', he received an income of £100 from the parish which had 400 families.[180]

In 1648–9 there are accounts of payments for the poor: travellers, soldiers, Irish, widows, a poor minister's wife with a child, a minister's wife out of the West Indies. The Puritan times and attitudes are not greatly reflected in the accounts, but one entry stands out as an example: in 1658 Robert Woodruff and Edward Trevis were fined 6s 8d for 'profaning of the Lord's day'; the fine was distributed to the Widow Mills and other deserving persons in the parish. In 1651 a new weathercock was bought for 2s. The church roof did not respect Cromwell's Protectorate and in 1652 £20.9s. was spent on leadwork by Thomas Avery the plumber, with a further £1.11s. on scaffold. Keys were bought for the church coffer (1652) and the church door (1653).

A 'table cloth' was bought in 1650, possibly for the communion table, it cost 8s.6d. An *ell* (c.45 inches) of cloth was bought in 1652 for 1s.3d. Francis Maning had a new cushion in 1650, presumably he was a church officer. In 1651 pupils were being taught in the chancel, which had a new stone chimney inserted for a fire.[181]

In 1651 there was an order that the parishioners of Rodborough paid 20s. *per annum* towards repairs of Minchinhampton church.[182]

Restoration: Charles II 1660–1685

The Restoration of the Stuart King Charles II was visibly celebrated in 1661 with the painting of the King's arms on the wall of the church by Richard Bayly, costing £2.15s.

There was repair work by Thomas Smith on the communion table in 1660 and a burst of acquisitions were made following the Restoration; in 1661 the parish bought two Acts of Parliament and prayer books, another copy of the *Book of Common Prayer* was bought in 1662, along with *the 39 Articles of the Church of England*, the Canons and a book from the paritor or visiting ecclesiastical official. The parish register was bound at a cost of 2s.6d. –registers were not kept during the Commonwealth so this may have been a new book, it was rebound in 1676 with more paper added, at a cost of 3s.6d.

An hour-glass was acquired for timing sermons (a replacement would be bought in 1669) and new plate was bought for communion. Bread and wine was listed as a purchase for the first time in years. The new rector Thomas Warmestree DD was to look his best: a new surplice was ordered using 10 ells of Holland cloth costing £3; it was made, washed and delivered for a further 12s.6d.

In 1662 the font was moved, and a new seat for the clerk built. The west door was repaired with new timber boards in 1663, and a new vane bought for the clock. The King's evil is first mentioned in 1663, when the child of Jonathan Harris receives a yard of ribbon, the next year he received 2 silk strings. The King's evil was a name for Scrofula, a bacterial infection of lymph nodes in the neck, and tradition held that the King's touch would cure it, aided no doubt by a gold coin worn around the patient's neck on a ribbon.[183]

Roof maintenance continued with 30 foot of timber wallplates and 70 foot of joists 'for the lead' in 1666. A new communion table was bought in 1669, along with a 'carpet cloth' costing £1. In 1671 the surplice was washed three times, and again the next year when a 'book of articles' –the 39 Articles- was bought. A desk was set up in the chancel 'where the two books are chained'. In 1675 another copy of the *Book of Common Prayer* was bought.

Entries referring to a visit by the bishop in 1676 may be for consecration of the bell brought from Beverston, but the visitation was surely for something more significant: a seat set up for the Bishop cost 19s.8d., and was hung with seven yards of linsey woolsey (7s.) a coarse twill with a linen warp and a woollen weft. The same year there was yet more leadwork, but also 'plastering over the gallery' presumably the ceiling above a first-floor gallery.

In 1677 a new copy of the *Homilies* was bought and 'a book for the keeping of the fast'. Another church register book was bought (10s.) in 1683, and a new copy of the *Book of Common Prayer* in 1687. In 1682 there is record of purchase of a new silver communion bowl and 'for changing the old one' at a cost of £4.12s.6d. The pewter plates were also changed. Two chalices survive from this date, each inscribed 'This with one more of the same belongs to the Parish of Minchinhampton in Glostershire 1681'.[184]

William and Mary 1689–1702

The accession was marked by the repainting of the 'King's arms' and new soft furnishings in the form of a new pulpit cloth and cushion, with 'flocks, galoon, looping and making' at a cost of £9.7s.6d. Flock work had been used for ecclesiastical drapery since the 16th century,[185] whilst galoon is a narrow braided fabric trimming usually with metallic threads; the new furnishings were clearly sumptuous. New candlesticks were bought at a cost of £3.5s. and the communion table mended.

A curiosity in the accounts is the payment of three shillings in 1694 'towards the redeeming of 6 men from the Turks' presumably captured by the Barbary corsairs.[186]

Queen Anne and the Georgians

THE PROCLAMATION OF Queen Anne was marked by eight shillings of celebratory wine, whilst the accounts show the proclamation and coronation of George I was marked by multiple celebrations with trumpets, bells, 'wine, beer and cider' and the building of a stage.

The 18th century church saw little change externally beyond the addition of at least three external stairs used to access the first-floor galleries that proliferated throughout this period.

The Hanoverian Royal coat of arms was painted on wooden boards and displayed in the church, the heraldry predates the Act of Union of 1801 and was used by Georges I–III (Fig. 57).

Fig. 57 The Hanoverian Royal coat of arms, from 1714–1800

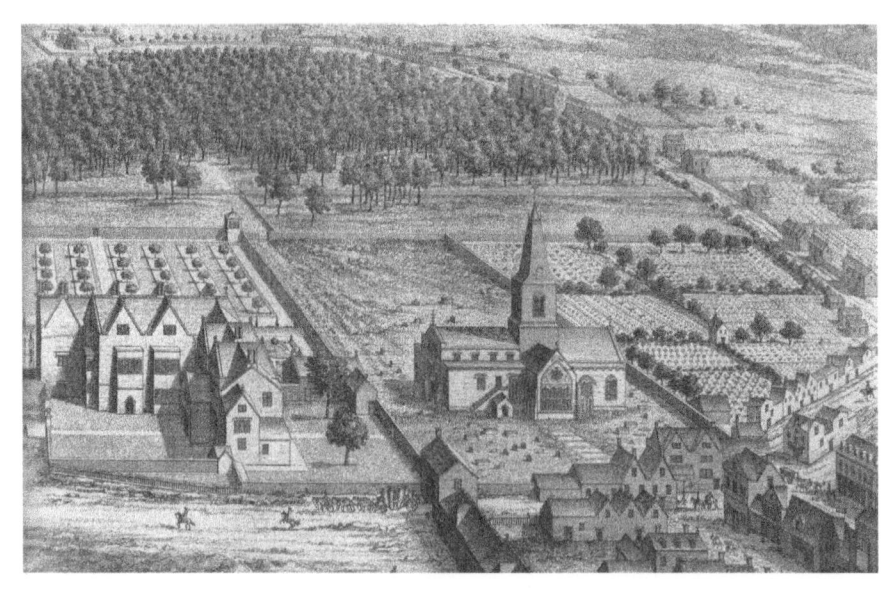

Fig. 58 Kip's Minchinhampton in 1712, showing the manor house, church and town

Fig. 59 Detail of the church from Kip's view of 1712

The manor had passed to Thomas Hickman, nephew of Thomas Lord Windsor, on his death in 1642, however he was forced to sell the manor and advowson, it being bought by Samuel Sheppard in 1651 who enlarged the steward's house next the church into a new Jacobean manor shown in Kip's engraving of 1712 (Fig. 58, Fig. 59). With the manor came the advowson -the right to present a candidate for rector- which was used to appoint Samuel's son Phillip Shephard as rector of Minchinhampton in 1720 (Fig. 60). The Sheppards prospered for nearly a hundred years before the collapse of the wool trade and the cost of construction of Gatcombe Park in 1771–4 caused increasing debts. The old manor house next to the church was sold to William Whitehead in 1804, who demolished it before himself getting in financial distress. The Sheppards sold Avening manor in 1812, and Minchinhampton manor was sold to the political economist David Ricardo in 1814.[187]

Fig. 60 The Revd Philip Sheppard 1695–1768

Pews, galleries and sittings

In the medieval period the congregation would have largely stood, with a bench around the nave wall for those unable to do so who would 'go to the wall.' Separate areas could be used by different groups: the north 'Rodborough's Aisle'[188] of the church was set aside for parishioners from Rodborough, who paid 20 shillings a year towards Holy Trinity,[189] and most parishioners would have their customary place.

By the 16th century it is likely that there would have been a large number of wooden benches, pews and seats inside the nave, at least for those that could afford them. From the early 17th century benches were replaced by pews, with box pews by the 18th century, including private seatings: 'Pews ran in all directions and the body of the church was full of odd corners and alleys.'[190] At the same time the focus of the church service shifted to the lengthy weekly sermon, delivered from a pulpit which formed part of the 'triple decker' along with the reading desk, and the clerk's desk. It was situated just within the nave by the northwest corner of the crossing but it would have been invisible, and perhaps the sermon and readings inaudible, to many in church. The sermon would have been a lengthy affair, timed with an hourglass, surely influencing the building of the numerous private and increasingly enclosed pews throughout the church.

The churchwardens' accounts contain several references to internal seating, and to galleries that were built to house an increasing population. A plan of the church at 1842 shows the layout of both pews and galleries some of which would have been hundreds of years old by then, having been built gradually to a variety of designs. The pews and galleries would have been constructed of timber by the town's carpenters, and many would have been carved or decorated, perhaps the earlier seats had linenfold panelling or carved bench ends, later on they would be in Jacobean or Georgian styles. Some pews would have required a Faculty from the Diocese. Seats would usually be assigned by the churchwarden, often to a property rather than a person, and the family and servants would sit together (as well as perhaps their dogs).[191] When a church was rebuilt the seating was often assigned as a reward to donors, whilst some pews or galleries were assigned to children, singers or other groups.

In 1563 nine pence paid for two seats 'and a panne', and two shillings paid for making Mr Vgnolles' seat in the church in 1565 may be for the church officials rather than private pews for parishioners, but we do know that by 1632 there were already private pews in the church. Surviving records of the sale and purchase of pews date back to the 1630s when there was a flurry of activity across the church that might indicate a concerted programme of seating. In these records a 'seat' is not an individual place, but a space that could accommodate several people, usually in an enclosed box pew. The wording of some records suggests that there were already rows of seats or pews: in 1632 four seats were purchased by individuals who each paid five shillings for them and their heirs 'for the next seat, except one, as we come in' the west door. In 1635 four more seats were taken on the right-hand side of the west door at a cost of 12d. each, and a seat was allowed next to the middle alley of the nave.

In the north aisle Jeremy Buck Senior, possibly the same that would later fatally attack the Revd Fowler, 'at his own proper cost and charge, built two seats for himself and his succeeding posterity on the north side of the church of Minchinhampton' in 1633, they cost Buck two shillings. At the same time Joan Fletcher had a new seat built for her and her daughter next to Buck's seats. Fletcher's seats were linked to her dwelling house near the market cross, a pattern that would be followed with private pews linked to a property as much as a family.

In 1634 the churchwardens' accounts had listed expenditure of 7s.4d. on timber boards, matting and 'marking of the seats at the lower end of the church for the officers to sit in,' this excluded the seats that had cost Francis Manning and three others 20s., suggesting that this was a block of seating or pews that was allocated partly for officials and was partly available for private purchase. In 1664 John Manning, possibly a relative of Francis 'hath erected and built one seat, upon his own cost and charge, for his wife and family, or any other persons as him shall please there being, and having the ancient rite and title to that seat. This seat standing and going to the pillar that stand near unto porch door upon the left hand as we do come in, and so reaches from that pillar to the font in that alley'.

By the mid-17th century it is likely that much of the interior of the church was largely divided up into pews, benches and seats, with the later plan of the interior suggesting a polyglot mix of different styles and types of pew, with many privately constructed box pews as well as seating for those without the wealth, or inclination, to buy a seating.

Disputes arose between parishioners over the seats as early as 1657, when Daniel Gilman and Antony Keene both claimed a seat and a hearing was held which resolved the issue in Gilman's favour. Many pews were marked by brass plates engraved with the names of the owners, although there were some 'Free Sittings'. There were sufficient transfers of pews and sittings between parishioners to make a Transfer Book necessary by at least 1821 -although sadly it has not survived. Concern and bickering over seats continued with the new church in 1841 when a great deal of time was taken to record who had which seat in the old church and attempting to mediate disputed claims (Appendix 3).

Space inside the church was clearly getting cramped, probably not helped by the division of the interior space into individual box pews. The solution, as in many churches, lay with the construction of timber galleries on the first floor. Galleries were also a solution to problems with raising capital at this time, providing a low cost way to expand room for increasing congregations.

At Minchinhampton these were largely accessed from external stairs which are shown on several views of the church and would have required doorways to be cut through the walls of the church. A 'new seat' recorded in 1637 cost the huge sum of £3.2s., this is unlikely to have been a single pew or seat and may be a first-floor gallery; the first definite reference to a gallery appears to have been built in 1670 by the churchwardens William Nickolls and George Smalle, 'at their own proper cost and charges, and is for their own use and those whom they let it unto for ever'. The next year Samuel Barnfield paid 20s. for the perpetual right of two persons to sit in the second seat 'at the coming into the gallery in Hampton church of the right hand', in 1680 John Fowler, 'broadweaver' paid for two seat rooms (box pews) in the gallery at Hampton, in the back seat. In 1716 two churchwardens, Daniel Clutterbuck and Jeremiah Day, built a small new gallery some 12 foot by 10 ½–14 foot in the 'east end' of the church. It was 'next the wall wherein they and their families and tenants may sit and stand and kneel to hear and attend divine service.' Later evidence suggests that the gallery was in the north transept by the tower stair.[192]

In 1841 Vestry clerk and schoolmaster Fenning Parke made carefully measured plans of the ground floor and galleries, marking each sitting, with dimensions, and the location of their doors and benches (Fig. 61, Fig. 62). There were large galleries in both nave aisles and at the west end of the nave, in both transepts -including one behind the organ which was housed in the north transept, and even in the chancel. Doors, accessed via external stairs, are marked in the south wall of the south aisle, and the south wall of the chancel, with two doors let into the windows on the east side of the south transept.[193]

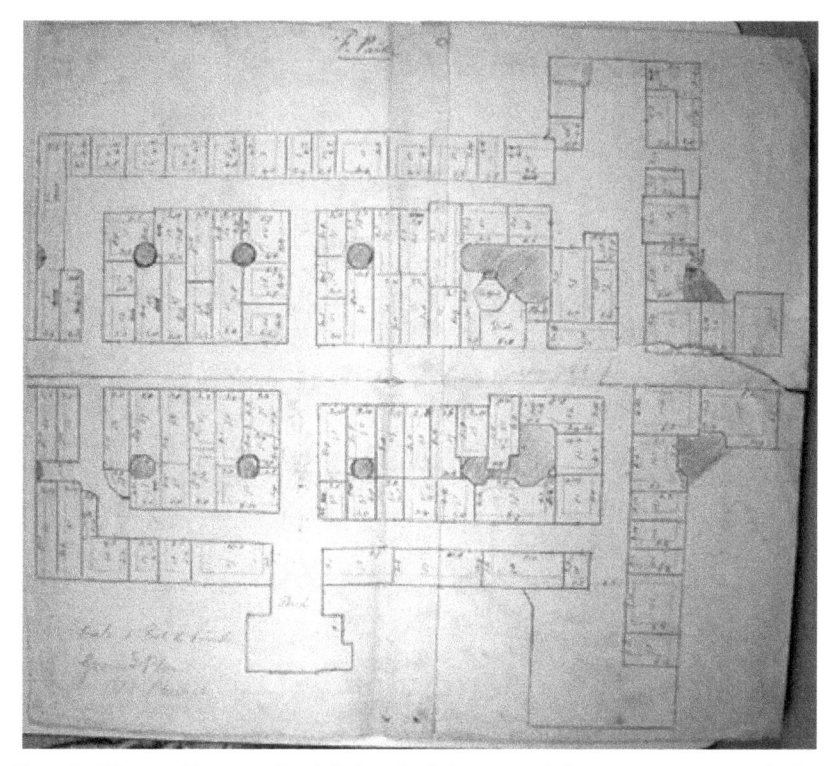

Fig. 61 Plan in Fenning Parke's hand of the ground floor seatings at 1842 P217 CW4/9

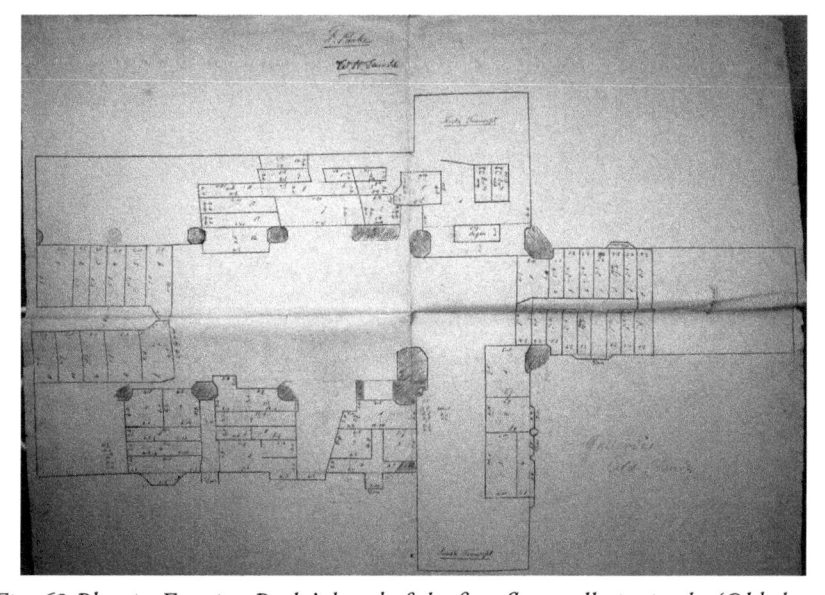

Fig. 62 Plan in Fenning Parke's hand of the first-floor galleries in the 'Old church' P217 CW4/9

Fenning Parke 1801–1872

Fenning Parke was the son of a wine merchant from East Smithfield, London. In 1818 at the age of 16 he was appointed by Ricardo Snr as Master of the school for boys and girls in the Market House, which was owned by Ricardo. In 1824 Parke married local girl Elizabeth Ogden and they lived at 33 Tetbury Street; a year later he was appointed Parish Clerk. Parke was very involved in town affairs and was a founding member of the Mutual Improvement Association, which promoted concerts, lectures and other public events in the Market House. Parke had a keen interest in local history, giving public lectures and recording local history,[194] starting in 1835 he collated the 'Minchinhampton Chronicles' a scrapbook of local history, lists, documents and newspaper clippings.[195] Parke was churchwarden from 1824 until his death in 1872. Playne records that it was Parke who rescued the churchwardens' accounts, which were in a neglected state and many other documents.[196]

HE Relton's engraving shows the very edge of a set of stairs leading up to a square headed door inserted into a window of the chancel, this would have been the access to a gallery that spanned the width of the west end of the chancel. There was another external stair on the west wall for the west gallery, and two stairs on the south wall for the south. Upstairs seating in the north transept and north aisle was reached by internal stairs in the northwest corner of the north transept and possibly another steep stair by the east wall; a stair must have existed in the south transept.

Although written in 1876, thirty years after the rebuilding of Holy Trinity, this description in the Church Times on the recently completed restoration of the nearby church of St George, King's Stanley, reflects the views of the Gothic Revivalists, probably the Revd John Gibson, but also paints an evocative pen portrait of a Georgian church interior church interior:

> Originally a Norman church, which, though small, was one of great beauty and dignity, it was enlarged in the fifteenth century by the building of an aisle, with an arcade of four arches, in the nave and two in the chancel. Suffering with hundreds of churches from the blighting influences of post-Reformation times, when the loss of definiteness of belief led to the cultivation of a comfortable religion, this church became gradually disfigured with huge pews, some being green-baized parlours, others resembling grim fortifications, with galleries, a three decker pulpit, monuments and hatpegs, a flat ceiling spanning the

whole length of the building, and reducing it in appearance to a Puritanical auditorium. Outside, the walls were flanked by numerous flights of stone staircases leading to the many gallery-boxes. The combined result of all this was a building which for unsightliness could scarcely be surpassed. All, however, is changed now, every disfigurement is removed.[197]

The proliferation of galleries and box pews would have led to a cluttered and labyrinthine interior with at least three separate external stairs leading to the upper galleries, a drawing of St Lawrence, Hurstpierpoint from 1799 gives an impression of how the space would have been divided and subdivided (Fig. 63). The pews of the wealthy could sometimes be a secluded haven, with high timber sides, plush cushions, drapes to keep out drafts, hooks for coats and hats and even heating. Most were far simpler and less comfortable places to listen to the lengthy sermons of the Revd Cockin, timed on the hourglass, where his identification of the sins of one's neighbours would perhaps form some amusement.

Fig. 63 Interior of the church of St. Lawrence, Hurstpierpoint in 1799 showing galleries and box pews (copied by Lydia Hamper in 1845 from an original by William Hamper, FSA)

The bells of Holy Trinity

Church bells were originally hung on a simple spindle and were rung by pulling a rope; later experimentation led to each bell being hung on a quarter wheel, later a half wheel. By the Reformation church bells were increasingly hung on a whole wheel, allowing the bell to rotate through 360° and offering both greater control and increased possibilities, especially when rings of bells were combined. In tandem with the development of bell wheels the methods and rules of bell ringing were also developed with increasingly complex patterns being rung, especially from the later 17th century.[198] Bell ringing became a popular activity with the bonus of a small payment for ringers, usually speedily converted into ale, and competitions sponsored by local taverns; the bands assumed a fair degree of autonomy up in the ringing chamber and heavy drinking and rowdiness was commonplace.

We do not know when the first bells rang out at Holy Trinity but whilst the Norman tower may well have been hung with one or more bells, the 14th century tower was certainly constructed with a bell-loft fitted with louvred baffles.

The oldest bell at Holy Trinity is not however in the belfry but set in the external corner of the chancel and south transept. A small bell, 17" in diameter, it is dated 1515. The bell is cast with IHS monograms, crosses and the legend 'Dame Alys de Hamton A°M^L V^E X^V', the 'de' being later struck through (Fig. 64). AT Playne relates that it originally hung in one of the

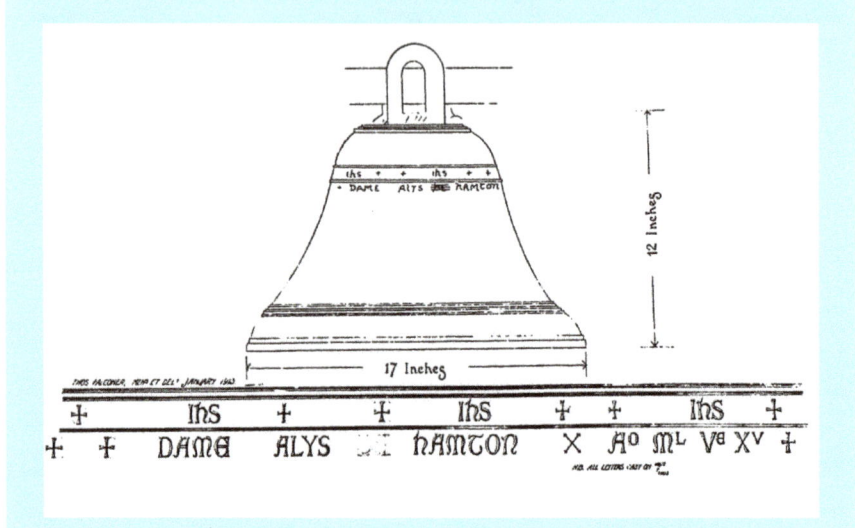

Fig. 64 Dame Alys de Hamton's bell, dated 1515[199]

market-houses, and when that was demolished in 1806 the bell moved to Longfords House as part of a turret clock; it was given to the church c.1920.[200]

Dame Alys died in September 1516 and she is mentioned on a memorial brass that is nominally to her father John Hampton. The Hamptons were a family of wealthy wool merchant: John's elder brother Sir William was a fishmonger in London, rising to become an Alderman, and was Lord Mayor in 1472. On William's death John inherited his considerable property, which then passed to Alys on his death. Dame Alys lived in Minchinhampton and was a Sister of the Chapter of the Abbey of Sion, where she placed her estates in 1508.[201]

It is probable that the bell was a gift to a chantry chapel the year before her death. As well as the bell, Alys left money for distribution to 'three poor persons in a certain almshouse' as well as for eight loads of firewood a year.[202] A 'saunte bel' (saint's bell) is mentioned in the churchwarden's accounts for 1555, and in 1560 the 'little bell', renamed for the Protestant times, was hung. Alys's bell appears to have originated as a chantry bell, survived the Reformation, the Marian revival, the return of Protestantism, and found its way -via a long stay at one of the market houses and Longfords, back to Holy Trinity some four hundred years after it was cast, and where it is still in use as the sanctus bell during communion (Fig. 65).

Fig. 65 Dame Alys de Hampton's bell, still in use after over 500 years

Bells are mentioned on an almost annual basis in the churchwardens' accounts, their maintenance, repair and replacement being a regular and sometimes considerable ongoing expense, although repairs could also be an opportunity to upgrade and improve the ring. Bells figure from the first year of the accounts: in 1555 the bellropes were shortened (5d.) and three new ropes and a 'saunte bel roppe' (possibly for Alys Hamton's chantry bell) were acquired at 6s.6d.[203] In 1558 the bells were overhauled: John Newman was paid 6s.8d. to make a new wheel for the second bell, fix another wheel and for 'trussing' the bells, other payments list nails, ironwork and timber for the bells. Later in the same year Newman returned and mended the 'grett belle whyelle', installed the third bell with a new bolt, and Phylyp Chamber made a 'boltt and a keaye for the same belle'. Clearly there was a ring of at least three bells hung on wheels in the belfry: the Great Bell -probably a tenor, and the second and third bells.

All that work was not the end of the expense and the very next year Wyllam Passelowe had to be called in to mend the clapper, with further repairs to clappers in 1560 and 1561. By 1559 two of the bell ropes had worn out and were replaced at 2s. a piece. Bell ropes are subject to a great deal of wear and although they could be locally repaired by splicing, they need (as is still the case) frequent replacement so it is no wonder they figure on a nearly annual basis in the accounts over the next three hundred years.

Another recurring cost was for the leather straps or baldricks that fit inside the iron strap which attach the clapper to the bell, these are subject to heavy wear every time the bell is rung and needed regular replacement. Baldricks were usually made of horsehide, which was bought in and made up locally; they are mentioned eight times in the accounts between 1555 and 1582.[204]

In 1562 a bell was mended and the clappers needed new rope and in 1567 a bell wheel needed repair and a bell was trussed by Thome Chambers (possibly a relation of Phylyp Chambers), helped by Edward Unnan.

A new bell was planned in 1568 -the bellfounder was paid an advance of five shillings of 'earnest money' to secure his services, with a further 20s. and a payment of 10s. 'for certain Iron aboute the belles' possibly for strapping up cracked bells. In 1574 a new clapper was bought.

The bell-loft needed repair in 1580, this required substantial timbers that had to be brought in by ox team -the ploughmen were paid with 20d. of beer. Once on site the timbers had to be hauled up the tower, costing a further 22d.

A clapper was repaired in 1583, and the clapper of the great bell replaced in 1610. In 1614 the clerk was paid 2s. for helping the bellfounder when he set up the bells, presumably this relates to another spate of work on the bells as in 1615 four new ropes were brought from Bristol, and three and a half days spent mending the bells. In 1620 the great bell needed repair once more.

In 1633 the costly decision was made to replace the bells and on 15th May Thomas Lord Windsor pledged £10 towards the new bells 'out of my rents of Minchinhampton', however raising the rest of the funds and engaging a founder took time and it was not until 1635 that five new bells were cast by Roger Purdey in Horsley, some three miles from Minchinhampton. The accounts show this expensive project in some detail: 'the macking of all the new frames and all other the appurtenanties belonging to the belles and frames' cost £60, with an additional 8s. going to 'Mr. Taylor, of Bristoll, for ropes'. Such a considerable expense clearly needed a proper contract and Purdey was bound by bonds and covenants prepared on parchment by a Mr Brothers. The churchwardens themselves rode to Bristol to purchase the 200 pounds of brass, hiring horses to bring it to Horsley where the metal was cast into the new bells whilst the clerks enjoyed 'meate and drinke for oure selfes'.

The new bells appear to have been trouble free for over thirty years which must have been both a great relief and vindication of the expenditure. Then in 1669 a bell wheel was made or repaired and in 1672 a new bell carriage was made up, in 1674 Samuel Cambridge was paid 'for timber to stock the great bell' with further payments for ironwork and other work about the bells. In 1675 a bell was exchanged with the church at Beverston, $4^{1/2}$ miles to the south; the Beverston bell was the heavier, so Minchinhampton paid £7.19s.3d. for the additional bronze. Carriage of the bell to Minchinhampton cost 5s. for transportation in 1676 when there was further 'worke about the bells', presumably the Beverston bell, and yet again new bell ropes purchased. In 1693 the casting of a new bell and a clapper by Abraham Rudhall of Gloucester cost £28.15s.6d.

In March 1825 the Vestry Minutes recorded that the tenor bell 'now lie split in the Tower' and needed recasting, which was done by John Rudhall of Gloucester.[205] Fenning Parke recounts that 'When the Bells were ringing at a Wedding 6th September 1824 the Clapper of the Tenor Bell fell out —One of the Ringers a Blacksmith procured a sledge hammer and struck the bell which of course split —It was recast at Gloucester in 1825 – at a cost of £39.0.0'.[206]

Fenning Parke recorded the inscriptions on the six bells in 1834:[207]

1 'Peace and good neighbourhood' Abraham Rudhall, 1719
2 'Prosperity to this Town and Parish' Abraham Rudhall, 1719
3 'John Rowden, Curate' Abraham Rudhall, 1719
4 'Prosperity to the Church of England Nath. Perks & James Parker Chwardens Abraham Rudhall, 1756
5 'A Townsend & G. Ralph, Churchwardens 1797 J Rudhall fecit' Abraham Rudhall, 1797
6 'Jos. Iles and Jacon Scuse, Churchwardens; John Rudhall Fecit' John Rudhall 1825

The 1756 bell did not survive the 1842 rebuilding, being replaced by a bell cast by T. Mears inscribed *'Geo Playne and Fras. Chambers (Churchwardens)'*. Currently the church has a ring of six bells, a D♯ of 1719 by Abraham Rudhall II, a B by Abel Rudhall (1756), an A♯ (1797) and an F♯ (1825) by John Rudhall, and a C♯ (1906) and a G♯ by John Taylor and Company (Fig. 66).[208]

Fig. 66 The bells of Holy Trinity

The first mention of payment for bellringing is in 1615 when the clerk was paid 13s.4d., presumably for the year. In 1655 ringing the 'winter bell' at 4 and 8 o'clock cost 15s. The bells rung out morning and evening, in

1833 this was at 8pm 'every Week day evening from Michaelmas to Lady Day: - The Bell to be rung at 5 o'clock in the morning on Week days and at 7 in the evening on Sundays'.[209]

As well as to ring the hours, the bells rang out to mark royal events, military victories and anniversaries including November the 5th, with many of these celebratory occasions recorded in the accounts. In 1666 the bells rang to mark Holmes' naval victory in the second Anglo-Dutch war, costing 2s., in 1705 ringing to mark the victory at the battle of Ramillis cost 7s.6d., whereas ringing 'at the Thanksgiving for the Union' only cost 5s. Major events such as the proclamation of George I in 1714 were clearly large festive and communal celebrations, the church paying for construction of a stage, the ringing of bells, a trumpeter and musicians.

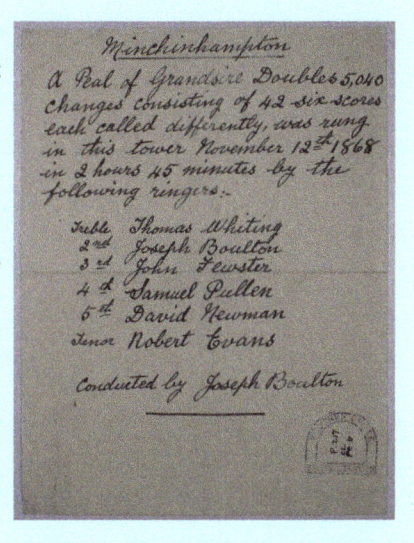

Fig. 67 Record of a peal of Grandsire Doubles from 1868 P217/CL/6

Minchinhampton in 1842

IN THE 18TH and early 19th century Minchinhampton's prosperity was largely based on wool and cloth and to a great extent the ups and downs of the wool trade dictated the town's fortunes. Whilst the market was the hub where sheep farmers would meet merchants, the wool and cloth industry extended into most corners of the parish. The clothiers drew on a web of workers: wool was put out to be spun into yarn which went on to be woven by hand in the cottages, returning to the mills to be dyed and finished. As the industrial revolution progressed new technologies were introduced and by the 1830s the use of automated looms began to make most of the hand weavers redundant. Strikes and unrest accompanied this advance -most notably in 1824 when the cavalry were called out.[210] In 1824 the Vestry estimated over half the population of Minchinhampton parish were employed in the wool trade and that the Poor Rate in the parish was ten times as high as in nearby arable parishes.[211] By the 1830s the wool industry in Gloucestershire was in severe decline and many weavers were in distress, leading to emigration to America, Australia, New Zealand and Bradford, often financially assisted by the Vestry.[212]

The population of Minchinhampton also followed the wool trade and increased rapidly in the 18th century from an estimated 1,800 inhabitants in c.1710[213] to 3,419 at the first census of 1801. The population then rocketed to 4,907 in 1821 before growth slowed with the declining wool trade. There were 5,114 people in 1831 and by 1841 the population had dropped slightly to 4,887.[214]

The increased population inevitably placed pressure on seating in the Old Church and the addition of galleries could be seen as a direct response. By the 18th century however Holy Trinity was not the only place of worship in Minchinhampton: there was a Quaker Meeting House by 1731[215] and a Baptist meeting house in Workhouse Lane was built in 1765, replaced in 1834 by a chapel (built on Tetbury Street on land sold by David Ricardo for a nominal sum of five shillings). The Baptists had a burial ground at Chapel Lane with the first burial there 20th April 1828. The Methodist divine the Revd George

MINCHINHAMPTON IN 1842　　　　　　　　　　　　　　　　　　93

Whitfield had preached at Minchinhampton, including to a crowd of about 12,00 on Hampton Common one evening in March 1743, however Methodists were not loved by all, and the house and person of Minchinhampton resident and preacher Mr Adams was repeatedly attacked by a mob in the 1740s.[216]

The Georgian church at 1842

Beyond the proliferation of galleries and stairs there was little development of the structure of the external church in the 17th or 18th centuries beyond the addition of a new porch in 1636 and the construction of several external stairs (Fig. 68). A number of early drawings and paintings show the outside of the church as it stood before the rebuilding of 1842 and the earliest, Kip's engraving of the manor house and church, dates to before 1712 (Fig. 58) and shows the church set in a large churchyard; the part of which furthest north appears relatively unused for burial, although with some memorials including table tombs. The southern part of the churchyard has numerous memorials and tombs, a wide, stepped path leads from the south transept down to Bell Lane and there is an open area to the west of the church. There are no trees shown within the churchyard which is bounded by a stone wall, with the manor house, its formal gardens and park to the west. There are

Fig. 68 Plan of the church in 1841. The plan also shows tombs and graves recorded in the watching briefs.

buildings shown along the southern side of the churchyard, possibly part of the butchers Shambles that had been located there since the medieval period.

The church is shown in some detail, and the engraving is an important source for the external appearance of the pre-1841 church. The church is cruciform in plan, with a chancel with two-light windows in the south wall, one set above a doorway. There is no buttress shown at the south-eastern corner of the buttress unlike on later drawings. The chancel ridge is shown at the same height as the nave ridge, which has a clerestory of four square-headed windows. The west end of the nave has two windows at height, with a stone stair leading up to a first-floor doorway for the internal west gallery. The corner of a north aisle is just shown. The south aisle has two windows, one a small two-light window, the other probably the large rectangular four-light window shown on later illustrations, and which would have flooded the pulpit in light. Both windows are set within square-headed hood moulds. On the south side of the south aisle there is a large stone stair leading up to a door above the porch which leads into the first-floor internal gallery.

Sadly there are no internal views of the church, and we must glean what information we can from the plans of the 'Old Church', surviving monuments and archaeological remains. Although mostly concerned with the internal sitting arrangements of the church, the plans –probably made by

Fig. 69 Painting of the church from before the 1842 rebuilding

Fig. 70 Engraving of 1838 by A. Smith, printed by George Rowe. From the collections of Museum in the Park, Stroud STGCM Y1992_112

Fenning Parke- do indicate the internal layout of the church and the location of windows and doors.[217]

Paintings and drawings from immediately before the rebuild are more detailed (Fig. 69) and show a church that has suffered numerous small and clumsily uncoordinated changes since the 14th century, especially the addition of the external stairs and inserted windows. Since the time of Kips' engraving in 1712 there is clear sign of structural distress, with the south-eastern corner of the chancel now supported by a massive buttress. A stone stair has been added along the west side of the south transept leading to another door into the church and the south gallery. A chimney is visible on the west side of the south transept, presumably from a stove or fireplace in the southwest corner.

Two engravings, by A Smith in 1838, and HE Relton in 1841, add further detail: the sun-dial set up on the south transept in 1833, a memorial plaque on the south wall of the chancel, another possible memorial by the door of the porch, the very edge of the steps up to the door to the chancel gallery, the detail of the lead rainwater goods and the apparent disrepair of the lead roof of the nave, a chimney in the south transept, and the graveyard with iron railings around a tomb (Fig. 70, Fig. 12).

The church in 1842 was showing its age, but it was also showing the minor accretionary developments of a medieval building that had evolved gradually to meet an expanding and changing congregation and the changes in rite from medieval catholic church to the Church of England. The building exhibits a somewhat jarring mix of medieval and 17th century, with the external stairs and the interior crammed with memorials, with signs and Decalogues, wooden box pews, galleries and the looming triple decker pulpit.

This is a very different church interior to the pre-Reformation building and its sumptuous decoration, its candles, incense and statuary, its streamers and processions, or to the early post-Reformation with the altars stripped and an austere plainness -where the changes to the church were in many ways an absence, a removal, rather than an addition. The 17th and 18th centuries had left the church with a cluttered accumulation of small changes, there had been no major unified campaign of rebuilding as with the previous Norman or Decorated schemes. The church interior would have looked very odd to many of us who are used to the Victorian Gothic Revival idea of a church, which harked back to the medieval church, but in 1842 those ideas had yet to take hold.

Reverend William Cockin †1841

Fig. 71 The Reverend William Cockin[218]

Originally the curate, William Cockin was appointed rector of Minchinhampton in 1806 by Joseph Pitt (Fig. 71). AT Playne tells a story that when the living became vacant 'Mr Pitt expressed a doubt, in Mr Cockin's hearing, as to whom he should appoint, and, as the story goes, Cockin immediately said: "I bet you £1,000 you don't appoint me"'. Cockin was also rector at the nearby parish of Cherington and would leave his horse outside Holy Trinity so he could gallop to St Nicholas for the next service.[219]

Cockin was described by AT Playne as being a 'very good natured, hospitable man, very charitable to the poor, and a great favourite with his parishioners, many of whom he used to rebuke by name in his sermons'. He lived at The Lammas, which had been bequeathed to him by two elderly parishioners, and on his death on March 3rd 1841, aged 75 leaving a large cellar of wine (Fig. 72).[220]

Fig. 72 Cockin's memorial in the church

The lead up to rebuilding

By the mid-19th century many of England's parish churches were physically in a poor state of affairs; the major church building and alteration programmes of the medieval period largely ended with the Reformation and many parish churches were showing their age. Holy Trinity was no exception with late 18th and early-19th century illustrations showing a church propped up by newly built buttresses and stairs, with a hotchpotch of inserted windows. As well as its physical state, and despite its many galleries, the church may have been inadequate for the expanding population of the parish, two factors that were largely behind the great wave of ecclesiastical rebuilding that swept through England in the Victorian period.

Following his father's death in 1823 David Ricardo the younger took up position as 'lord of the manor,' organising and funding many local projects including new churches, schools and almshouses. Whilst Holy Trinity was in poor repair, Ricardo built a new church at Amberley in 1836 and at Brimscombe in 1839–40,[221] the parish was subdivided into four benefices in 1840.[222]

As early as November 1836 wide-ranging repairs to the church were being actively planned, and alongside this ran a subscription for a new organ. A proposed increase in the Church Rate to fund the repairs had been voted down by parishioners, leading to the churchwardens distributing a printed leaflet setting out the 'FACTS' -as they saw them: the rate was intended for repairs to the church, and not for a new organ, re-pewing the church, or erecting a new gallery as had been stated in 'VERY EXAGERATED statements (Fig. 73).' On the reverse of the copy of the leaflet in Gloucestershire Archives are hand-written extracts from a speech by Lord John Russell on the Rate and a quote from the Christian Advocate: 'Dissenters should put forth their whole strength on the occasion: The Church Rate gone, the Establishment will be an easy prey'![223]

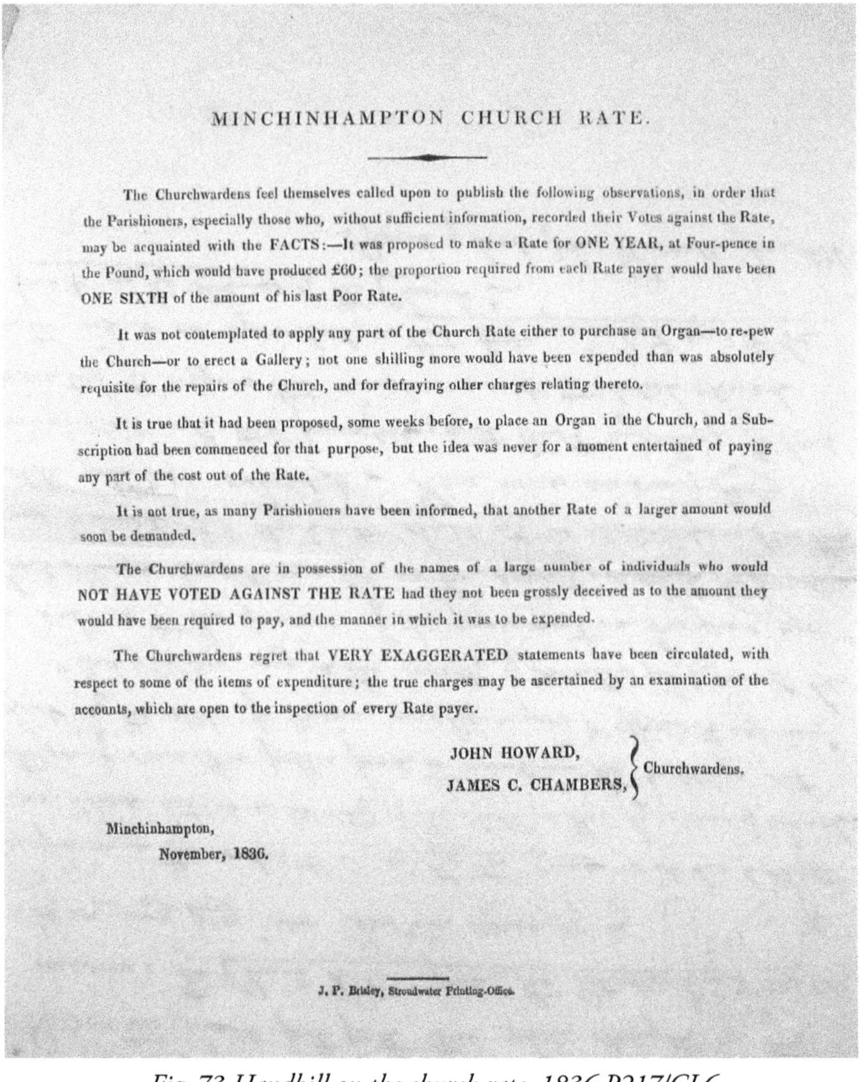

MINCHINHAMPTON CHURCH RATE.

The Churchwardens feel themselves called upon to publish the following observations, in order that the Parishioners, especially those who, without sufficient information, recorded their Votes against the Rate, may be acquainted with the FACTS:—It was proposed to make a Rate for ONE YEAR, at Four-pence in the Pound, which would have produced £60; the proportion required from each Rate payer would have been ONE SIXTH of the amount of his last Poor Rate.

It was not contemplated to apply any part of the Church Rate either to purchase an Organ—to re-pew the Church—or to erect a Gallery; not one shilling more would have been expended than was absolutely requisite for the repairs of the Church, and for defraying other charges relating thereto.

It is true that it had been proposed, some weeks before, to place an Organ in the Church, and a Subscription had been commenced for that purpose, but the idea was never for a moment entertained of paying any part of the cost out of the Rate.

It is not true, as many Parishioners have been informed, that another Rate of a larger amount would soon be demanded.

The Churchwardens are in possession of the names of a large number of individuals who would NOT HAVE VOTED AGAINST THE RATE had they not been grossly deceived as to the amount they would have been required to pay, and the manner in which it was to be expended.

The Churchwardens regret that VERY EXAGGERATED statements have been circulated, with respect to some of the items of expenditure; the true charges may be ascertained by an examination of the accounts, which are open to the inspection of every Rate payer.

JOHN HOWARD,
JAMES C. CHAMBERS, } Churchwardens.

Minchinhampton,
November, 1836.

J. P. Brisley, Stroudwater Printing-Office.

Fig. 73 Handbill on the church rate, 1836 P217/CL6

There was clearly widespread discussion (however erroneous) of the future of the church throughout the town, and this was linked by the establishment to radical ideas. The timing of the vote could not have been worse: the Church Rate Abolition Society had been founded that year and feelings were running high across the country. Concern was clearly high on both sides, a majority of the parishioners felt that they would be asked to pay increasing amounts for repairs and improvements to the church, whilst the churchwardens -and presumably the Revd Cockin, Ricardo and the gentry- were aghast at their plans being voted down by these 'abolitionists'.

All the while the major repairs were planned, minor alterations and repairs continued: in 1834 a sun dial with inscription 'momento mori' had been set up by Edmund Carrad 'over the buttress at the large South window' of the south transept,[224] it is shown on Relton's engraving (Fig. 12). In 1837 the stone tiles of the south transept were repaired[225] and in 1839–40 there were payments to a plumber for leadwork, and a mason for work in the tower.[226] These ongoing costs were clearly exercising the churchwardens and in July 1840 the Vestry met to consider the repairs of the church and the churchwardens were tasked with forming an estimate of all the expenses connected with the church for the ensuing present year and to report back, it is clear that all options for the future of the church were being seriously considered.[227]

And then the Revd William Cockin passed away. He died on the 3rd March 1841, a day shy of his 76th birthday; he had been rector for over 34 years. His replacement was Charles Whateley, who had been appointed by Ricardo as curate at the newly consecrated Brimscombe church. Whateley was inducted into the rectory on 29th March and his first dramatic action was to enter the church 'by the side door of the Porch, locked himself in the Church, passed through a door that was in Mr Clutterbuck's Pew to the Belfry stairs and tolled one of the bells 4 or 5 times'. For his first Sunday sermon Whateley read the 39 Articles of Religion from the Book of Common Prayer and preached from Luke 19 v13 - the parable of the Ten Minas.[228]

Matters suddenly started moving extremely swiftly: on the 12th April 1841 a committee was established 'with power to call in an Architect to examine the present state of the Church and Church Yard and to report the same to a general Meeting of the Parishioners to be called for that purpose and also to suggest the most eligible method of providing for the decent and comfortable accommodation of the whole Parish inhabitants'.[229] Within just three days the committee had reached their decision: 'we are unanimously of opinion, that the best and most satisfactory plan for the due accommodation and comfort of the inhabitants, would be to take down the Nave, and rebuild the same.'[230]

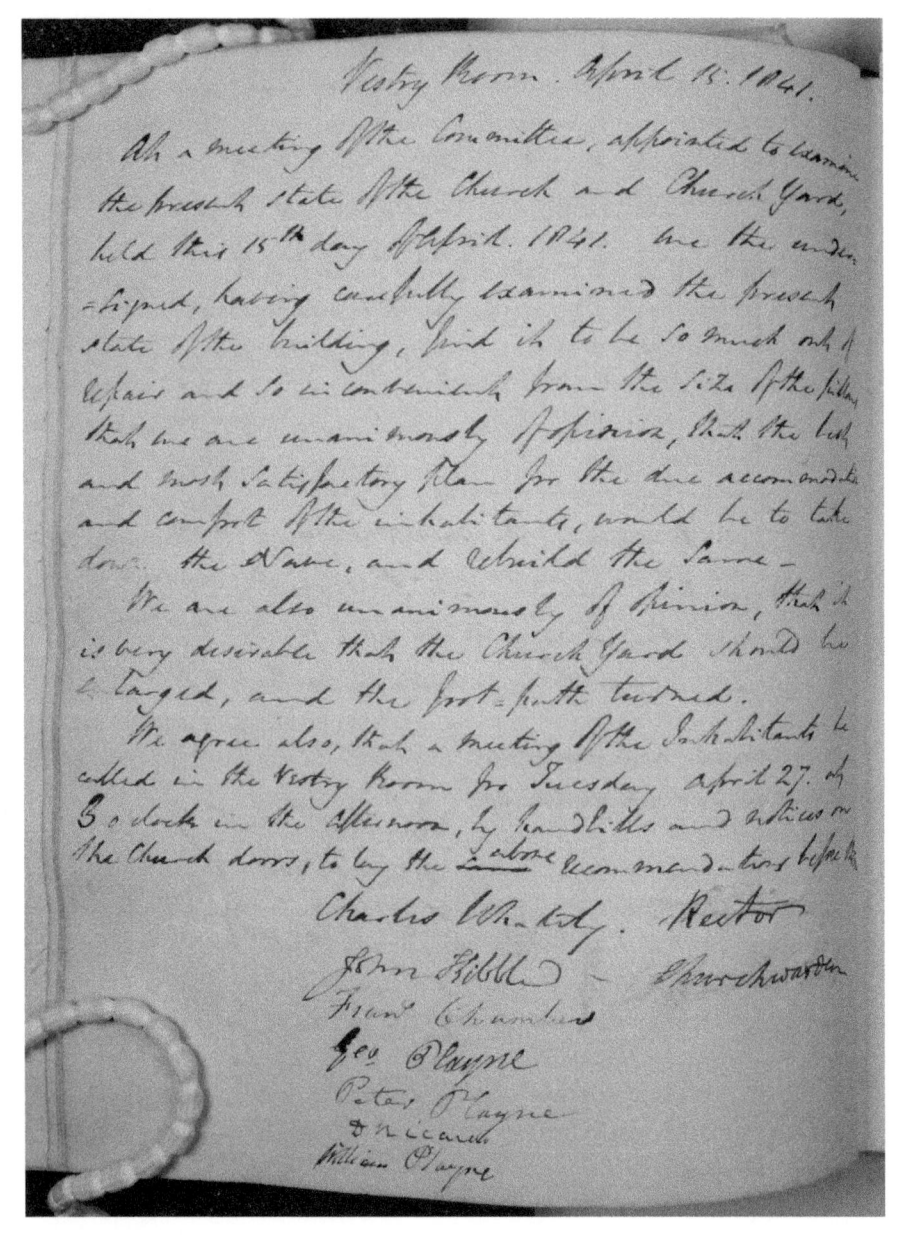

Fig. 74 Extract from Vestry minutes April 27th 1841 on the decision to demolish the church[231]

It is tempting to cast the Revd Cockin as an obstacle to this radical plan, his death allowing Ricardo to carry out an ambitious rebuilding of nearly all the church –originally only the tower would remain. Ricardo had extensive experience of the costs of constructing new churches and would have understood the relative and ongoing costs of repairs, compared to those of a near total rebuild. Ricardo was clearly behind the new plan and with Cockin gone and Whateley in place, the way ahead was now clear.

Confidence in their decision was high, that same day the committee called for a 'Meeting of the Inhabitants be called in the Vestry Room for Tuesday April 27. at 3 o clock in the afternoon, by handbills and notices on the Church doors, to lay the same above recommendations before them.'[232]

The meeting went ahead on the 27th: 'At a Public Meeting of the Inhabitants of Minchinhampton, convened together by public notice, It was resolved unanimously That the Report of the Committee, appointed on the 15th April, to examin into the state of the Church of the and Church Yard be adopted; and we consider it expedient to take down and rebuild the Nave and side aisles of the Church, and we give our Consent thereto. We also agree that the Church Yard sh^d be enlarged, and the footpath turned (Fig. 74).'

David Ricardo pledged £2000 and the Revd Whateley £500 -on the condition that £1000 match funding be raised within six months. At the meeting it was revealed that as well as the nave, 'the Chancel be pulled down and rebuilt, the Amount of Dilapidations being thrown into the general fund'.[233]

The committee was renamed a Building Committee, and tasked 'with full power to call in an Architect and to proceed to the pulling down and rebuilding the Body of the Church and the Chancel and to make other such alterations as may be required.'[234] Whateley had been in post less than a month. Planning progressed with the appointment of Thomas Foster of Bristol as architect and William Shepstone as builder. A survey was carried out by a Mr Franklin, costing the committee £2,[235] producing a scale plan of the church. In addition a detailed enquiry and record was made of the pews and seating so that they could be transferred across to the new church.

Foster drew up his plans for the new church, no doubt aided by David Ricardo, but the plans were not without opposition: the original plan included to pull down the south transept however this was dropped after protestations led by Dr Edward Dalton LL.D FSA, who lived in the parish at Dunkirk Manor, Nailsworth and held a pew in Holy Trinity.[236] Although saved, the masterful south window was somewhat hubristically altered by the removal of a transom which spanned the window just below the springing, and by the

Fig. 75 Oil painting of Foster's church soon after completion, but before the alterations to the south window of the south transept

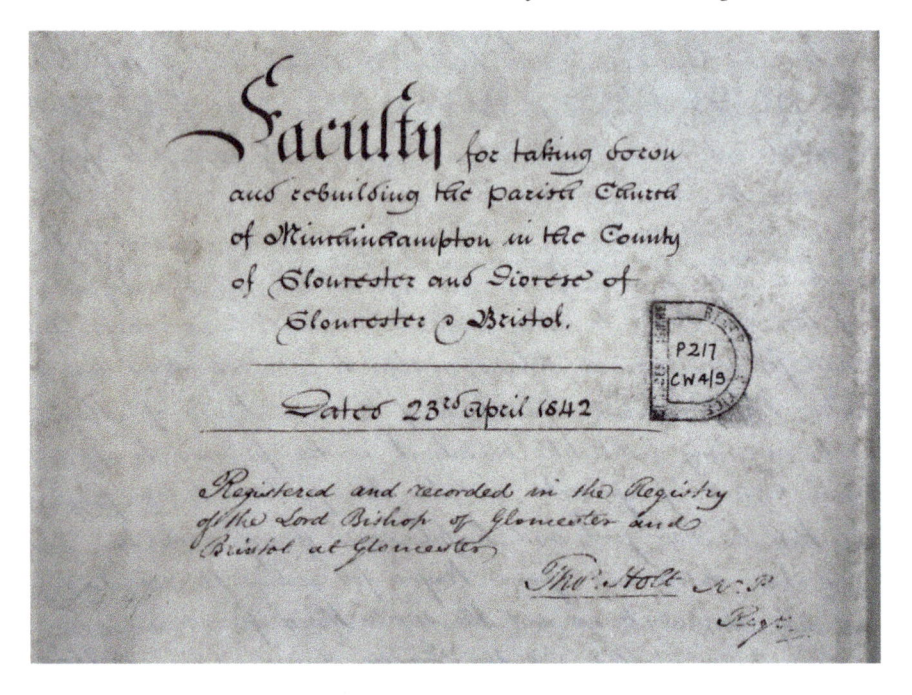

Fig. 76 Faculty dated 23rd April 1842, over a month after demolition started

alteration of the mullions.[237] That action cannot be laid at Foster's door with any certainty as an oil painting in the Church House shows the new church with the old tracery, complete with transom[238] (Fig. 75).

The plans were finalised: the nave, aisles and chancel would be taken down and rebuilt, only the medieval tower and transepts would survive. On Sunday 13th March 1842 the last sermon was preached by Whateley in the old church: Matthew 25 v10 'And while they went to buy, the bridegroom came; and they that were ready went in with him to the marriage: and the door was shut'. The next Tuesday demolition started,[239] the Faculty allowing this was not signed until over a month later (Fig. 76).[240]

Charles Whateley 1795–1865

Born in London 19th February 1795, Whateley lost his mother aged 11 and was sent to Eton and then to Trinity College Cambridge. He took Holy Orders as a curate in Banwell, Somerset and then Trinity church Weymouth, from where he was selected by Ricardo for the new curacy at Brimscombe, before being moved to Holy Trinity on Cockin's death. Whateley died 24 March 1865 in London, five days after his last sermon (Fig. 77).[241]

Fig. 77 The Revd Charles Whateley's memorial in the Chancel

Demolition

'1842: March 15th: The Demolition of the Church was commenced this day: the Nave, aisles and Chancel to be rebuilt: The Tower & transepts remain'[242]

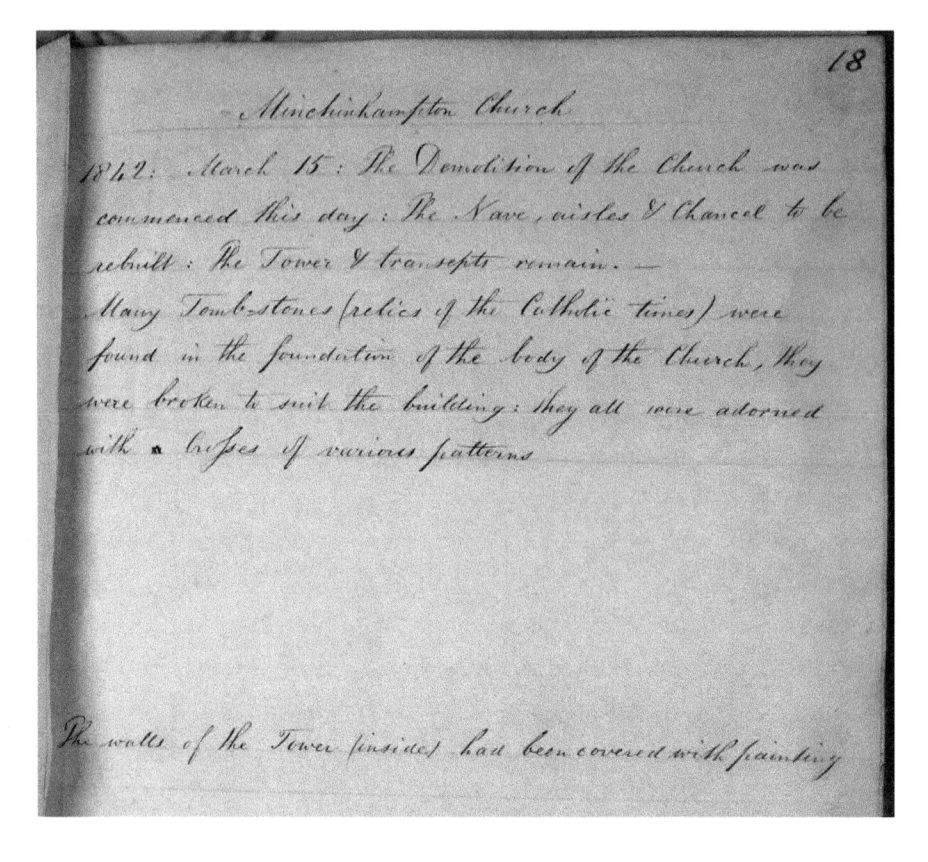

Fig. 78 Extract from Fenning Parke's scrapbook the **'Minchinhampton Chronicles'** *on the demolition*

And so the churchwarden, schoolmaster and local historian Fenning Parke recorded the end of the old church in his *'Minchinhampton Chronicles'* (Fig. 78). The demolition of the old church was comprehensive, the recent excavation showed that the nave and aisles were razed to the ground with little surviving, even of the foundations. Shallow internal burials were nearly all removed, although deeper graves and tombs were left *in situ*, sealed under a demolition and construction layer of trampled lime, dust and dirt. Despite largely surviving intact, the transepts were stripped internally and the upper gable end and roof of the north transept was rebuilt.

Direct physical evidence for the medieval nave, aisles and chancel is therefore scarce. Fortunately the builder, William Shepstone, wrote his detailed letter describing the fabric of the old church that he had pulled down, it is highly likely that this would have been at the request of Fenning Parke. Shepstone had also made sketches of some of the Norman architectural fragments and had kept an ornamented capital in his possession, although sadly these are all lost. His letter however, combined with the surviving documentation, scale plans, illustrations, the surviving medieval fabric and the excavated evidence does provide an abundance of evidence of the appearance of the old church.

Some materials were clearly set aside for reuse in the new church and it is likely that much of the building stone was reused in the new walls, although the external facing stones were all newly quarried. Oak timbers were salvaged, with some of the timbers used in the 1909 lychgate said to be from the old church. Medieval cross-slabs found in the church walls were taken away and at least one can be found reused in an outbuilding in Minchinhampton.

The area around the church, especially to the north and at the west end, was terraced with many burials being exhumed. AT Playne is quite scathing of the exhumations where 'no care whatever was taken' and hundreds of loads of the dark soil, mixed with bones, was simply piled up in adjoining fields 'for any one who cared to use it to carry away. Some was spread on pasture land or taken away and used as garden manure'.[243]

There were local cases of typhus in 1844 and then a large but localised outbreak in 1846. The deaths of the Revd Whateley's wife, one of his children, and his gardener, who had used the soil in their garden and shrubberies, from typhus were linked by the local doctor Daniel Smith to the cemetery soil, an accusation fiercely denied by Ricardo and leading to a series of acrimonious letters in the local and London papers, the fever becoming a well-known controversy across the country and beyond.[244]

David Ricardo the younger 1803–1864

David Ricardo was the second son of the wealthy financier, political economist, abolitionist and MP David Ricardo (1772–1823) who was a Sephardic Jew who had converted to the Unitarian faith on his marriage to the Quaker Priscilla Anne Wilkinson. Ricardo senior had bought Gatcombe Park in 1814 from local clothier Edward Sheppard. Gatcombe had been built in 1771–1774 as a replacement for Minchinhampton manor house[245] and was inherited by David the younger after his father's death in 1823, his elder brother having died in childhood. Ricardo the younger was also a prominent figure in local affairs, appointed High Sheriff of Gloucestershire for 1830–31[246] and elected as Whig MP for Stroud in 1832 although he "took the Chiltern Hundreds", a parliamentary mechanism allowing MPs to resign, in 1833.[247]

Unlike his father, who does not seem to have distributed his largesse locally, Ricardo played a prominent, active, and largely improving role in the town and outlying villages, instigating and funding a spate of public and private projects using his inherited wealth. Projects include new alms houses built at Minchinhampton's West End in 1833[248] and in 1849 he led the formation of a local board of health.[249]

Fig. 79 Monument to David Ricardo Senior outside the east end of Hardenhuish church, Wiltshire

Ricardo directed his considerable energies to the provision of churches in the parish. In 1836 he established a new church, with basement schoolrooms and adjoining glebe house, at Amberley, also funding a new church and school at Brimscombe in 1839–40 immediately preceding the rebuilding of Holy Trinity.[250] As well as Holy Trinity, Ricardo held the avowson of the new rectorship of St Mary Magdalene at Rodborough, previously a chapel-of-ease to Minchinhampton, and may have funded some of its rebuilding in 1842–3. The parish was formally subdivided into the four benefices of Minchinhampton, Amberley, Brimscombe and Rodborough in 1840.[251] Not restricting his munificence to the Church of England, Ricardo also donated land and gave stone for Minchinhampton's new Baptist Chapel in Tetbury Street in 1834.

Ricardo had bought back the advowson of Minchinhampton -the right to present the bishop with a candidate for a vacant post of parish priest- in 1836.[252] Ricardo presented the Revd Whateley first to Brimscombe parish and then to Minchinhampton church as a nominee who presumably was largely aligned to his beliefs. Although it is not known if he was a Unitarian like his father, Ricardo the younger is said to have objected to Tractarian principles and at Brimscombe the chancel is at the west end[253] whilst at Amberley the church was built in a plain and unadorned Early English style at Ricardo's request; it is intriguing to consider the interplay of personal beliefs in the appointment of the vicar and the rebuilding of Holy Trinity at such a time of change in the Church of England.

Foster's church

A MONTH AFTER demolition started, the foundation stone was laid by David Ricardo on Whit Monday, 16th May 1842, following hymns and an address by the Revd Whateley to the assembled crowds.[254] It is not known where the large congregation gathered between the closure of the old church and the consecration of the new church in 1843.

The church was rebuilt in a 'solid' Perpendicular style to plans by architect Thomas Foster of Bristol, who had just finished building Brimscombe church for Ricardo (Fig. 80). The builder, William Shepstone, claimed that the new church was '…although by no means rich in detail yet its architecture throughout with respect to arrangement proportion and finish has its claims for correctness simplicity and elegance equal to any of the modern built churches.'[255] Later commentators, many looking through the prism of the Gothic Revival, would reflect less kindly on the design.

Fig. 80 Postcard of Foster's Holy Trinity, dating to before 1909. From the collections of Museum in the Park, Stroud STGCM 2018_16_170

Thomas Foster

Thomas Foster (†1849) was born into a Bristol architectural family: his father James (†1823) and his brother James were both architects. Thomas and James set up a practice in Bristol with William Ignatius Okely; James died in 1836 and Okely left in 1840, after which Thomas' son John joined his father.[256]

Foster had a strong connection with the area, and the late 30s and early 40s was a busy period with work on several new churches in the wider Stroud area including the Early English style Holy Trinity, Stroud (1837–9),[257] the 'bold' neo-Norman Holy Trinity Brimscombe (1839–40) for David Ricardo,[258] the neo-Norman St Paul's Whiteshill (1839–41),[259] the remodelling in Romanesque style of Christchurch Chalford,[260] the Early English style Christchurch Hanham (designed 1837, built 1840–1),[261] alterations at St Mary Olveston (1840–1),[262] a new Decorated style north aisle at St Andrew Whitminster (1841–2)[263] the rebuilding of St Mary Magdalene Rodborough for Ricardo (1842–3), and in secular buildings the Cotswold Tudor style Old Vicarage, Randwick in 1844.[264]

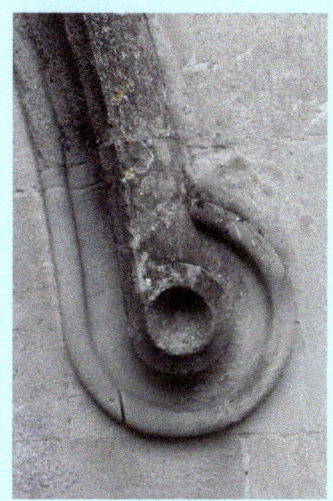

Fig. 81 Labelstop by the southwest door

Foster's new design did not include for retention of much of the medieval fabric and the whole of the nave and aisles were taken down including their foundations. Burges noted that 'The only attempt at restoration being the two-light Decorated windows – one in the North Chancel wall and the other in the south – from careful examinations it appears that a few pieces of the ancient tracery have been reused.'[265] Slightly later parish church restorations, increasingly influenced by the Oxford Movement, Cambridge Camden Society and the Gothic Revival in valuing medieval architecture and craftmanship, would often painstakingly retain or copy ancient features, with varying success, but 1842 was right at the start of the influence of the Revival, and neither Foster nor Ricardo were inclined to retain or restore anything much of the old church in the newly built parts. Little is known of William Shepstone, the builder who took down the medieval church, and built Foster's plans, bit he had a good knowledge of medieval architecture, and his letter describing the old church is an invaluable record of what was lost[266].

The church was constructed on its newly terraced site, the churchyard to the north of the church held back by a new dry stone retaining wall with a stone-lined drain at its base to carry water around the north side of the nave and chancel (Fig. 82). The new church largely adopted the footprint of its medieval precursor: the widths of the chancel, nave and aisles were dictated by the retention of the tower and transepts, and the arcade bases were reused. The chancel however was reportedly shortened.[267]

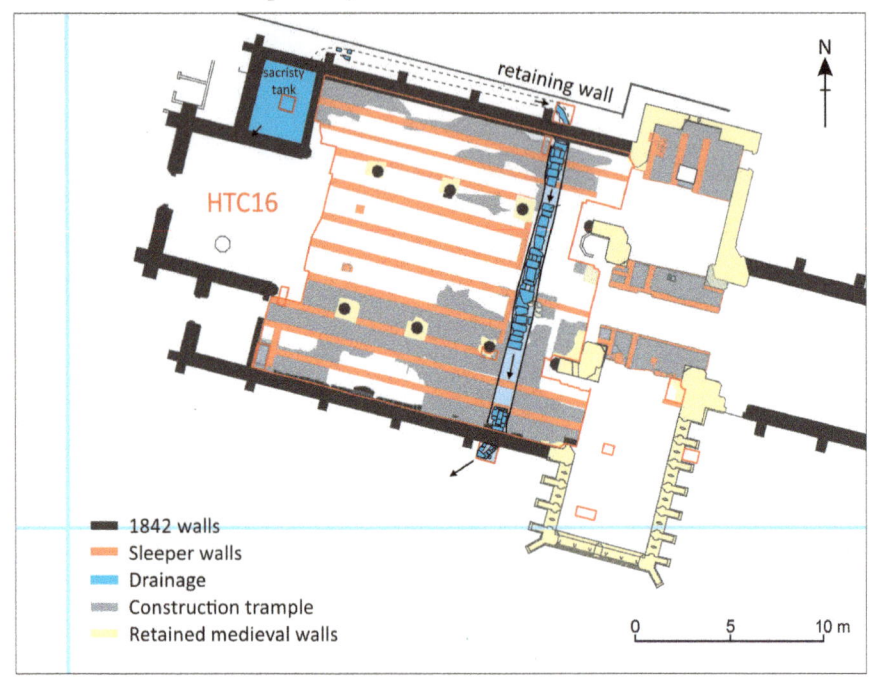

Fig. 82 Plan of Foster's church and the excavated features

The church was laid out and the foundations built directly on the limestone bedrock. New walls were of rubblework with Painswick Stone ashlar cladding and Minchinhampton Weatherstone details.

The chancel was knocked down and rebuilt, Burges noted its appearance in his letter of 1869 before he remodelled it once more. 'The plan of the Chancel is also said to have been shortened. The present East window [of 1842] is a comparatively small one of four lights, the North and South walls are both alike and contain the perpendicular lancets with tracery in the heads. The roof has two framed principals but no tie beam, the plaster ceiling taking the form of a 4 centred Arch.'[268] The original Decorated windows in the north and south walls were retained. An engraving published in The Builder in 1858 shows a two-light window above the hooded Priest's Door; there is a string course around the chancel, but no buttresses (Fig. 83).[269]

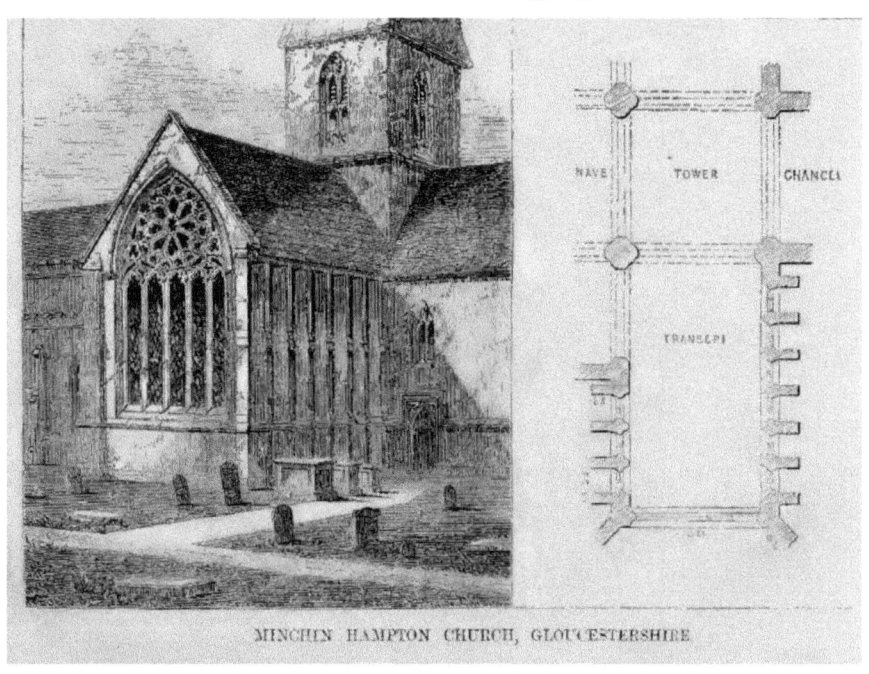

Fig. 83 The south transept and west end of the 1842 chancel, showing the window above the Priest's Door; published in **The Builder** *in January 1858*

The nave and aisles retained the arcade spacing and size of their predecessors, with four bays and tall octagonal piers. At the west end was the narthex, with memorials reset in the floor and against the walls. Two lobbies in the north and southwest corners could be accessed by external or internal doors and contained stairs to the first-floor galleries. The new church was to seat an increased congregation -despite the new churches at Amberley and Brimscombe, and the rebuilding and uprating of St Mary Magdalene at Rodborough into a parish church.

The new west end was embattled, with crocketed pinnacles and a niche (since 2000 containing a statue of St Francis of Assisi with a wolf carved by local sculptor Rory Young (Fig. 84)) the embattling continuing along the top of the aisle and clerestory levels. The west window is rather undersized, it has four cinquefoil lights with a hood terminating in figurative stops.

The arched west door sits between a pair of low small single-light windows, all under a heavy hood mould. The Ricardo coat of arms is carved on the left-hand side of the west door. The main windows of the aisles are of three cinquefoil lights, with the upper clerestorey windows of twin cinquefoil lights under flatter archs.

The South transept was largely unchanged externally, aside from the alteration to the transom, but the north wall and perhaps roof of the north transept appears to have had structural problems and was rebuilt from wallplate level up, with a new triple-quatrefoil occulus window sporting grotesque labelstops added above the original reticulated window (Fig. 85).

Fig. 84 Statue of St Francis of Assisi and a wolf on the west wall

Fig. 85 Oculus window in the north wall of the north transept unserted as part of the 1842 rebuild

The design and construction of the church was eminently practical as well as liturgical, with a system of stone-lined drains to divert and harvest rainwater from the roofs: two cast iron downpipes took all the water from the roofs of the northern nave and aisle; the western pipe fed into an underground water cistern beneath the northwest lobby where there was a hand pump to raise the water to ground floor; an overflow on the cistern drained excess water away to the south. The eastern downpipe fed into a stone culvert —constructed of reused medieval architectural fragments- that took the water underneath the nave and aisles and out to the south of the church (Fig. 86). It was the collapse of this drain, subsiding into earlier graves under the nave, that contributed to the issues with damp that led to the 2016 reordering (Fig. 87). Intriguingly no such system of drains appears to have served the north side of the chancel where the downpipe appears to have discharged via a gully and a pipe directly into the ground just 2m from the north wall, causing damp problems inside the chancel. A pit, probably from this date, had been filled with tightly packed architectural fragments (Fig. 88).

left: Fig. 86 The 1842 culvert under the north aisle, collapsing into underlying graves in the nave; scale 0.5m and 1m
top right: Fig. 87 The nave looking south-east, with voids from collapsed graves; scale 1m
right: Fig. 88 Pit by the south arcade backfilled with closely fitted architectural mouldings; scale 0.5m

A boiler room lay under the southwest lobby, accessed by an internal stone stair and with iron heating pipes leading off under the church floor, where they were covered by iron grilles.

Once the walls were up and the roof on and slated, a series of low sleeper walls were laid across the interior to carry the stone slabs of the aisles and the softwood timber pew bases, each base raised above the surrounding stone and red and black tile floor. The sleeper walls were built of reused stones from the medieval church, odd-sized blocks that were left over from the rebuilding (Fig. 89). These included architectural mouldings, fragments of ledgers, and a series of five fragments of a carefully prepared limestone slab which bears the inscribed design of a medieval window tracery. Excess rubble and dust was left between these walls and sealed by the timber pew platforms (Fig. 90).

Fig. 89 The sleeper walls of the nave and south aisle being cleaned up during the 2016 excavation; scale 0.5m

Fig. 90 Rubble and dust filling the voids beneath the pew platforms; scale 0.5m

Evidence for the builders was preserved under the new pews, the impression of a hobnailed boot found in a layer of mortar (Fig. 91), and curled softwood planings from the pews nestling in the rubble and accumulated dust.

Fig. 91 Impression of a builder's hob-nailed boot in the mortar of the pew sleeper walls; scale 5cm

The internal walls were plastered and whitewashed. The lower part of the aisle walls were panelled and the new pew bases and pews were built in four blocks across the nave and aisles, all to the same simple design. Foster's plans showed the transepts with pews, however it seems that the south transept never received its pews, although sleeper walls and the remains of a stone slab aisle in the north transept suggest it was seated at the rebuild.

The 14th-century font was removed, only being replaced in 1915. Many of the original wall-mounted memorials were reset on the new walls. A new stone pulpit was fitted at the east of the nave.[270]

The internal layout of the church looked back to the previous church, rather than forward to the Gothic Revival, it was built as a new auditorium, with the pulpit still largely the focus of the church.

Pews, galleries and sittings

At first floor level timber galleries seating 354 worshippers were constructed over the aisles and at the west end of the nave over the narthex (Figs. 92, 94). The west gallery was the 'Singing Gallery' also originally housing the organ.

As part of the planned rebuilding work, the Committee prepared a register of 'Particulars of Claims to Pews & Sittings In the Parish Church of Mn: Hampton' (Appendix 3), taking evidence from parishioners as to the

Fig. 92 The nave and aisles of the 1842 church; originally a first floor gallery would have filled the upper part of the aisles

ownership of the existing pew sittings and settling disputes over ownership -at least in the minds of the Committee- and purchasing some pews for the church. Disputes were recorded and judged, the Committee also purchasing many sittings from the claimants, evidence was provided for claims, with references to the Transfer Book, the brass plates, and to exchanges between parishioners. The pews and sittings, many of which were held by women, were often attached to and transferred with properties, and the record of their ownership and transfer holds valuable evidence for the links between many families of the parish.[271]

The plans of the Old Church made in 1841 show all the pews and galleries in the church and this appears to have been cross-referenced, with the pew numbers recorded in the register (Fig. 93, Fig. 94).

Pew sittings were a major consideration in 1841 when the church rebuilding was announced. David Ricardo's donation of £1000 was on the condition that he had 80 pews to hand out for houses in his estate:

1 Pew for ~~Self~~ Gatcombe House to hold   6
2 Pews for ~~servants~~ Gatcombe   "   10
1 Pew for House occupied by Mrs. Gee   5
1 Pew for House occupied by Mr J Kibble   5
1 Pew for House now void behind Mr Kibble's 5

1 Pew for House now occupied by Mr Turner	5
1 Pew for House occupied by Mr R Chandler	5
1 Pew for Crackstone Farm	5
1 Pew for Peaches Farm	5
1 Pew for Horse & Groom Farm	4
1 Pew for House occupied by Chas Jones	4
1 Pew for ~~Tobacconist~~ Barcelona Farm	5
1 Pew for Bubblewell Farm	5
1 Pew for House occupied by Geo Simpkins	4
1 Pew for Shard House	4
	80[272]

Ricardo also expected 400 Free Sittings to be appropriated: one half given to the Sunday School Children and 'the remainder for the use of the Poor generally' with 'all present pew rights should be respected.[273]

Originally each sitting was to be 20 inches by 35 inches wide, however this was soon cut to 33 inches width, presumably to fit more seats. The Building Committee had power to appropriate and allocate seats in the 'New Church'. Foster's plans show that the new church was originally to have a capacity of 1091 seats, despite the subdivision of the parish and the new churches at Brimscombe and Amberley. The seats were divided between the ground floor and the galleries, including the girls' and boys' seats in front of the organ in the west gallery. The north end of the north transept was partitioned off as a '*Robing room*' but otherwise the transepts were down to have pews, which would partially extend into the crossing. In the nave and aisles the free sittings were at the east end, including around the triple decker of pulpit, reading desk and clerk's desk, whilst the main body of pews were '*appropriated*' to households, and the sponsors' pews were at the west end. The font was intended to be in the central aisle, towards the west of the nave, it had moved to its present location by 1870.[274]

Appropriated sittings in pews	(below)	496
Appropriated sittings in pews	(Gallery)	194
Free sittings	(below)	103
Free sittings	(Gallery)	50
Singers		12
Sponsors' pews		26
Children		210
Total		1091

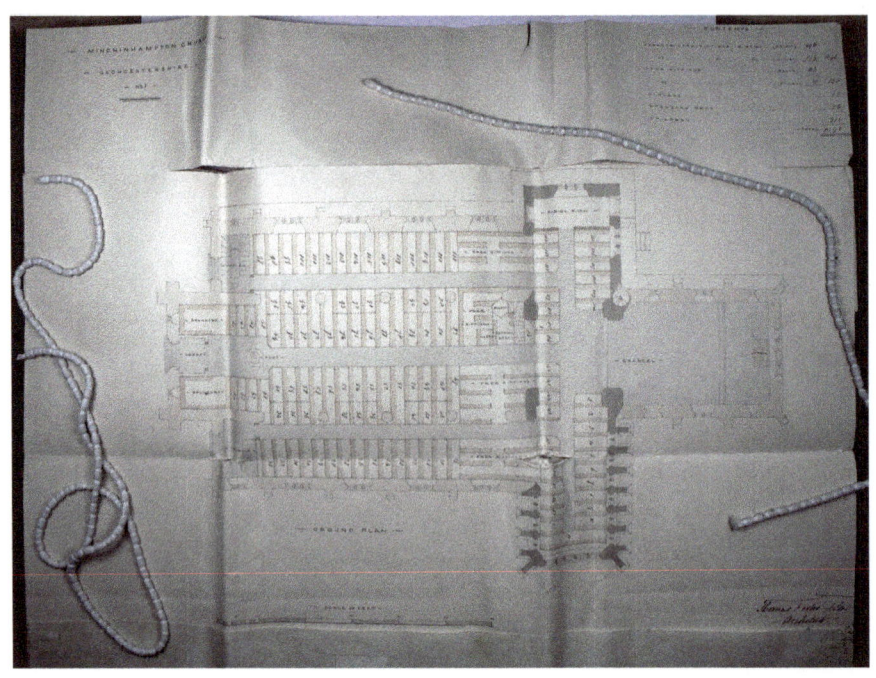

Fig. 93 Ground floor plan of the new church P217 CW/4/9

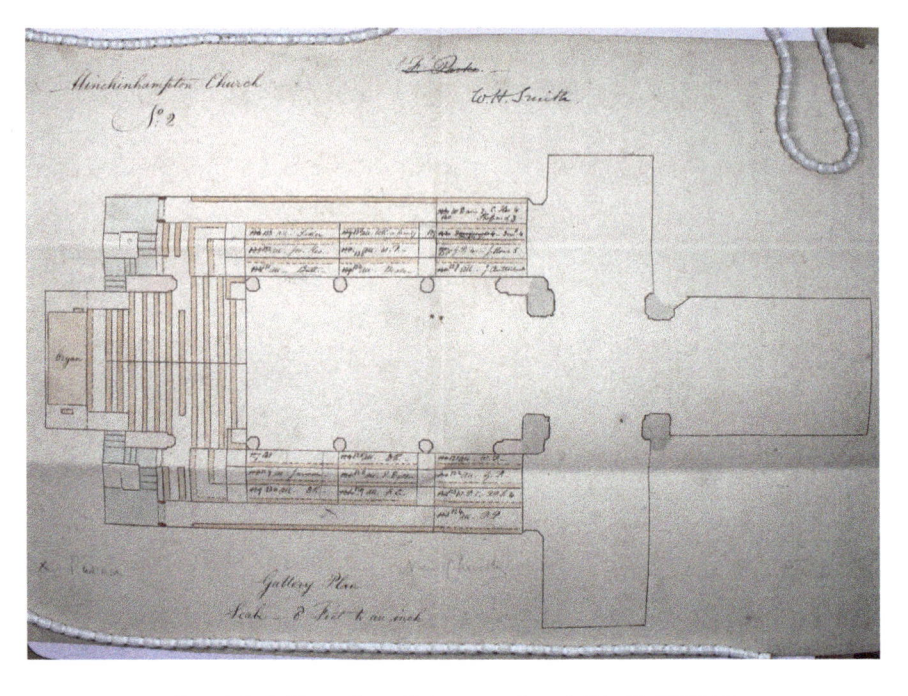

Fig. 94 Gallery plan of the new church P217 CW/4/9

The new galleries were of dark wood, extending from the outer walls in to the arcades, and would have reduced the light levels within the new church considerably, sitting above the dark pitch pine pews of the ground floor (Fig. 95, Fig. 96) however the unified design and ordered layout would have been a marked change from the accretion of Jacobean and later box pews and galleries that they replaced.

Fig. 95 Foster's pews in the north aisle; scale 0.5m

In 1858–9 Pew no 88 in the North Aisle was bought back by the church, the accounts for that year note that the churchwardens were buying the seats held by non-parishioners, so that they might be used by parishioners with nowhere to sit. Pew 65 was bought back in 1861–2, Pews 109 and 111 in 1863–4 and three sittings in Pew 105 in 1864–5.[275]

In 1870 the churchwardens had wanted to reconcile the existing situation with legal opinions that pews should be freely available to every parishioner without

Fig. 96 The nave pews with heating pipes

payment, and that letting pews was illegal. As we have seen the practice for some time, consolidated within the new church, was that pews were seen as the property of individuals and could be bought, sold, or let. The churchwardens produced a printed leaflet setting out their case that this was not the case, and asking all those with a sitting to register those.[276]

Two plans of the ground floor Sittings survive, annotated with names in a faint pencil, slight differences between the two copies possibly showing the occupants or households before and after the changes (Fig. 97). The pew numbering and layout differs from Foster's proposed plan, some names are legible, others sadly not, the Rectory household was in pew 52 in the nave, whilst their servants were at the back of the south aisle in pew 3. Gatcombe held on to pew 24 and the Playne households sat in pews 21 and 49. 'Boys' occupied the back seats of the north aisle. The south transept is filled by rows of chairs rather than pews, the plans also show chairs at the east end of the south aisle and two rows of chairs in front of the nave pews, and further chairs and at least one new pew at the rear of the nave.[277]

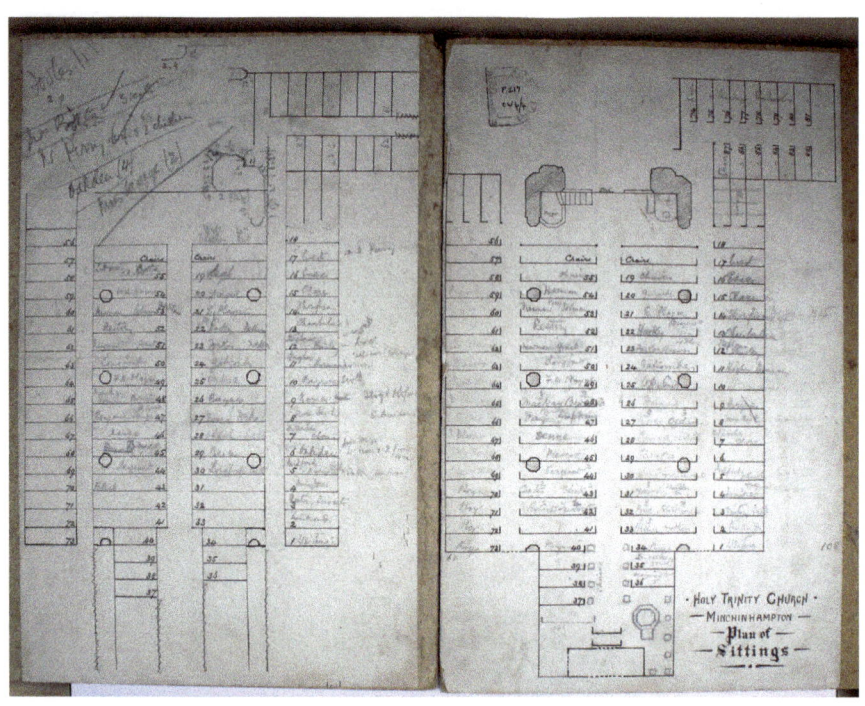

Fig. 97 Plan of Sittings, 1870 P217/CW/4/4

The changes must have caused some unhappiness and there appears to have been an ongoing dispute; in 1881 the churchwarden WH Smith wrote to the Stroud News that parishioners should keep their existing seats, but should register then with the churchwardens of them (as had been requested in 1870). Finding seats for all the parishioners, let alone outsiders, was a clear problem and appears to have been cause of many a headache for the churchwardens who stated a 'firm belief in the principle of unappropriated sittings, with the church entirely free to parishioners', i.e. a simple life![278]

Maintenance and upkeep in the Victorian church

Building work on the new church might have been completed but repairs and replacements were still needed and the day-to-day costs of running the church are listed in the printed accounts of the new church, many of the entries echoing the expenses and issues faced by churchwardens three hundred years before, and some to this day.[279]

For the Communion, 'Tent' wine - a Spanish red, usually from Galicia, and bread was purchased, whilst candles were now of whale oil: '6lb of Sperm Candles' at 2s.6d. in 1843–4, and 6lb of 'Mould' candles at 8d., the next year more candles were bought, but also 12 gallons of 'Sperm Oil' and 8 gallons of 'Seal Oil' for oil lights in the church, which also needed lamp cotton for the wicks and new glass globes. Gas lighting came to the Market House in 1859–60, but not apparently to the church as oil continued to be purchased until 1866 when the first payment for gas is listed.

Heating the church using the new boiler used 193 bushels of coke in 1843–4, whilst the next year 402 bushels were bought. The boiler heated the church via a 'hot water apparatus' using steel pipes set into the ducts within the floors. The system seems to have often needed repair, and a new high pressure 'Perkins hot water apparatus' was purchased at a cost of £29.10s.2d. in 1867–8.

Furnishings included coconut matting for the floors, and in 1852–3 the 'Ladies of Hyde Court' raised money to carpet to the stairs to the Reading Desk and Pulpit. Blinds were purchased for the windows, which often needed repairs. In 1852–3 'the best Church Bible and Prayer Book' was purchased from the Society for Promoting Christian Knowledge.[280]

The bells needed repair in 1843–4, and new bellropes were still a common expense. The church clock was painted and gilded in 1849–50 and needed repair and cleaning every few years. The organ also needed attention, with occasional payments for cleaning and tuning.

The church building itself needed plastering and painting, doors were varnished, flues swept and stoves cleaned. There was an annual payment for cleaning the church; mops, brushes and dusters were bought most years, and surplices were sent to be washed. The weather also created costs for the parish, in 1853–4 the church roof needed to be cleared of snow after heavy snowfall, and the next year snow was cleared from the churchyard.

1868–9 Oldfield, Burges and the new chancel

THE REVD CHARLES Whately died in 1865, shortly after the death of David Ricardo who was succeeded by his son Henry David. The new rector was the Revd. EC Oldfield and again a changing of the guard coincides with further change to the church as Oldfield recast Foster's church, leaving it in largely the form we have today. Oldfield was largely following the ideas of the Oxford Movement, with its rejection of the post-Reformation model of a church as an auditorium, dominated by the sermon and preaching from the pulpit, and a return to the church as a building that was designed around the primacy of the Eucharist.

In 1869 Oldfield invited the renowned Gothic Revivalist art-architect William Burges to inspect the church and offer his suggestions for altering the chancel, Burges received a copy of Shepstone's report and visited the church,

Fig. 98 Burge's chancel with its double-plane east window, with the later ceiling painting by FC Eden

drawing up a number of options for which he prepared detailed drawings which sadly do not survive. His letter of 28th April 1869 sets out his own valuable contemporary opinion on the quality and significance of the remaining medieval parts of the church, and on Foster's 1842 work (Appendix 2). Burges was disparaging about Foster's design, writing 'In 1841 the nave and chancel were entirely rebuilt in a very unsatisfactory version of the perpendicular style'.[281] The Gothic Revival did not approve.

Burges' work at Minchinhampton was restricted to the chancel; although it is highly likely that much of the chancel was retained there were many structural alterations, especially to the windows and roof, and buttresses were added to the chancel walls. Burges removed the small two-light window above the Priest's Door but his principal contribution was a five-light east window whose double plane tracery has a circular design intended to echo the south window of the south transept (Figs. 98, 99). The main lights of the window feature scenes from the crucifixion, with the cartwheel window above featuring angels around Christ enthroned. The chancel became a memorial to Mary, wife of William Playne of Longfords who had died in a fall from a carriage the previous year,[282] with Playne paying the entire costs of the new chancel and the glass (by Hardman to designs by Powell).[283]

The chancel also contains a highly polished encaustic tile pavement by William Godwin of Herefordshire, chosen by Burges to reflect the light entering by the east window (Fig. 100). Archaeological work shows that Burges moved the Sanctuary step westwards, creating more space in front of the Communion Table, which would soon be once more referred to as an altar.

Oldfield instituted further changes in the nave: by 1870 the font had been moved to the west end, and Foster's triple decker (if it had ever been built) had been replaced by a new pulpit sited against the northwest crossing pier, with a slightly raised lectern against the southwest pier.[284]

Fig. 99 View of Burges' double plane east window

Fig. 100 Burges's highly polished chancel floor of Godwin tiles

William Burges 1827–1881
Although largely forgotten for nearly a century, William Burges was one of the greatest architect-designers of the Gothic Revival. Born in London he left his engineering studies at King's College School after a year and took a position with architect Edward Blore at the age of 17. Burges travelled widely in Europe and Turkey, and developed his own very eclectic and possibly over-decorated style that combined Gothic Revival architecture and Pre-Raphaelite decoration, influenced by Pugin, Islamic architecture, and opium. Burges called himself an art-architect, and was an accomplished and prolific designer. He helped create the Ecclesiological Society's Mediaeval Court at the International Exhibition in London in 1862, the same year as Burges' first major commission at St Fin Barre's cathedral in Cork. His outstanding work continued with Cardiff Castle for the Marquis of Bute, and smaller, but still expensive, commissions.

Removal of galleries
In 1873 the south transept window was re-glazed with coloured glass by Messrs Hardman depicting scenes from the life of Christ.[285] The western first floor 'Singing Gallery' was removed in 1878, and the choir relocated to the crossing and furnished with new choir stalls, now removed, the design of which cannot be related to Burges's work (Fig. 101).[286]

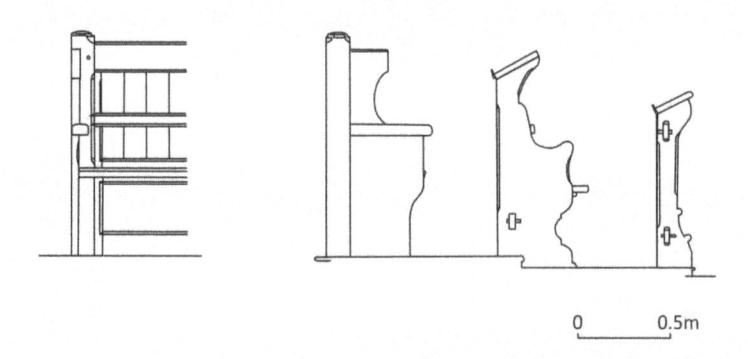

Fig. 101 Drawing of choir stall in crossing

The organ was moved at the same time (that instrument was replaced in 1887 by the present organ). The north gallery, which was in the way of the organ, was removed in 1887, and the south gallery in 1888.[287] The extant southern stairwell now leads up to a blocked doorway at first floor level.

The VCH alludes to some further restoration work being carried out in 1884 and the walls of the south transept and nave were scraped (Figs. 102, 103) but were later re-plastered and whitewashed at some point after 1919.

The pulpit is of alabaster, decorated with statues of St. Peter, St. John and St. Paul, and erected by local subscription as a memorial to the Revd EC Oldfield who had died in 1885. This replaced one in stone which presumably dated from 1842.[288]

Fig. 102 South transept in 1901 showing the walls scraped and with chairs rather than pews

1868-9 OLDFIELD, BURGES AND THE NEW CHANCEL

Fig. 103 The nave, with scraped walls, taken after the removal of the south gallery in 1888

Stained glass

The chancel and south transept glass is by Hardman, part of Burges' work, with most of the later windows in the nave and aisles by Herbert W Bryans, brother of the then rector and partner to Webb who designed the new altar. Bryans' windows are signed with a greyhound (Fig. 104).

Fig.104 Herbert Bryan's signature greyhound on the glass of the south aisle

The organ

A church organ is first mentioned in the churchwardens' accounts for 1556, when 12d was spent on repairs; organ music would have ceased under the Protestant reforms so perhaps the old organ was brought out of safe keeping with the return of Catholicism under Mary.[289] In 1644 organ music was banned in churches and the organ may well have been vandalised by

Fig. 105 The organ sits in the north transept

the Roundhead Captain Jeremy Buck who attacked the Royalist rector Henry Fowler. There is no further mention of an organ until 1836 when a subscription raised the required funds and the, presumably second hand, organ was housed in the north transept, marked on Fenning Parke's plan of the old church by the Singing seat.[290]

The organ was moved to the western Singing Gallery in the new church, a reference to 'the purchasing and putting up of Mr Allen's organ' suggests there may have been a new organ with Jim Portbury suggesting that an existing two manual instrument was acquired and installed by Charles Allen, complete with eighteenth and some seventeenth century pipes.[291] In 1878 the Singing Gallery was taken down and the organ moved back to the north transept, by 1887 it was however 'in such a frail condition, that it is absolutely necessary to take it immediately in hand, or else there may be sudden collapse. The tuner, indeed, said that it was useless to tune it anymore in its present state. Under these circumstances the opinion of an expert was taken, and he strongly advised that the Organ should be re-built, and that the Old Pipes should be used again.' [292]

Messrs Nicholson and Lord of Walsall were approached to provide a specification for a new organ costing £350, an appeal fund was started and as it was progressing well the organ was ordered, however the total cost was not reached so the new organ, whilst incorporating some of the old organ's pipes, lacked several components on its installation in 1887. Plans to complete the organ rumbled on, in 1893 Nicholson and Lord quoted £104 to add the Choir Organ, but this could not be afforded; in 1904 £89 had to be spent on repairs, and it was not til 1937 that the Choir Organ was added by Messrs. Hill, Norman and Beard, although not to the desired specification. Further works were carried out in 1956, with repairs and improvements failing to keep up with increasing problems before a major overhaul was carried out in 1969 by John Coulson of Bristol at a cost of £1914 (Fig. 105).[293]

In 2021 an appeal to refurbish and enhance the organ was opened and at the time of writing the organ has been fully dismantled and is being restored off-site by Martin Goetze and Dominic Gwynn Ltd. The works include a careful restoration of the main divisions of the organ along with some augmentation of the pedal organ, including a Pedal Trombone to Nicholson and Lord scales, and a new mechanical action Choir Organ. The tonal scheme will be based on the Nicholson and Lord as left by Norman Beard in 1922, alongside research into other similar size Nicholson and Lord organs of the time.[294]

The stained glass
Dan Humphries ACR

John Hardman & Co. (1838–1908) was commissioned by Gothic Revivalist William Burges to create the chancel and the south transept glazing, although the designs were by Powell. Hardman was one of the pioneers of the stained-glass revival of the nineteenth century. His Birmingham-based firm started out as an ecclesiastical metal works and, following the suggestion of AWN Pugin, the business expanded into stained glass production in 1845. Pugin designed for the firm until his death in 1852 when this role passed to John Hardman's nephew and Pugin's son-in-law John Hardman Powell. John Hardman was a Roman Catholic, and his association with Pugin assured their popularity among Catholic patrons well into the twentieth century[295].

Nearly all of the glazing of the north and south aisles, and the west

Fig. 106 'Ghosting' of a face on the stained glass

window is by Herbert W Bryans (1856-1925), brother of the rector, whose work can be identified by his running greyhound rebus. Bryans trained under CE Kempe, his style here almost identical. Two windows have the initial JW for John Wimbolt (1867–1952) alongside Bryans' greyhound; Wimbolt joined Bryans in 1898 also after training and working under Kempe. The western two windows of the north aisle are by H Vernon Spreadbury, 1935 (also worked with Kempe), and Edward Payne 1959.

At the time of writing a new project has been launched for the conservation of the stained glass. Much of the glass is affected by severe paint loss, compromising the legibility and resulting in 'ghosting' of faces (Fig. 106) as

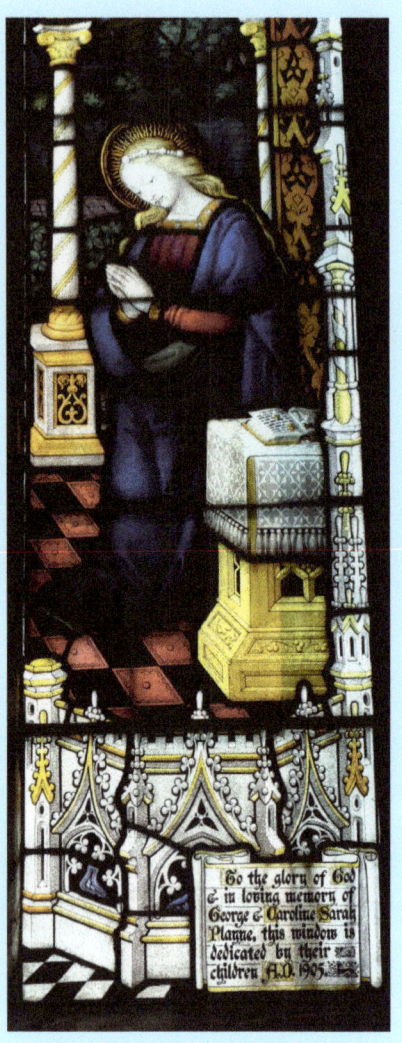

Fig. 107 Stained glass in the south aisle by Herbert Bryans, in memory of George and Caroline Sarah Playne, 1905

well as accumulated dirt which obscures clarity and colour. For many panels the only surviving painted detail is now confined to a few border pieces or decorative strap work. In many instances, reading the images depicted in the windows has now become difficult. In addition, several of the Hardman windows are bowing and have ferrous bars that are spalling the stone in places. While some of the paint loss may be attributable to a flawed firing process, the repeated condensation events over many years within the building has been the main mechanism for damage, as may be seen in the condensation run-off, staining stonework below the rose window in the Lady Chapel.

Fig. 108 The south transept window

The earlier stages of the recent re-ordering greatly improved environmental conditions inside the church, resulting from the enhanced heating system (underfloor), raising the baseline temperature of the interior and creating a much more stable environment for the conservation work on the windows, in the knowledge that it will be consolidated and maintained by the now stable temperature

The Twentieth century

IN 1909 THE old double gate into the churchyard was replaced by the present lychgate, built by Minchinhampton builder William Harman using oak apparently salvaged from the church and Market House (Figs. 109, 110, 111). The lychgate was dedicated to the memory of Edward Playne (†1907), a former county

Fig. 109 Postcard of the 1909 lych gate by Comley. From the collections of Museum in the Park, Stroud STGCM 2007_183_2022

Fig. 110 Postcard of Holy Trinity and the lych gate. The photograph was taken between its construction in 1909 and the installation of Kempe & Co's war memorial in 1919. From the collections of Museum in the Park, Stroud STGCM 2018_16_171

Fig. 111 The lychgate on Bell Lane in 2022

councillor and chairman of the Parish Council and of the Stroud Board of Guardians.[296]

Minor alterations continued throughout the 20th century: a new altar, riddle posts and hangings were designed by Geoffrey Webb in 1911, shortly

Fig. 112 The new Lady Chapel in the south transept, photographed by EP Conway between 1911 and 1914. Some of the furnishings may have come from the chancel

before his conversion to Catholicism. As part of Webb's changes the top step of the sanctuary was removed and the old altar table moved to the south transept, now referred to as the Lady Chapel (Fig. 112). The 14th-century font was returned from the rectory garden in 1915 and mounted on a stone base in the narthex; it was re-dedicated to the memory of Second Lieutenant Geoffrey Robert Johnson of the Gloucestershires, who fell fighting at Gallipoli August 7th 1915, aged 22 (Fig. 113).

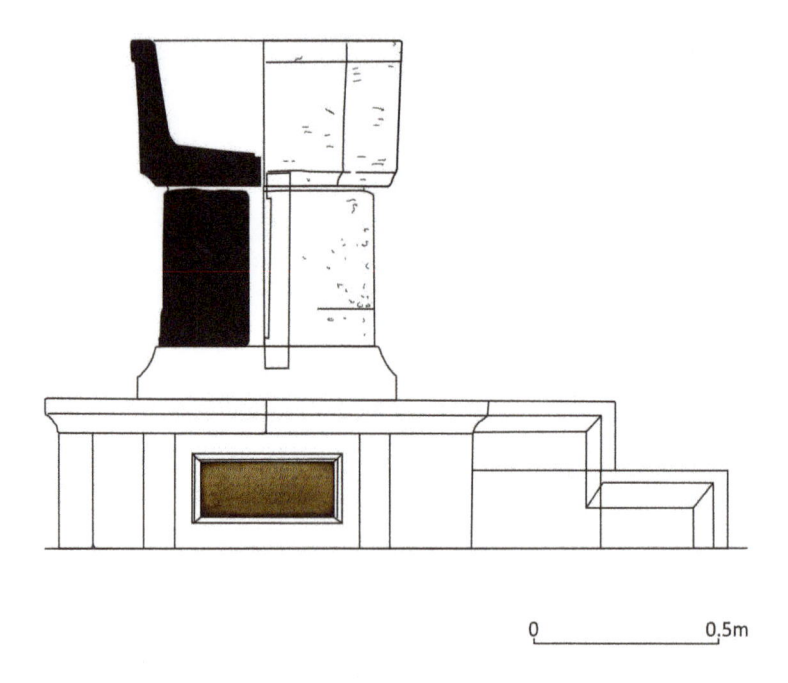

Fig. 113 Cross-section of the font and its early 20th-century stone base, the dedication brass to Lt Johnson is now mounted on the narthex wall

The Great War was also remembered in 1919 with a churchyard cross by Kempe & Co (Fig. 114), and an ornate carved rood and screen by FC Eden -who originally intended them to be painted but the parish would not allow it. The rood forms a memorial to Lieutenant Harold Courtenay Woollcombe-Boyce, the commander of HMS Ghurka which was sunk after striking an enemy mine off Dungeness on 7th February 1917 (Fig. 115, Fig. 116). The screen itself is a memorial to the fallen of the Great War (Fig. 117, Fig. 118).

Fig. 114 Kempe's graveyard cross of 1919, a memorial to the dead of the Great War

above left: Fig. 115 FC Eden's rood screen, in its new position south of the crossing

left: Fig. 116 Detail of FC Eden's rood and the chancel arch with its medieval painted decoration

above: Fig. 117 FC Eden's carved rood, set within the crossing arch with its medieval red painted foliate decoration

    FC Eden returned to Minchinhampton in 1931, adding an aumbry in memory of the Revd Thomas Hodson, curate at Holy Trinity 1875–77, and painting the chancel barrel ceiling as a memorial to Sarah Louisa Woollcombe-Boyce, which has since been restored (Fig. 119).[297] The altar rails were set up in memory of Violet Hylda Eton, after her death in 1933. The encaustic tile steps to the chancel were removed in 1946.[298] Several pews were removed under Faculty, the first in 1961. In 1962 the nave ceiling was painted by Campbell Smith of London to designs by Peter Falconer.

Fig. 118 Detail of EFC Eden's carved oak rood screen

Fig. 119 The chancel ceiling, designed by FC Eden and painted in 1931

Porch Room 1973

The hexagonal multi-purpose space of the Porch Room was added to the west end of the church in 1973 to the design of Peter Falconer (Fig. 120); the design was inspired by a traditional Tanzanian house, harking to the ministry there of the vicar John Cornwall. A further physical expression of Holy Trinity's African links is the crucifix above the pulpit; a gift from the Diocese of Masasi in the south of Tanzania.

Fig. 120 Peter Falconer's Porch Room with the new lantern and doors: the church is open!

The Porch Room was further altered to include toilet and kitchen facilities to designs by Toby Falconer in 2014, and new glass doors and a glass lantern have been added to the connecting link by Antony Feltham-King in 2020.

The 2016 re-ordering

THE 2016 REORDERING provided the churchwardens and Parochial Church Council (PCC) an opportunity to reassess the use of the church at every level, with consultation with the congregation and every user-group, and the preliminary work encompassed every aspect of use, from the damp, to seating, heating and public address systems. This largely mirrors the process carried out in 1842, when Ricardo, the Revd Whateley and others would have sat down with the architect Foster to work through what they wanted for the new church: what worked in the current building, what didn't work, what could be saved, and what could be afforded. Of course they felt far less constrained by the existing building than the 21st-century PCC, and their consultation with the congregation was perhaps more one-sided, but accounts of the run up to the re-ordering of 1842 make fascinating reading from the perspective of the modern day and highlight the need to preserve minutes and opinions for

Fig. 121 Clearing out the rubble and dust from beneath the pew platforms of the nave

Fig. 122 Shuttering work for the new floor slab and underfloor heating

future historians. The research to write the Statement of Significance needed to support the application for a Faculty revealed the breadth of historical sources, and ignited wider interest in the history of the church and has led to this publication.

Fig. 123 The chancel arch, rood, crossing and Burge's chancel

THE 2016 REORDERING

The recent reordering has seen the removal of some of the 1842 structures and the installation of underfloor heating and drainage to combat the damp that previously affected the building (Fig. 121, Fig. 122), caused by the failure of an 1842 culvert under the church.

The most visible change has been the removal of the nineteenth century pews and pew bases and the laying of a new limestone floor across the main body of the church. FC Eden's rood screen, but not the rood, has been translated by 90 degrees to now stand between the Lady Chapel and the Choir (Fig. 123, Fig. 124). Following further issues with damp under the chancel that were causing Burges' tiles to crack and split, a new soakaway was excavated in the churchyard to take the water from the north chancel roof, which previously had just run out of the end of a shallow underground pipe!

The opportunity was taken to address many long-standing problems and upgrade the infrastructure of the church, in some ways the 2016 reordering has seen the most significant changes to the church since 1842, however the fabric of the 1842 church remained almost entirely intact.

The organ is currently being restored and the next phase of works is to repair and enhance the stained glass. As the 16th and 17th-century accounts show so clearly, a church is never static, and there is always something to do!

Fig. 124 The view down the nave into the chancel

Under the floorboards

The removal of the timber Victorian pews revealed a number of items that had ended up in the dust and rubble beneath the floorboards. Several of the items are likely to have been dropped by children, suggesting their attention may not have been wholly on the service in hand; a 'Players

Fig. 125 Cigarette cards and a cardboard milk bottle top from under the pews

Cigarettes' card of St Laurence's Gate, Drogheda is No 42 in a series of 50 'Celebrated Gateways' cards and dates from 1909. Cigarette cards stiffened packets of cigarettes and from the late 19th-century sets of themed cards were printed, with albums produced for card collectors. A 'Barratt & Co LTD' cigarette card from 1955 was aimed at a slightly younger market, this card was included with confectionary cigarettes. The card is from a pack of 'Mickey's Sweet Cigarettes' featuring the character Tinker Bell from Disney's film of Peter Pan (released 1953), number 32 of a series of 35 cards. A card milk bottle top stating 'PURE NEW MILK AS THE COW GIVES IT' is a fairly common design in the 1950s, just before aluminium foil started being used as bottle tops; these tops were used in games, latterly re-emerging as 'Pogs' in the early 1990s (Fig. 125). Other items found loose included a 1937 George VI halfpenny, a copper alloy thimble, a cockleshell and a number of clay tobacco pipes, one dating from the 17th century.

The finds

Barring architectural fragments, only a very limited amount of artefactual material was recovered during the evaluation and watching brief, this no doubt is largely due to the scraping of much of the inside of the church down to bedrock at the 1842 demolition. Descriptions of finds have been integrated into the main text wherever they add to the narrative. A full quantification and description is available in the post-excavation reports.[299]

Only 28 sherds of pottery were recovered from the site: two sherds of Roman 'Severn Valley' pottery hint at early occupation and there is a single sherd of 11th–12th-century Oolitic Limestone Ware pottery from the churchyard, as well as four sherds of early/mid-12th–16th-century Minety-type ware and two sherds of 14th–early 17th-century Oxidized glazed Malvernian Ware. The rest of the pottery is post-medieval, much of it probably introduced during the 1842 rebuild.

Four fragments of greenish window glass were recovered, two from a layer of rubble and dust beneath the pews, probably from the removal of windows in 1842, whilst the others were found in grave backfills in the soakaway excavation.

A surprisingly small number of fragments of medieval floor tiles were recovered from the watching brief, these were largely undiagnostic although one can be reconstructed as part of a 16-tile design that would have formed part of a complex pavement.

Twenty-seven fragments of clay tobacco pipes were found in the evaluation and watching brief, with seven partial or complete pipe bowls found. There are three decorated pipes but no maker's stamps, the pipes represent a small group of largely locally made pipes and range in date from c.1600 to the mid-19th century.

Pins included copper alloy pins with heads formed from wound wire, common from the medieval period until the 19th century. The Gloucester pin industry produced pins by hand from the late 16th century until well into the 19th century; by 1763 Gloucester was probably the largest production centre of pins in Britain before declining during the Napoleonic Wars with Bristol, Bath and Birmingham all taking market share.[300] Stroud was a production centre for pins in the 19th century, utilising waterpower from the disused textile mills to power newly invented pin making machines from 1834, commercial electroplating was developed shortly after and four such pins were recovered.[301] The pins are likely to have been used as shroud pins and to fasten funeral clothes, although given their small size some could also be casual losses within the church.

<SF2>

Fig. 126 Copper alloy button from a grave

A two-piece brass button from a grave backfill is made from a domed front clasping a flat back with a separate loop or shank which has been swaged onto the back (Fig. 126). Some silvering remains on the dome, which is decorated with a raised emblem of St Edward's crown on a background of radiating 'starburst' lines; the form of the crown indicates it is of Victorian date. The button falls into a large group known as 'Patriotic' which were issued periodically c.1780–1910 and is likely to be from the uniform of a civilian and be of mid 19th century date (Pickup *pers. comm.*); such small buttons were used on peaked caps to secure the chinstrap, and on waistcoats. It is likely to have been a casual loss in the churchyard, rather than from funeral clothes.

A copper alloy lace-tag or aglet was recovered from a grave fill, it is made from an undecorated sheet of copper alloy rolled into a tapered tube, which tapers gradually along its 42.4mm length. The lace-tag would have been fixed onto the end of a thin cloth or leather cord or ribbon used to tightly tie up clothing; lace-tags are known from the Saxon period being more often found from at least the 14th century to the early 17th century;[302] the excavated example is a Livings Type I lace-tag, most commonly found in 15th and 16th century contexts.[303] Lace-tags have been found in burial contexts however this example is likely to be residual in this context and represent a casual loss above ground rather than be from burial clothes.

Cross-slabs

Whilst most medieval graves would have had simple wooden marker crosses, wealthier parishioners including gentry, merchants and priests might be afforded a stone memorial. In the medieval period the most common surviving form of memorial was a *cross-slab*: a flat or coped stone slab that was set over the grave, or less often formed the lid to a stone coffin, and was decorated with a form of cross. Cross-slabs would have been found both inside the church, and in the churchyard, and are the precursors of the later ledgers and memorial slabs we are more familiar with.

During the 1842 rebuilding more than twenty of these cross-slabs, and numerous fragments, were recovered from 'the foundation of the body of the Church, they were broken to suit the building: they all were adorned with Crosses of various patterns.' [304] Although broken they were in a 'remarkably fine state of preservation, –the incisions of some of them being almost as sharply defined as when they were first made' (Fig. 127). Most of the slabs are of late 12th to 13th century date but were found within the 14th-century walls of the nave and chancel, presumably disturbed from their original settings and reused in the new walls. As flat slabs they were useful building material and one cross-slab had been re-used as a sill for the east window of the chancel, whilst another was used in the north end of the ceiling of the 14th-century south transept, where it is just visible with a very powerful torch and good eyesight.[305]

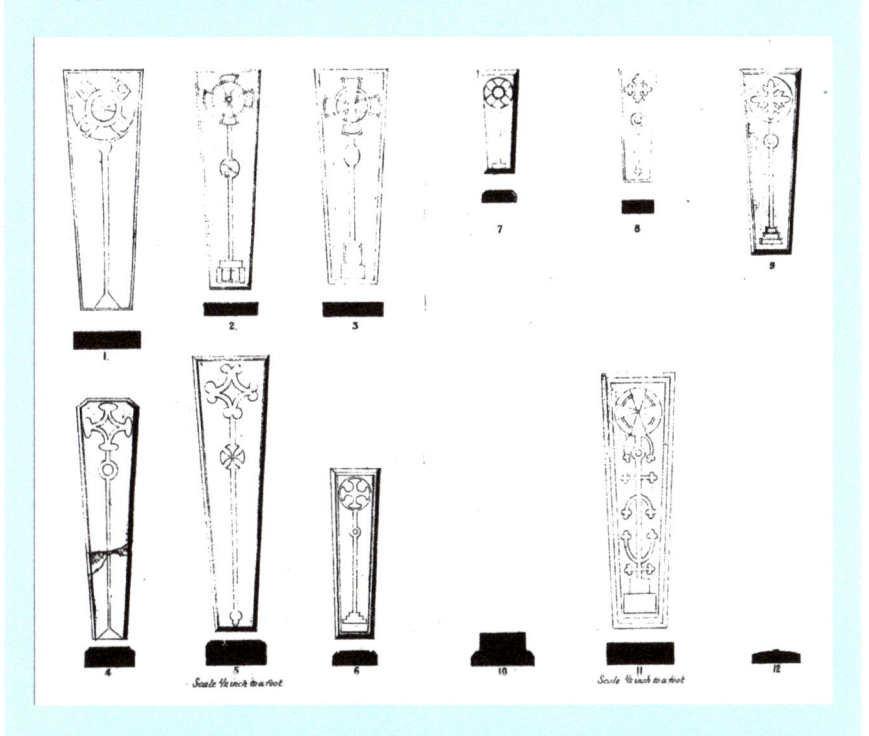

Fig. 127 12th- and 13th-century cross-slabs found during the 1842 rebuilding[306]

GF Playne relates how the slabs were appropriated by the contractors, presumably amongst them Shepstone, and given to 'anyone who cared to have them' ending up in 'rockeries and ferneries, or lying in neglected corners of pleasure grounds'.[307] At least one slab was transported to Stonehouse Manor, nearly seven miles by road, where within a few dozen years it had acquired a local myth that it was the gravestone of Cromwell's horse. A further cross-slab of similar date has been found set into a Victorian outbuilding in town and more almost certainly await rediscovery. GF Playne illustrates twelve of the cross-slabs, including the cross-slabs which survive to this day in the church and churchyard.[308]

DEATH, BURIAL AND MEMORIAL

Death, burial and memorial was a preoccupation for the medieval population; anticipated during life, this final episode was marked by the funeral mass and burial, but beyond that point prayers and intercessions for the dead were a major concern and a key part of the role of the medieval church.

As with most parish churches, nearly all baptised parishioners would have been buried in the churchyard, with a far smaller number buried within the church itself -generally those from the wealthier and more socially important families. By design the recent work at Holy Trinity had a very limited impact on the burials within the church with only one burial requiring exhumation; following osteological study this individual has been reburied in the graveyard. Excavation for the new soakaway outside in the graveyard required the recording and exhumation of thirteen burials; again these have been studied and reburied in the churchyard.

Burials within the church

Graves in the excavated areas of the church were concentrated in front of the crossing and in the aisles, with most surviving graves being deeply dug into the bedrock. The backfill of several of the graves was very loose, with frequent voids suggesting that the deceased had probably been buried within coffins which had subsequently rotted away and collapsed.

Whilst Shepstone only records burials outside the church (with one in the west doorway) he most likely removed shallow burials from the interior of the church when it was stripped down to bedrock prior to rebuilding. That extremely shallow graves had been present inside the church is demonstrated by the burial of a young man[309] in the south aisle who had been buried in a coffin immediately below the pre-1842 floor level (see below). We cannot be sure how many similarly shallow internal burials Shepstone removed, but the 2016 excavations revealed at least eight further graves and five tombs within the church, all of which predated the 1842 rebuild. Further graves and tombs are likely to be present in the north transept, crossing and chancel in areas that were not excavated in 2016.

The date of these graves and tombs is uncertain, although many are likely to be post-medieval in date; interment within the church would have been made far more difficult once the interior was filled with box pews, however the floor plan of the church in 1841 shows that although many internal graves were placed within the aisles, many graves and tombs were in fact beneath pews (Fig. 128).

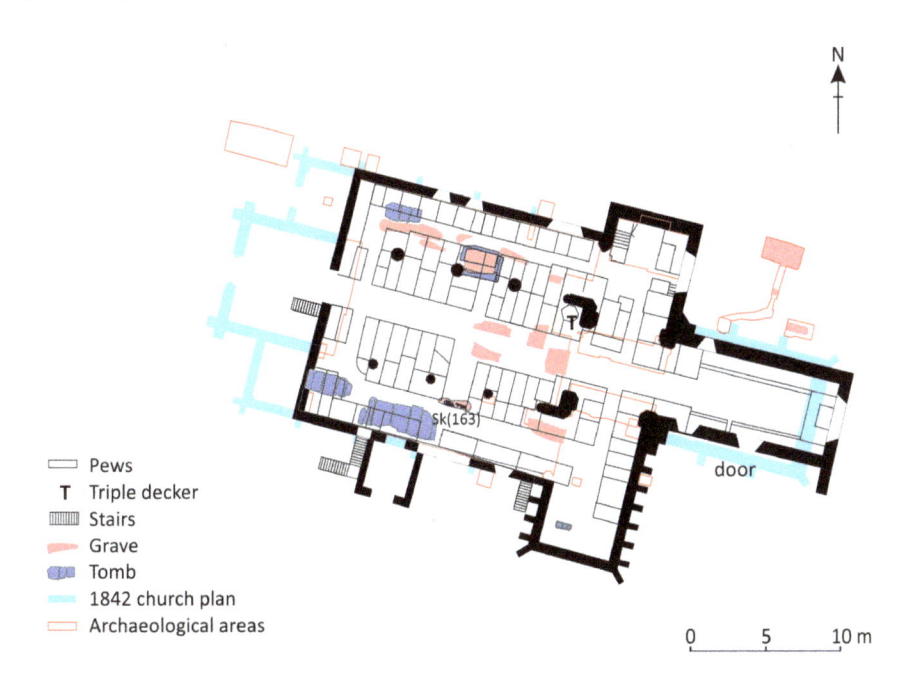

Fig. 128 Holy Trinity in 1841 showing the pew plan superimposed over recorded burials and tombs.

During the 2016 works all surviving graves were undisturbed, with a single exception; along the line of the south arcade a thin strip of brashy soil had survived to a level just below the 1842 floor level, this area needed to be dug down to allow for the new underfloor heating system, and within this strip lay a very shallow grave which was excavated. In 2021, the excavation of a new soakaway in the churchyard led to a further 13 burials being exhumed.

Tombs

Five tombs or vaults were recorded during the archaeological works in the nave and aisles, each probably used by an individual family and marked by a memorial slab set in the floor, or possibly on a nearby wall. The earliest tomb was a wide, kite-shaped tomb in the north aisle lined with faced limestone

Fig. 129 The kite-shaped masonry tomb by the north arcade, the dark soil is from a later interment; scale 0.3m

Fig. 130 Massive limestone slabs covering burial vaults in the south aisle; scale 0.5m

blocks, originally it would have been covered with large stone slabs, however these had been removed and the tomb had been infilled, with graves then dug within the tomb (Fig. 129). Large stone slabs sealed two tombs or vaults in

DEATH, BURIAL AND MEMORIAL 149

the south aisle; smaller tombs were present in the north aisle and in the south transept, these are likely to contain several coffins each stacked one on top of each other.

Burial in the church was a disruptive event, requiring the floor to be taken up and relaid, often with a new ledger or memorial set over the grave, and from 1575 to at least 1687 the church charged a fee of flat 6s 8d for each such burial. The remains of such burials were seen across the nave and aisles, with large limestone slabs sealing tombs (Fig. 130).

The Churchwardens' Accounts record several internal burials in the 16th and 17th centuries and often emphasise the physical impact of such burials: in 1575 for 'the seueralle buryalles of Walter Payne, Thomas Kynne, and Rychard Sewelle, buryed wythin the churche', in 1593 'for breaking up of the churche for Mr. Carpenter's graue', in 1595 'for breakinge the churche pavement for the buriall of William Millward', and in 1635 'for breaking up of the church for Hancockes grave'. In 1650 there was 5s 'for one grave beeing made in the church'. In 1653 the fee of 12s 8d which was received from Edward Arndell and Will. Perrie, 'for breaking open the church' may be for two burials, although the fee is lower than would be expected. In 1686 and 1687 Mr Driver and John Iles each paid 6s 8d for 'breaking the church'.

It does not appear that any burials were interred within the church following the 1842 rebuild, certainly there were none in the nave or aisles, although the ashes of the former rector Rex Hodson (1887–1976) and Mollie

Fig. 131 The northern churchyard, a peaceful haven of reflection and nature

Hodson (1897–1988) were interred beneath the floor of the Lady Chapel.
Burial in the churchyard

The vast majority of parishioners were buried in the churchyard, and over the thousand or so years that Holy Trinity has stood, many thousands of individuals have been interred there, the graveyard being extended northwards at least twice (Fig. 131). The surviving gravestones and memorials only mark a small fraction of those graves -there are none earlier than the 17th century for example, and the ground around the church is likely to have been dug over many times as new generations of parishioners were interred.

Indication of the density of burial was given by the excavation for the new soakaway immediately north of the chancel. Thirteen burials were exhumed from this trench, with several more individuals left *in situ*, with a burial density in excess of 2 burials per cubic metre.

All of the excavated individuals had been laid in graves aligned east–west, with their head laid at the west end as is standard Christian practice. The earliest burial was also one of the deepest, it was of a young, possibly female, adult and the body had been surrounded by rough slabs of limestone to create a cist around the body.[310] This burial had been cut through by the grave of an infant who had died aged 6–8 months and who had possible metastatic neuroblastoma, a form of cancer.[311] Two of the limestone blocks from the earlier grave had been appropriated and used to mark the head and foot of the grave (Fig. 132).

Fig. 132 Photo of cist burial in the centre between the two upright slabs, and infant burial to the right; scale 0.2m

Stone-lined or 'cist' burials are known in England from the Roman period onwards, and are fairly common in the Anglo-Saxon period, however they are also a known burial practice in medieval graveyards where they have been well documented in monastic cemeteries.[312] The location of Holy Trinity on the Cotswold limestone would ensure that the digging of most deep graves would generate the thin limestone blocks, so it is perhaps not surprising that stone-lined graves were found.

During the 1842 rebuilding works the ground at the west end of the church was terraced, and Shepstone the builder reported that 'On excavating… to form the new approach to the entrance we found to the number of eight or ten graves of a very simple but curious description containing generally skeletons of full grown persons. These had been interred without a coffin the rock had been excavated to the depth of a few inches affording little more than room enough to receive the length and width of the corpse, undressed stones from two to three inches in thickness were fixed on edge intirely [sic] rounded sufficiently high to receive a rough flat stone covering to clear, the bones were remarkable clean the teeth in beautiful preservation. One of these graves may be found under the large entrance door, there is also a stone coffin without a lid in the immediate neighbourhood of these near the S.W corner of the S Aisle'.[313]

The other individuals excavated for the soakaway were buried in simple graves, with the body laid to rest in either just a shroud, or within a wooden coffin. The earliest excavated burials were laid in cloth shrouds, which can be demonstrated by the position of the bones compared to coffin burials -where the shoulders and pelvis have space to 'relax' as they are not held in place by the soil around them. Pins found associated with the skeletons and redeposited in graves are probably from fixing shrouds or burial dress in place, some may be of medieval or post-medieval date, whilst two are electro-plated and are Victorian. Burials would have been made in a simple shroud in the medieval period, made of wool after 1667. Later burials were increasingly dressed in linen or cotton clothes and with bonnets which were fixed with pins, with the coffins having elaborate linings.

Other, stratigraphically later burials, may be medieval but cannot be dated except by the lack of coffin nails and furniture, which suggests the earlier date. Later graves containing *in situ* or redeposited coffin nails and grips/handles are likely to date to the 17th century or later. Five burials within soakaway excavation were in coffins, with a further two individuals possibly buried in coffins. The latest grave, the coffined burial of an elderly woman, almost certainly postdates the rebuilding of the church in 1842: the backfill of the grave contained two electro-plated pins and a Victorian button

None of the excavated graves were still marked by headstones at the time of excavation and no trace of any markers was found, however it is likely that some of the burials would have been marked by a marker of some sort, some may have been cleared during the 1842 rebuilding, or may have been in wood or stone which had decayed over the centuries. Headstones immediately east of the excavated trench, including a reused 17th-century headstone, are from the mid-19th century and indicate that there were burials in the immediate area after the rebuilding of the church.

In contrast to burial within the church, burial in the churchyard could be a far cheaper option, although only recorded twice in the accounts. In 1598 the cost of shrouds for Eisame and for an unnamed man 'that died in the church purche' the fee 'for makinge their graues' and a payment to Marget Mallard and Goody Swaine for a sadly undecipherable service was only 3s 4d, whilst in 1635 'the bur[y]ing of the straing man, y^t dyed in ye feilde' was 1s 6d. The burial of the unnamed man in the porch and the 'strange man' are probably references to vagrants where the burial costs would fall on the parish. After laying in, the deceased would be carried to the church on a wooden bier; this was mended in 1617, and in 1634 four shillings was paid for 'macking of the cover of the bier and the timber'.

Burial costs are not often mentioned in the Churchwardens' Accounts, except where the parish paid for them; in 1830 Workhouse overseer John Rudge was contracted 'to make the Coffins and find the Dresses at the sum of 12s 6d each one with the other' possibly for deceased inmates of the parish workhouse.[314]

Burials were made on all sides of the church, with the burial ground extending to the north for some distance due to the constraints on other sides. The north side of churchyards has sometimes been thought of as a less popular choice for burial, or been used for lower status burials than the southern sides,[315] however at Holy Trinity there was a high density of burials and there is no indication that, at least in the post-medieval period, this area was used in any way differently to the other areas of the churchyard with numerous elaborate memorials across the northern churchyard dating from the 18th century, including that of James Bradley, Astronomer Royal who died in 1742. The finding of decorated coffin furniture and the proportion of coffins from the excavated burials confirms that this was not an area used exclusively for pauper burials (who might be buried solely in a shroud), or for those of a lower social or economic status, although this may be due to the proximity to the church.

The churchyard was extended to the north in 1832, the land being sold by David Ricardo at £60 an acre. The new churchyard was enclosed in a mortared wall 8 feet high using the old coping, presumably taken from an old wall in poor repair, and with a doorway onto Bell Lane.[316] The churchyard was not solely used for burials, it was also used for unofficial activities and in 1841 the churchwardens had to be instructed to stop clothes being hung out to dry.[317]

During the 1842 rebuilding, external terracing, and the widening of Bell Lane graves would have been disturbed and the cemetery soil was piled up and made available to be taken away by parishioners. An outbreak of Typhus in 1846 was linked, by some, to the cemetery soil.[318] An additional area was consecrated for burial on August 19th 1843, this may have been the southwestern corner of the present churchyard, which had previously been occupied by buildings.[319]

Shrouds and burial clothes

In the medieval period the deceased would have been prepared for the grave and wrapped in a simple linen sheet, tied at head and foot and with copper pins sometimes used to close the front seam of the shroud. Shrouds are mentioned in the Churchwardens' Accounts in 1598 when two shrouds are bought 'for him that died in the church purche and an other for Eisame'.[320]

To protect the wool trade and reduce imports of foreign linen, Acts of Parliament were passed between 1666 and 1668 requiring all burials to be in an English wool shroud, on pain of a fine of £5. The onus was on the parish to witness and record compliance in a register and the Churchwardens' Accounts for 1678 lists a payment of 2 shillings 'for a booke to enter ye burialls in woolen'.[321] The rich would occasionally pay this sumptuary tax, but in a wool town like Minchinhampton it is likely that nearly all would be buried in wool. The act was repealed in 1814.

From the 18th century the body was usually placed in a shift and bonnet -the latter tied in place under the chin, and coffin sheets were pinned in place to the side of the coffin. 'Shroud pins' could be used to tack the shroud or coffin sheet in place, pin a bonnet onto the deceased's hair, or fix the burial clothes in place. Several copper pins were recovered from both grave backfills, and from close association with individual burials

Pauper burials would have been in a simple shroud and would have been transported to the graveside in the parish coffin, a simple re-useable coffin that afforded some dignity, but which in the early 18th century fell out of favour as a potential cause of contagion.[322]

Coffins and coffin furniture

Prior to the 18th century the majority of individuals were wrapped in their woollen shroud and placed directly into the grave with no coffin, but increasingly coffins became the norm in most burials. At first the coffins, made by the local joiner, would have been simple boxes of planks fixed with wooden pegs, and with the lid nailed on. Later they would have coffin grips (handles) and possibly coffin plates in varying numbers around the coffin and would be nailed together and so easier to identify archaeologically. Even when not excavated, coffined burials can sometimes be identified by the voids caused by the collapse of the coffin, it is likely that most of the burials left *in situ* within the church were of coffined burials.

The excavated coffin furniture includes examples of these decorated coffin grips (handles), grip plates, escutcheons and metal coffin 'lace.' The finds show that some Minchinhampton burials were decorated with coffin furniture produced by specialist manufacturers many of which were in Birmingham, with the same designs found as on burials excavated in Gloucester and London. Coffin lace gets only a passing mention in Tuesby and Cooper's catalogue of 1783, but there are 33 designs of coffin lace in a pattern book of *c.*1826 (Fig. 133, Fig. 134).[323]

Fig. 133 Tin-plated coffin lace from the graveyard excavation; coffin lace was tacked on as decoration and to hold fabric covering the coffin in place

DEATH, BURIAL AND MEMORIAL

Coffins became increasingly decorated and might be covered in fabric which was held in place by small tacks or by decorative 'coffin lace'. Patterns of studs could be used to mark out patterns on coffins, and in the 18th century tin escutcheon plates were often nailed onto the lid and sides.[324]

Coffins for adults usually had eight grips or handles, three to each side and one at each end, whilst children's coffins had only two per side, although at the Quaker burial site of Coach Lane, North Shields over half the coffins only had two grips: one at each end, possibly reflecting

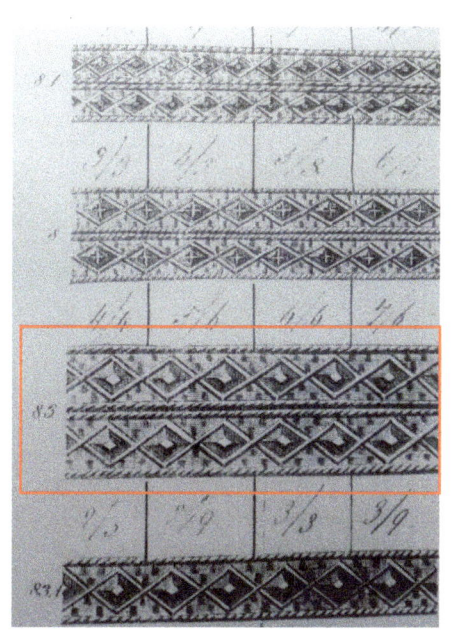

Fig. 134 Coffin lace with diamond lozenge decoration from the 'AT' catalogue

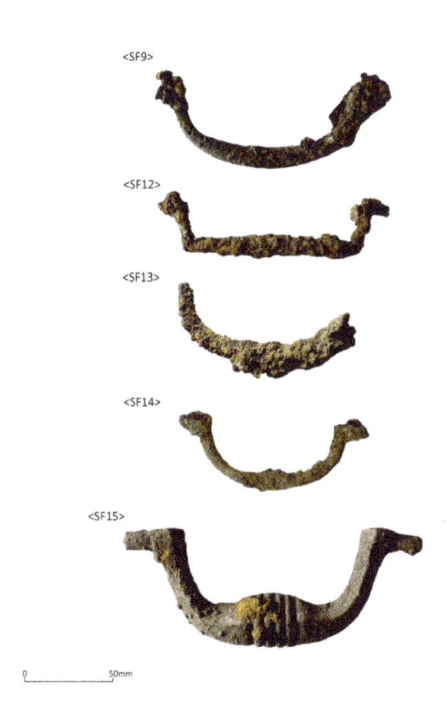

Fig. 135 Cast coffin grips from the churchyard excavation

a simpler burial rite.[325] Grips were attached by bent iron loops or rings to the coffin and given the weight of a full coffin the grips may have been largely decorative.

The grips can be divided into two main groups, wrought-iron fixed grips very similar to handles used on contemporary furniture and which would have projected out from the coffin at 90° (Fig. 136), and hinged cast iron handles that may have been made in the specialist coffin furniture factories of London, or Birmingham where the trade moved in the early 19th century (Fig. 135).[326] Blacksmith made wrought iron grips are essentially identical in form to handles from contemporary furniture and are hard to date precisely on the basis of their stylistic features, although they appear to be used in funerary contexts between 1650 and 1750 after which they were superseded by cast hinged grips.

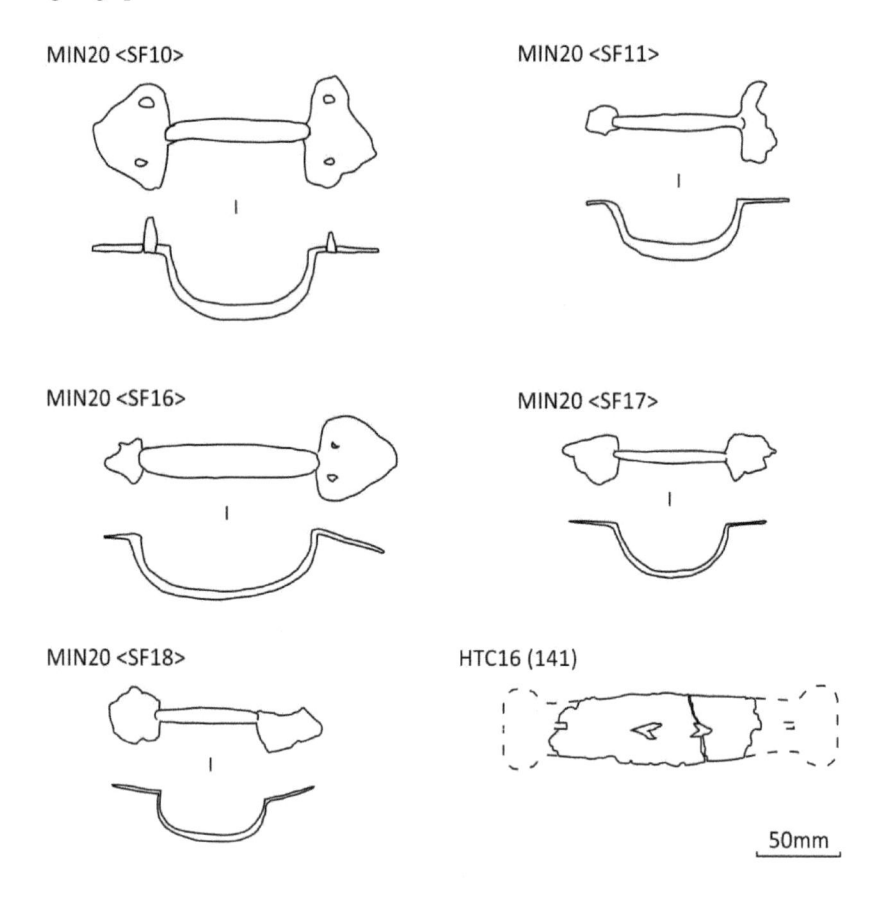

Fig. 136 Wrought iron coffin grips from the churchyard excavation, and a grip plate from inside the church

Grips were often used in conjunction with grip plates which could be a simple thin strip of sheet iron like the plate perforated by two 'V' shaped holes and one rectangular hole; similar examples are known from the late 17th century onwards and have various forms of terminal; this grip plate is likely to date from the early to mid-18th century and is very similar to an example with double lobed terminal from St Oswald, Gloucester.[327]

Grip plates could be elaborately decorated, especially die-stamped tin-plated iron grip plates with matching escutcheon plates. They would be sold 'white' (unpainted) or could be japanned in a variety of finishes[328]. Two matching decorated tin-plated grip plates <SF7–8> were recovered from the backfill of a grave in the churchyard; they are decorated in *bas relief* with an opposed pair of winged putto heads above an empty cartouche with decorative palm foliage; the background has radiating lines and there is a laurel border (Fig. 137). The design is extremely similar to examples illustrated in the Tuesby and Cooper trade catalogue of 1783 (Fig. 138), where four sizes were available for between 3s 2d and 7s 6d[329] and to grip plate design no 3 from the crypt at Christchurch Spitalfields, London where it is dated between 1768 and 1842;[330] a similar grip plate was found with an ornately decorated grip during recent excavations at Gloucester cathedral,[331] and the design is described as 'ubiquitous' at St Augustine the Less, Bristol.[332] Both <SF7> and

Fig. 137 Late 18th century coffin grip plate with attached grip <SF8> from the backfill of a grave excavated in the churchyard

Fig. 138 Grip plates of the same design as the excavated examples in a coffin furniture trade catalogue of c.1783[333]

<SF8> have their coffin grip still attached (these were sold separately), these are of Spitalfields type 2a (1763–1837); a further coffin grip <SF9> in the same form was attached to a small fragment of attached plate was recovered from the same context, and may be part of the same disturbed coffin.

Decorative grip plates were mass produced with a centre of production in Birmingham. The only surviving catalogue for funerary goods from the 18th century, that of Tuesby and Cooper from 1783, includes elaborate designs of puttees, urns and flowers however such designs do not appear in a pattern book of 1826 by which time they appear to have fallen out of fashion, and it is likely that the grip plates date from the later 18th century or early 19th century.[334]

All this is tantalising evidence for the development of the undertaker's trade, with more affluent families perhaps using undertakers and ordering fashionable coffin furniture, whilst poorer families selected locally made, or cheaper, handles. By the 18th century specialist coffin furniture was certainly accessible to Minchinhampton families, however without a larger sample, or closer dating, it is hard to unpick the influences of social status, trade and availability and compare it with the more closely studied cities.

Memorials

From its first consecration the churchyard would have been the burial place for the vast majority of parishioners, and whilst there is no surviving memorial to nearly all these individuals, a large and important group of 17th, 18th and 19th century memorials still survive both inside and outside the church. As well as these extant funerary monuments, there is an important assemblage of *ex situ* earlier memorials which demonstrate the diversity and development of some of the main types of medieval and post-Reformation memorial over the centuries. Memorials can be found not only in the churchyard but also on the walls and floor of the church with several curated together in the narthex of the church. Many local families are represented on the memorials, although it must be remembered that most burials would have had just a simple marker, and that only the wealthy or well-connected would be likely to get a memorial inside the church.

Cross-slabs

The earliest surviving memorials are known as cross-slabs, these are a type of medieval stone grave marker common in Gloucestershire from the Norman conquest through to the later 15th century. They are usually a flat or coped slab with carved decoration in the form of a cross, the style of which can be broadly dated. Cross-slabs would have been placed over stone coffins but also simply over a backfilled grave, with the slab set flush or slightly proud of the floor or

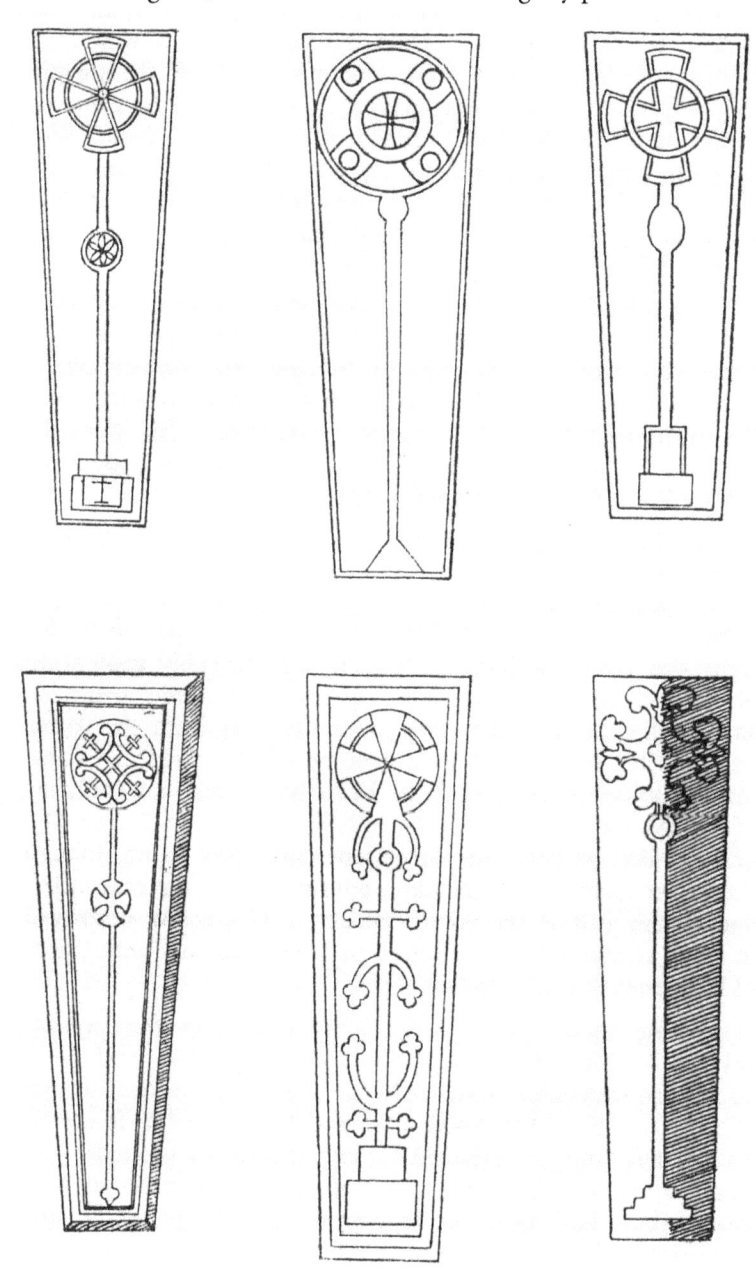

Fig. 139 Illustration of cross slabs found in the walls of the 14th-century church during the 1842 rebuilding[335]

the earth. Cross-slabs were set both inside and outside the church and were occasionally adorned with a motif such as a chalice, shears or sword which is taken to indicate the deceased's occupation or rank. Cross-slabs were rarely inscribed and very seldom bear the name of the deceased, although some later examples have inscriptions in Lombardic script.

During the demolition of the medieval church many cross-slabs, mostly of 12th or 13th-century date were found reused in the core of the 14th-century church walls 'all were adorned with Crosses of various patterns' (Fig. 139),[336] they had presumably been disturbed and reused during the construction of the south aisle in the mid-14th century. A further cross-slab had also been reset in the stone vault of the South Transept, where it is still just visible with a torch and good eyesight. More than twenty complete cross-slabs and many fragments were recorded in 1842, and two of the cross-slabs found in 1842 have been reset in the narthex wall, with a further fragment of a cross-slab may be found placed against the cemetery wall east of the chancel.

No definite cross-slabs were recovered during the watching brief, although a fragment of a coped, tapered slab executed in the local Minchinhampton Weatherstone may be from a cross-slab.[337]

Some cross-slabs acted as lids for stone coffins, and a stone coffin, with no lid, was found in 1842 near the southwest corner of the south aisle.[338] The stone coffins, often equipped with drainage holes to allow the liquids of putrefaction to drain away, might be buried below ground, the lid being flush with the ground, or be above ground as in wall tombs. The tomb niche in the north transept contained a stone coffin, with a cross-slab lid bearing an inscribed cross; the coffin 'contained a skeleton of an adult, together with traces of habiliments and clouted shoes' and was destroyed in 1842.[339]

Effigies and wall tombs

The south transept was rebuilt as a chantry chapel in the early–mid 14th century and is home to the recumbent stone effigies of its founders, John and Lucy de la Mare. The effigies are set within a pair of ogee-arched tomb recesses set into the south wall beneath the window. A wall niche is also present in the north transept which was constructed at around the same date and was also a chantry. A third wall tomb was noted in the chancel, probably on the north wall.[340]

Brasses

By the late 15th and 16th century engraved brasses, set into stone slabs, started

DEATH, BURIAL AND MEMORIAL

to replace cross-slabs as memorials. Three medieval brasses survive and are now set up in the narthex. The brass of the merchant John Hampton (†c.1461) and his wife Ellen, shown in burial shrouds with their daughter Alys and other children was in the north transept according to Bigland and Rudder, the latter stating it was 'fixed on a flat stone' (Fig. 140).[341] This brass may be that mentioned in the late 17th century by Wantner, although the description does not match the surviving brass.[342]

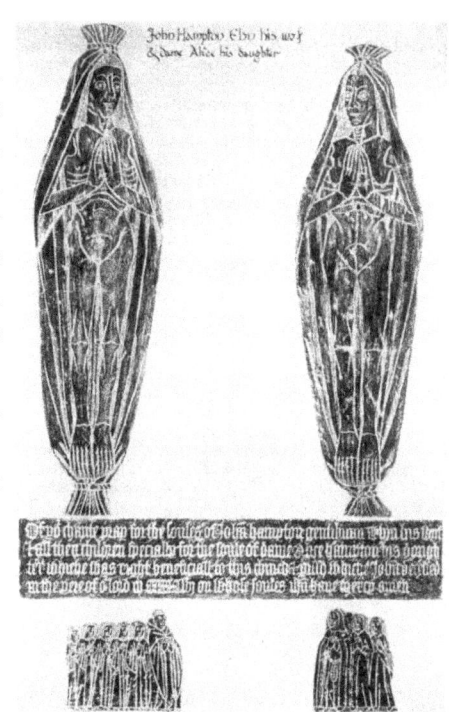

Fig. 140 The brass of the merchant John Hampton (†c.1461) and his wife Ellen in shrouds, with their daughter Alys, and other children (from Playne 1915 opposite p69)

A brass of c.1500 to a man and his wife has lost its inscription; the third brass is to the cloth merchant Edward Halliday (†1519) of Rodborough[343] and his wife Margery and includes Edward's cloth-mark (refitted upside down), this is reported by Wantner as being set in a large stone slab in the south *alley* or aisle, but by Bigland as in the south transept (Fig. 141).[344]

Fig. 141 Brass of Edward Halliday (†1519) of Rodborough and his wife Margery[345]

Ledgers and memorials

Stone ledgers were a slightly later type of memorial and usually bore an inscription, sometimes in Latin script, on a flat stone slab. Fragments of five late 16th to late 17th-century ledgers were recovered during the archaeological works although all of their inscriptions were too worn or fragmentary to decipher. Two larger, and slightly later, limestone slabs would have held engraved copper plates, similar to those found in the churchyard, whilst another large slab was simply inscribed 'MV 1710'.

Eight large stone memorial slabs are now set in the floor of the narthex, these would have originally been set into the floor around the church, many sited over the family vault, and would have been moved and reset during the 1842 reordering.

Bigland records ten engraved brass plates in the nave, all dating from the late 17th and 18th centuries, the wording of five plates indicates that they lie above the deceased. All were probably set in stone ledgers.[346]

Wall-mounted memorials

The church contains a number of wall-mounted memorials which were re-erected after 1842. They range from simple plaques to ornate classical memorials in imported stones such as marble. At least two wall-mounted memorials are shown on HE Relton's sketch of the south side of the church, with Antiquarian Ralph Bigland recording a freestone monument to Elizabeth Chambers †1725 on the south side of the chancel, and Elizabeth Deane †1640, and Martha †1684 and William and Nathaniel Webb †1742 on the south wall.[347]

Anne Baynham

Removal of the organ for its renovation in 2023 revealed a wall mounted memorial high up on west wall of the north transept (Fig. 142). The memorial is to Anne Baynham, who died in 1632. A recumbent effigy of an infant, dressed in a ruff and dress, lies with their right arm on a skull – a *momento mori* or symbol of mortality, in her left hand is a lily branch representing purity. The inscription tells that Anne died at less than 30 days of age, and was daughter of Alice and Joseph Baynham.

Here lyeth the Body of
ANNE, Daughter to
JOSEPH BAYNHAM,

> Who was second Sonne to
> JOSEPH BAYNHAM, of Westbury,
> Esquire.
> Her Mother was ALICE,
> Fourth daughter to
> ROBERT FREAME, of Lypeat, Esquire.
> She died the 16 Day of August
> Anno Domini 1632.
> She had not spun out thirty days
> but God from paine took her to ioyes
> Let none then trust in worldly bliss
> all youth and age must come to this
> but manner how place where time when
> is knowne to God but not to men
> Watch pray, repent and sinne forsake
> lest unprepard Death thee should take
> Then happy thou that so shall dye
> To give with God eternalye

The effigy is a rare example of a memorial solely to a child, and it is intriguing that such an accomplished (and expensive) monument was set up to a baby lost so young. The sculptor is not known, it is unlikely to have been by the pre-eminent Stroud mason Samuel Baldwin, but was certainly from a specialist workshop.

Ralph Bigland recorded the memorial as being in the chancel and having the Baynham coat of arms above the surviving monument.[348] The monument was also recorded in the chancel by HE Relton in 1843, so must have been moved at the rebuilding.[349]

Anne's grandfather, Joseph Baynham Senior (c.1548–1613) was a staunch Calvinist and attended church in Westbury on Severn as little as possible, worshipping instead in a barn -for which he was prosecuted. This had little effect on his standing as he was High Sheriff of Gloucestershire from 1594 –5 and held Westbury manor until his death in 1613. The family had long had strong Protestant beliefs, one member being burned at the stake in 1532.

Intriguingly Joseph Senior's first wife was Ann, daughter of a man named Hampton (we do not know his first name). Until relatively recently Minchinhampton was often known as Hampton, and there was a family

Fig. 142 The memorial to Anne Baynham, recently moved to the narthex

of that name -in the narthex is the medieval brass commemorating John Hampton who died in 1461, and his wife Ellen and their children including Alys. It was Dame Alys who gave what is now the Holy Trinity sanctus bell in 1515. Could there have been a longstanding family connection between the Westbury Baynhams and Minchinhampton?

Anne's father, Joseph Jr was born in 1590 and was the fifth child, the indebted estate having been sold by his elder brother Alexander (born 1589) in 1625. Joseph Jr moved from Arlingham to Lypiatt, near Stroud) after 1619, and married Anne Freame at Holy Trinity Minchinhampton on 12th September 1625.

Anne's maternal grandfather Robert Freame died in 1599; the family had held Nether Lypiatt manor since probably the 12th century. Both Freame and Baynham families were linked by marriage to the Clutterbuck family of Bisley and Minchinhampton, who held a pew in the north transept and have memorials in Holy Trinity.[350]

The Baynham and Freame families were of some standing, and although perhaps fallen on tougher times, would have held status within their communities, part of this status was reinforced by memorials in prominent positions and it is intriguing, and touching, that little Anne was memorialised at such a young age.

DEATH, BURIAL AND MEMORIAL 165

Fragments of memorials were found during the archaeological work, suggesting that there were many more such memorials in the pre-1842 church, as reflected in Bigland's survey. Sixty-four fragments of hand-moulded Plaster of Paris are probably from a single wall-mounted memorial, the acanthus foliage surrounding a plaque which would have borne the details of the deceased (Fig. 143). The group probably dates from the later 17th to 18th century, certainly pre-dating 1842.

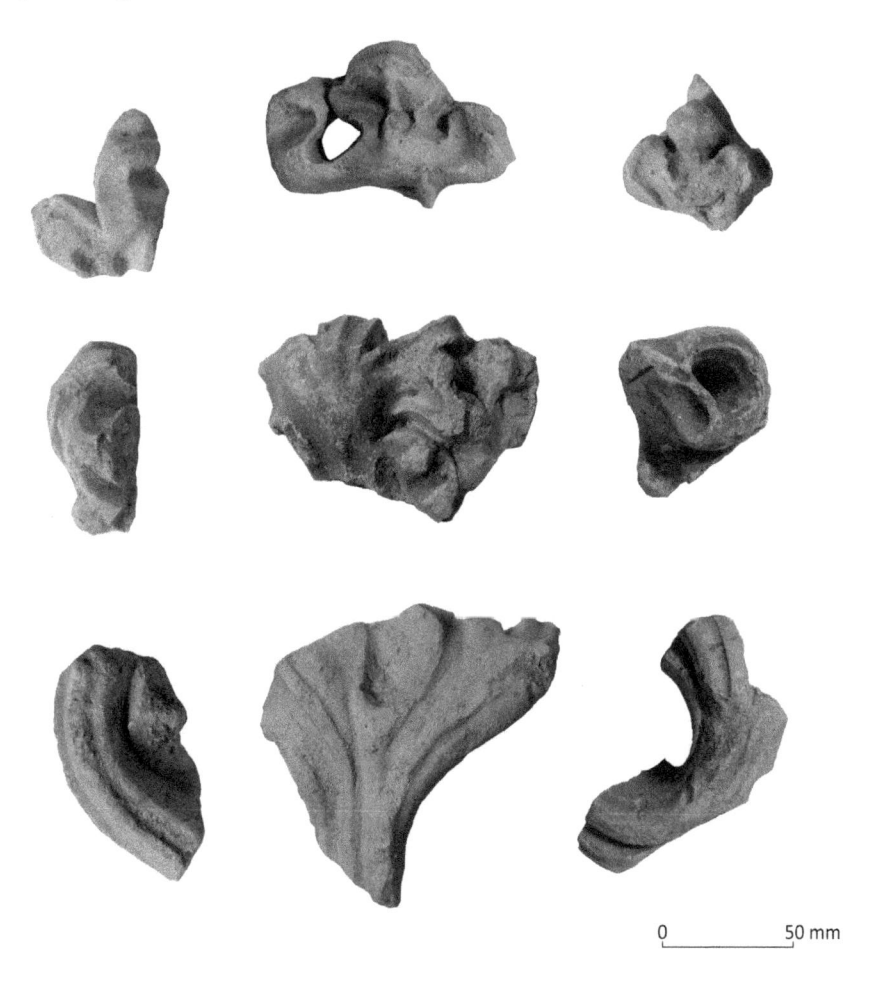

Fig. 143 Hand moulded Plaster of Paris acanthus foliage

Churchyard monuments

The churchyard contains a large and important group of post-reformation tombs, memorials and headstones dating from the 17th to 20th centuries which mark the changing styles and fashions of memorial; several monuments are

*Fig. 144 18th-century tombs decorated with **momento mori** and puttis*

individually Listed by Historic England. Bigland recorded memorials in the church and churchyard, apparently shortly after 1789, the date of the latest headstone in his list. The earliest surviving memorials are headstones dating from the 17th century which often bear '*momento mori*' motifs such as deathsheads, winged *putti* or cherubs, urns and drapes; these motifs also appear on some upstanding tombs (Fig. 144). The vast majority of memorials recorded by Bigland date from the 18th century a bias reflected in the current survivals.[351]

Fig. 145 A late copperplate plaque for Samuel Cosburn Pimbury† 1864 and his wife Alice†1869, inscribed by 'PARKE ENG.'

In the 18th and 19th century many large recumbent memorial slabs were affixed with small copper alloy plates bearing the elegantly inscribed details of the deceased, often signed by the engraver (Fig. 145). A number of these copperplates from the churchyard are set up on the wall of the narthex, whilst the inscribed brass from the tomb of Dr James Bradley (Astronomer Royal from 1742; Fig. 146) was removed from his tomb and set up in the church in the 19th century. By the 19th century headstones had become increasingly popular; the northern extension of the graveyard contains many late 19th-century memorials.

Fig. 146 Dr James Bradley, Astronomer Royal, who is buried in the churchyard[352]

The burials
Gaynor Western

AT THE HEART of the Holy Trinity Church, of course, lie the people. The people who built the church, the people who worshipped here, found comfort and solace, the people who got married and had their children baptised here. Generations of people spanning centuries, indeed throughout the entire history of the Church, would eventually come to be buried here. Fundamentally, the history of the people of Minchinhampton themselves is encapsulated by the congregation who had their funerals at the church and were buried there. Today, these survive as burials of archaeological human skeletal remains, each one telling a unique story of life in the past.

The manner of Christian burials has changed over time as the beliefs and practices within the Church have evolved. Cyst burials enshrining the body with stone, shallow graves with bodies wrapped in shrouds and even the exhumation of older burials, where the traditional 'skull and cross bones' of a person were stored in ossuaries or crypts, were all accepted practices within the medieval Church. Christian burial grounds were more a communal mishmash of human skeletal remains than perhaps we would think of today, with earlier burials being regularly cut through by later ones, and disturbed remains being rather haphazardly deposited in the nearest convenient spot. The Reformation brought about a move away from the Catholic belief in purgatory, whereby souls went through a process of purification before entering heaven. Purgatory went hand in hand with the attention necessarily placed upon a person's soul rather than the physical remains after death; Christian liturgies of prayers for the dead were sung in the chantry chapel and the disturbance of the mortal remains in churchyards was considered no bad thing.

Once the Church of England denounced purgatory in the 16th century, realised lawfully by the Abolition of Chantries Acts in 1545 and 1547, the ensuing belief in glorification shifted the emphasis of treatment of the dead onto the physical body itself and its resurrection to reunite with the soul after death. Increasingly from the 17th century, the intactness of the body in Christian burials became of paramount importance. Investment in protecting the body after death became a core feature of burials. It became the norm for each individual to be interred in a coffin, for example. Graves started to be marked by what were hoped would be permanent headstones and, latterly, footstones. The requirement for individual bodily intactness sat well with Victorian aspirations during the Industrial Revolution, whereby individual ingenuity and prosperity were rewarded with grandiose funerary monuments to be gazed upon in posterity. However, the population was also increasing exponentially during the Victorian period, and very soon churchyards were overflowing with burials, making it impossible to avoid disturbing earlier burials. As a result many churchyards were closed to further burials by law in the mid to late Victorian period on public health grounds following the Burial Acts of 1852, 1853 and 1855. Latterly, belief in the link between the physical body and the resurrection also waned, resulting in the formal introduction of cremation in 1902.

The burials excavated at Holy Trinity Church represent a cross section of these practices, from the earliest phases of burials likely dating to 13th century, including graves furnished with stones, to the final phase of burial in the mid-late Victorian period, including bodies placed in coffins and dressed with pinned shrouds, gowns and head cloths binding the jaw. While the Church today recognises that burial is final, in conjunction with English Heritage, it allows the archaeological investigation, recording and retention of human remains over 100 years old, where construction work will unavoidably disturb any burials within its grounds. This allows the skeletal remains to be studied to develop new understandings of life in the past from the unique scientific evidence they provide, whilst being treated with dignity and respect, archiving each individual skeleton separately in controlled conditions to protect them any further decomposition or disturbance. Osteological analysis of human remains can not only provide information about an individual regarding age at death, biological sex, stature, origins, migration, diet and disease but also information about the community as a whole; how the wider living environment has impacted on human health, how that compares with other communities, and also how that has changed over time. Scientific methods are rapidly developing and we are also just starting to learn how to capture wide-ranging evidence from DNA, providing conclusive evidence of diet and disease, and this is sure to expand in the future.

Construction work was once again undertaken at Holy Trinity Church in 2016 and 2021, representing another phase in its long history of renovations. This time, however, it provided the first opportunity to glimpse into the past lives of the inhabitants of Minchinhampton based on the osteoarchaeological analysis of their skeletal remains. The remains of 14 individuals were exhumed and recorded, though only three were complete due to the intensity of the burial. One burial was excavated from inside the Church and likely represented a higher status individual whereas the remaining thirteen individuals were located in the churchyard and were more likely to be lower status. A very large amount of disarticulated skeletal elements arising from this disturbance of earlier burials were also recovered; despite the small area investigated, a total of 912 individual bones and bone fragments were also scanned for evidence of pathology and supplementary evidence for age, sex and stature where possible. The bone was in excellent condition, meaning that the impact of preservation issues on the analysis was minimal and it was possible to make observations regarding the age and the sex of the exhumed individuals where sufficiently complete as well as observe any pathologies affecting the bone that had occurred during their lifetime.

Of the fourteen articulated individuals that were exhumed, ten were adults and four were sub-adults, suggesting that the areas investigated were used for burial of both adults and children. Three of the adults were male and four were female or possible female. Five of the adults could be assigned a more specific age range; two had died as young adults, between the ages of 20 and 24 years, one had died in middle age, between the ages of 34 and 49 years, and two of the adults were old age, i.e. over the age of 50 years at death. Similarly, a wide range of ages were seen in the remains of the sub-adults. Two were teenagers, aged between 13 and 14 years, one was a younger juvenile aged between 7 and 9 years and one, sadly, was only aged between 6 and 8 months old at death. Prior to modern medicine, improved sanitary conditions as well as living and working conditions, deaths of younger individuals was much more common than today, although some people did live into old age, which is reflected in this small assemblage from Minchinhampton. Despite its small size and rural location, life in the town could be hazardous and subject to disease, as well as being affected by local economic conditions. Rural populations dependent on local harvests could be subjected to frequent intermittent famines, causing sharp rises in mortality rates, and many rural agricultural workers had little money to spare. During the Victorian period, between two thirds and three quarters of the family income was spent on food; half of the family income was spent on bread alone, as a hand-made item.[353] It times of financial crisis, it was commonplace for children to endure hunger and malnourishment, exposing them to fatal acute infectious diseases such as measles.

In human skeletal remains, we only see the effects of diseases that are primary diseases of bone or those conditions that are chronic and long-standing enough to affect the bone in some way as part of the course of the disease. This means that many acute infectious diseases that would have been rife such as cholera, typhus, scarlet fever, measles, smallpox and plague leave no trace on the skeleton. It is relatively unusual, for example, to see pathological changes in the skeletons of sub-adults, who are very likely to have succumbed fairly quickly to acute infectious disease. However, evidence for childhood physiological stress from malnutrition and febrile diseases may be present in the dentition, where arrested tooth crown development results in enamel defects called dental enamel hypoplasia. This was present in four individuals in the assemblage, both in the low and high-status individuals, indicating that childhood illness was not circumvented by wealth. Also present in another two individuals was *cribra orbitalia*, which creates a porotic appearance to the roof of the eye orbits caused by childhood megaloblastic or haemolytic anaemias.

In contrast, some individuals were much wealthier and lived a privileged existence, such as the Sheppard family who are buried in Holy Trinity Churchyard and built the fine mansion at Gatcombe Park in 1774. One disarticulated bone element displayed evidence of a condition called diffuse idiopathic skeletal hyperostosis (DISH), which is associated clinically with obesity and diabetes, and more common in older adult males. Some individuals in Minchinhampton were evidently not averse to fine dining and overindulgence! Another young female individual, despite her age, had numerous extensive caries indicating a diet high in sugar, a relatively new commodity to the English diet in the Georgian period, though quickly gaining popularity among the working classes during the Victorian period as a ready supply of calories.

Old age adults are more likely to accumulate a number of conditions over the course of their lifetime that may leave traces on the bone. Evidence of physically intensive activity that could well be associated with a more rural life was present in two post-medieval individuals, both of whom had a condition called *os acromiale* of the right shoulder joint, in addition to some ossifications at the sites where the muscles attach to the shoulder joints indicating increased physical stress and soft-tissue trauma to the joint. *Os acromiale* consists of a continued separation of two bony parts at shoulder that would normally fuse together during adolescence as the scapula is developing. It is thought that an increased stress on the joint caused by an intensive and repeated throwing type motion of the arm during adolescence can lead to the bones not fusing together. Both the old adult male and old adult female affected also had secondary degenerative joint disease and osteoarthritis of the shoulder, likely occurring as a long-term consequence of this condition and the activity underlying it.

Old age had similarly affected both these individuals about the joints of the spine, hip, wrists and knees, where either age-related degenerative joint disease or osteoarthritis could be seen. The old age female also had osteoporosis, an age-related disease affecting post-menopausal women that leads to a decrease in bone density and makes the vertebrae of the spine prone to collapse. This is a disease that appears to have increased in prevalence over time, as more women started to live into old age following industrialisation. This is also true of cancers. While cancers were present in the past, recent research suggests that cancer incidence has risen over time, likely due to age being a primary factor in it causation, as well as modern lifestyle factors. Not only suffering from osteoporosis, this old age female showed signs of a rare possible case of metastatic cancer, that consisted of a marked destructive lesion in the jaw accompanied by bone inflammation in the area that was active at the time of death.

The old age male had also endured some rib fractures during his lifetime, quite likely caused by an accidental fall or strike to the chest. Trauma was a common theme in the lives of individuals from both rural and urban settlements in both the medieval and post-medieval periods. Low status individuals tended to be more at risk of fractures given the more dangerous work roles they undertook, particularly involving manual labour and construction. Today, fatalities within the agricultural industry are the highest and are 16 to 18 times higher than average. Nonetheless, in the past, unregulated sporting hobbies and road accidents involving horses were also a perpetual hazard for rural and urban populations alike.

As noted earlier, not everyone was lucky enough to live into old age. Air pollution in the form of occupational dust was commonplace prior to a series of Health and Safety Acts introduced during the Victorian period, recognising the link between certain occupations and disease. One young male individual, likely aged 25-35 years at death and interred within the Church possibly indicating a higher social status, had gross erosive and inflammatory changes to the left side of his face that originated from the maxillary sinus and affecting the surrounding bones and tissues, leading to pain and swelling at the area. These changes could have been caused by an extensive maxillary infection but a likely cause was also maxillary sinus carcinoma. Clinical symptoms can include bloody nasal discharge, bulging of the eye, double vision and ulceration of the palate. Today the condition is linked to cigarette smoking but also has a much-increased rate amongst those chronically inhaling toxins or irritants as might be found in woodworking, in particular hardwood dust. Furniture and cabinet making was recently classified as 'carcinogenic' by the International Agency for the Research of Cancer. Other causes might include inverted papilloma or chronic invasive fungal sinusitis. It is interesting to note that by 1880, Tetbury Street in Minchinhampton was home to a master cabinet maker and his two apprentices. Earlier historical records from 1831 record that 38.8% of the Minchinhampton male adult population were involved in the manufacturing industry and a further 24.2% were employed in the retail and handicraft trades.[354] It would be unusual for a manual labourer to be interred within the Church, which was a burial rite usually reserved for higher status individuals. Nonetheless, skilled labourers such as cabinet makers or clerks in a factory of the 'middling' class may have been chronically exposed to the carcinogenic or infectious conditions associated with such nasosinal pathologies.

Evidence of chronic lung inflammation was present in a young adult possible female. Chronic inflammation of the lungs leads to new bone formation on the visceral or inside surfaces of the ribs, which is where the lining of the lung attaches to them. It represents chronic lung inflammation, such as might occur in pleurisy. The rib lesions present in this individual were active at the time of death. From a study of known individuals, it has been demonstrated that rib lesions were present in 62% of those that had died from tuberculosis and in 70% of those that had died with tuberculosis and a co-occurring pulmonary condition, in comparison to only 22% who had died of a pulmonary disease other than tuberculosis and 15% of those who had died of a condition not related to pulmonary diseases. Tuberculosis primarily affects young adults. However, the presence of rib lesions is not absolutely indicative of tuberculosis, and differential diagnoses including other respiratory conditions should be considered. Air pollution in industrial urban environments is a likely contributory factor of the considerably higher rates of visceral surface lesion in its post-medieval skeletal populations, particularly in areas of run down, ill-ventilated housing. Any individual who had spent a long period of time inhaling polluted, smoky air in low status housing would have been at risk of developing chronic lung inflammation.

Skeletal analysis can give us a picture of what life in the past was like in Minchinhampton, not only from the perspective of the individual but as a community. The pathology observed in the skeletal remains to some degree reflect the surrounding living environment, a small town in a green and leafy location that has seen economic ups and downs. A few higher status individuals no doubt benefited from the boom that the local wool trade brought along and were perhaps able to afford a richer, more affluent diet and lifestyle. However, the majority would have been working hard, physically labouring, sometimes in hazardous environments, in order to put food on the table. Even the 'middling sorts' were not shielded from disease, though they may have been buffered from the effects of malnutrition to some degree. Childhood mortality was high and even in adulthood, some individuals in Minchinhampton died of possible occupational related diseases and chronic infections, perhaps increasing during the 19th century when the population was growing but the wool industry was on the decline in the town. Those that survived into old age by the Victorian period were starting to suffer the diseases typical of old age that we see today, such as cancer, osteoporosis and osteoarthritis. Although a small assemblage, the individuals present in the skeletal assemblage point to how the local living conditions have influenced their health and the diversity of their experiences of health outcomes in Minchinhampton according to their individual age, sex, status and occupation.

Architectural fragments and building stone

The 2016 reordering works required the demolition of a series of low stone walls which had supported the 1842 pews. 110 architectural fragments were recovered from these walls, from rubble left between the walls by the Victorian builders, and from the lid of the drain under the nave and aisles. These fragments are all reused from the pre-1842 church, and provide important clues as to past appearance and internal decoration. The stone was assessed by Chiz Harward and Dr James Wright.[355]

Minchinhampton is situated on the top of the Cotswold limestone plateau, with abundant natural resources of limestone available both on the plateau and on the steep scarp slopes to the north and south. Formal quarrying for limestone has been carried out in the area out since the Roman period, however limestone was used as a building stone in Neolithic long barrows, and Iron Age earthworks such as The Bulwarks would have also produced stone which could have been used for making structures.[356]

Stone extraction is documented in Minchinhampton and the surrounding area from the medieval period onwards, in particular for Minchinhampton Weatherstone, a very hard-weathering fossiliferous, cross-bedded, re-cemented, ooidal limestone that was used on Gloucester Cathedral and which was quarried from a series of quarries on Minchinhampton Common up to the 1950s.[357] The quality and bed thickness available declined over time and Shelly Painswick stone was sometimes used as a substitute in the Victorian period.[358]

Perhaps surprisingly there is relatively little Minchinhampton Weatherstone amongst the excavated architectural fragments, perhaps due to selective reuse of the stone. Minchinhampton Weatherstone was generally chosen for external, exposed elements such as door and window surrounds, copings, chamfered string courses and parapets, a pattern of use that appears to be followed at Holy Trinity, with Minchinhampton Weatherstone used in the medieval north and south transepts and tower.

Further local quarries produced a range of limestones, from fairly poor quality local shelly limestones of the Athelstan Oolite Formation (most suitable for rubble infill), to the massive and uniform oolite of the 'Painswick Stone' (Painswick Freestone, Whitestone) of the Cleeve Cloud member of which so many medieval and post-medieval Gloucestershire buildings are constructed. Painswick Stone is a general name for stone quarried from the member, which is over 50m thick in places, with quarrying by galleries in the Chalford and Nailsworth valleys.[359] The stone is generally free of fossil, although it can become shelly, especially when poorer quality stone was quarried in later centuries.[360] Local variations abound, with a particularly fine and clean white oolite quarried at Nailsworth, which permits great detail and fine workmanship.

Painswick Stone is the most common stone type in the assemblage, and it appears that it was used for the majority of stonework at Holy Trinity, especially for finer internal work where the finest, whitest stone is often selected, although some mouldings are in a yellowish shelly limestone of unknown provenance.

The Througham Tilestone formation occurs at the top of the Fuller's Earth around Minchinhampton, it consists of fissile sandy limestones which would be split to make roofing tiles commonly known as Cotswold Stone slates and which are used to tile the church roof, with three such slates found during the evaluation.[361]

All the recorded stone is of fairly local origin, with no stone imported any great distances. A single fragment of a paver in the fissile blue-grey Forest (Pennant) Sandstone similar to that found in Great Berry Quarry, Forest of Dean, hints at wider trade in stone, but more exotic imports are missing, perhaps as the local quarries could supply most needs.

Fig. 147 Framed oil painting of Minchinhampton Church and Market Square by W. Brigad, 1890. From the collections of Museum in the Park, Stroud STGCM Y1992.78

DISCUSSION

The church of Holy Trinity has stood for over 900 years, serving the community and town of Minchinhampton and in that time the church has seen and embodied great changes in architecture, religion and society. From the building of the Norman church by a foreign monastery to the comprehensive rebuilding of the 14th century, through to the Reformation, the War of the Three Kingdoms, Commonwealth and Restoration, the rebuilding of 1842, and the alterations of the Gothic Revival, the physical church can be seen as a cipher for trends which run through the history of both England and the church. The building that we have today is an amalgam of centuries of alteration; it is not a static structure and never has been: the details visible in its walls and windows combine to illustrate a history of the church and its community.

Fig. 148 The early 14th-century south window of the Lady Chapel is one of the unsung glories of the Cotswolds

Fig. 149 The tower and south transept from the High Street, photographed by EP Conway between c.1905 and 1914

DISCUSSION

Although the broad development of the church has been previously chronicled, the recent archaeological investigations at Holy Trinity have hopefully illuminated parts of that history that were previously little understood and have provided a valuable opportunity to go back to the original sources and draw together much of the available information. Although the excavations revealed that, outside the tower and transepts, the 1842 rebuilding had stripped away nearly all of the medieval church, they have still provided important information on the appearance of the church and more importantly provided the opportunity to carry out the research that has led to this paper.

From the outset it was felt that a traditional archaeological report on the works would not be the best platform for the results, both as the purely archaeological findings were perhaps outweighed by the historical evidence, but also as it was felt that the results should be published in a more accessible form so that they could be read by as many parishioners and visitors as possible. This then has not been a traditional archaeological report, nor a standard church guide, but a hybrid.

The standing fabric, the excavated remains and the artefacts have been combined with the historical documentary sources and illustrations to attempt to reconstruct the development and history of the church. This combined approach has aimed to detail not only the main evolution of the church building, but also to draw out the often tiny but tantalising artefacts and observations which each open up a window into an aspect of the past life of the church and its community (and have led the author down many a rabbit hole). The Covid 20 pandemic hampered research, but luckily most relevant sources kept at the Gloucestershire Record Office had been copied before the first Lockdown, although sadly the library of Minchinhampton Local History Group was not available to consult and local historian Diane Walls sadly passed away before this paper was written.

The survival of the churchwardens' accounts has given a very practical insight into the ebb and flow of the Reformation, particularly the Marian reversion, the dry lists of purchases and expenses hints at the religious turmoil of this time, and the upheavals that were taking place. The records also record aspects of the rebuilding of 1842 and show the level of planning and record keeping associated with such an endeavour -something the present day churchwardens can identify with only too well. The role of Fenning Parke, schoolmaster, parish clerk and local historian is central at this time, he has maybe a supporting role to the greater actors in the drama of his time, but the legacy of his work as record keeper, collator and inquirer was crucial in reconstructing the later church. His activities almost certainly extended

Fig. 150 Postcard showing Minchinhampton Church and War Memorial, postmarked 1954. From the collections of Museum in the Park, Stroud STGCM 2018_16_180

beyond his official roles, he preserved the Churchwardens' Accounts, but also had them transcribed by Bruce; he also saved some of the medieval cross-slabs and one suspects it was Parke who asked the builder Shepstone to write up his discoveries from when he demolished the medieval church. Without Parke we would know so much less about the Victorian church, but also about the church that came before.

The surviving medieval and later documents have not only allowed us to reconstruct lost aspects of the church building and contents, but they also add in detail on the characters involved. Usually this is the great and the good: the rector William of Prestbury and his Lady Chapel, John and Lucy Ansley and their effigies, the Hamptons on their brass. These are the class we know from the traditional 'Kings and battles' school of history, but from the mid-16th century other, less privileged characters appear, and the repeated lists of work done for the church provide a rare glimpses of the network of local and specialist craftspeople, traders, officials and passers-through that supported or needed the church, and hint at the complex web of parish life that continues to this day.

Female protagonists are seldom visible in the documents even though the church was held by the Abbess and nuns of Caen; Dame Alys Hampton – herself a nun who donated the sanctus bell in 1516 is very much the exception but was from an important and wealthy local family. There are very few mentions in the churchwardens' accounts of named women: in 1600 'Good wife Hall' sold wine to the church and in 1633 Joan Fletcher had a new seat built for her and her daughter in the church. Other women are not named and the documents must underplay the many roles of womenfolk in the daily life of the church and its community. In later years women become slightly more visible in the church records: in 1841 a good proportion of the pews were claimed by women, many of whom are clearly the heads of households, owned property and could sell or pass it on. Whilst a few are anonymised as 'Samuel Jenkins' widow' or 'William Nicholls and sister' most are named in their own right.

The lives of individual parishioners are also brought to us through the osteological analysis of the excavated burials. Whilst many large urban cemeteries have been excavated across England, there are fewer examples of churchyard excavations from small urban cemeteries. The fourteen individuals studied at Minchinhampton are a small but important group and illustrate the lives, and deaths of parishioners through the centuries.

In the absence of any surviving Norman architecture, Holy Trinity's story is dominated by its two massive rebuilding projects –that of the early-mid 14th century, and that of 1842. The 14th-century programme of works was ambitious in both its scale and in its modernity: a plan to tear down and rebuild much of the church in the new Decorated idiom and project that glory onto the town below. The work was probably carried out successively on each part of the church with the works funded by at least two major local patrons and potentially with more than one team of masons.

The crowning glory is the south transept, this under-recognised gem was a key part of the new scheme, jutting proudly out towards the marketplace; a chantry chapel rivalling the chancel in its glory which would not be out of place in a far greater church. As Jon Cannon has showed, the patrons of the south transept, probably John and Lucy Ansloe, deliberately sought out a mason who was actively pushing the boundaries of the Decorated form and style, and who had a detailed knowledge of contemporary and innovative work across the region. The mason, possibly the same mason that inscribed his design process onto a limestone slab, brought the latest ideas to the transept and achieved a structure that is superlative and deserving of far more attention than it currently receives; we are all indebted to Dr Edward Dalton who spoke up and saved the south transept from demolition in the 1842 rebuilding.

The south transept, like the north transept, was built as a chantry chapel, a memorial to the benefactors that was aligned with the current ideas of contemporary ideas of Purgatory and the intercession of saints. The church was remodelled as a memorial, and also as an engine for redemption, primarily for the benefactors, but also the wider congregation. That medieval, catholic, outlook was to be cast away with the sixteenth century Reformation, whose effects on the church can be deduced from the Churchwarden's Accounts.

The Georgian church, of galleries and long sermons, was captured in a series of external illustrations, but also in the plans and records made by Fenning Parke just before the 1842 reordering. The medieval church had been largely stripped of catholic ornamentation and was an austere box: an auditorium for the preacher. In 1842 the chancel, nave and aisles were demolished and rebuilt in a Perpendicular style. The reasons for the 1842 rebuilding are not entirely clear, although there were clearly structural issues with the medieval building, the role of David Ricardo cannot be understated. It can be no coincidence that the church was torn down almost as soon as the Revd William Cockin died.

Holy Trinity was rebuilt at the start of the Oxford Movement, but the rebuilding looks back, not forward: it was a new auditorium centred on the pulpit. It is easy to chart the Oxford movement in new churches, but less so in old ones. Does Ricardo retain the medieval tower and transepts due to a respect for the Gothic, or due to cost? The fact that originally the transepts were meant to be rebuilt suggests the latter. How far the extensive writings of the Oxford Movement had reached Ricardo or Foster is unclear however as with the Reformation,

Fig. 151 The chancel arch, rood and crossing

Minchinhampton may have remained a slightly conservative town. One focus of the Oxford Movement was the abolition of assigned pews, but this did not happen at Holy Trinity which remained low church and traditional.

Whilst England in the 1840s and 1850s still harboured anti-papist feeling -with riots at some churches- there was a gradual move to a more High Church approach in many parishes spurred on by the Oxford Movement and the Gothic Revival.[362] By 1869 Minchinhampton was fully signed up to the

Gothic Revival, employing one of its foremost designers, William Burges to glorify the chancel in an appointment that may reflect increasing ritualism in the church (possibly continuing in the early 20th century with FC Eden's rood and the consecration of the altar in the south transept 'Lady Chapel'). The galleries were removed at around the same time, the church was now fully focussed on the altar and the sacrament.

The recent re-ordering has changed the church physically but will also maybe change the church as a community and as a place for the congregation and other groups. The role of a parish church in its community is one that has changed time and again over the centuries, the building responding to often rapidly developing beliefs and liturgies. Sometimes the changes were relatively superficial and could be stripped away, others like the massive rebuilding programmes of the 14th and mid-19th centuries would leave a far greater mark. The recent reordering of the church has been light touch compared to those, but has addressed long term problems of the physical church and made it fit for the present congregation and community.

APPENDIX I
SHEPSTONE'S 'BUILDER'S REPORT' OF 1845

Report on the old church by the builder William Shepstone to Fenning Parke, March 5th 1845, transcribed into the 'Minchinhampton Chronicles':[363]

(Presumed) report of the Old Church by William Shepstone architect[364] of the chancel, nave and aisles which were rebuilt in 1842 to 1843.

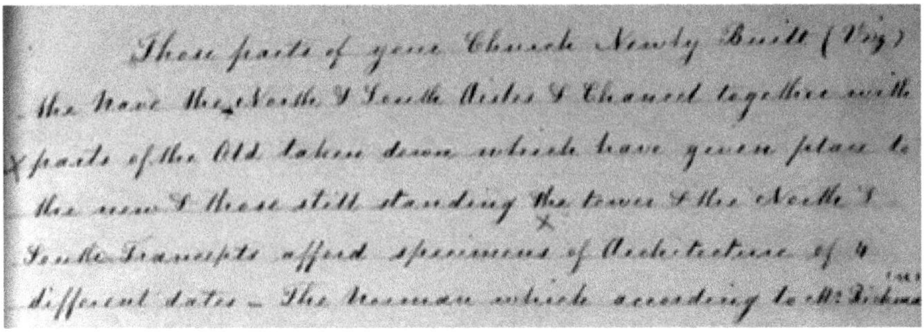

Fig. 152 Extract of Shepstone's report transcribed by Fenning Parke in the Minchinhampton Chronicles

'Those parts of your Church Newly Built (viz) the nave the north and south aisles and chancel together with parts of the Old taken down which have given place to the new and those still standing the Tower and the North and South Transepts afford specimens of architecture of four different dates – the Norman which according to Mr Rickman[365] continued from William I to the end of the reign of Henry II -1189. The transition or Early English Gothic to Edward I 1307. The Decorated to the end of Edward III – 1377. The Perpendicular

English Gothic reaching to 1630 or 1640.

The principal parts of Norman origin were the range of piers and arches on the north side of the Nave the piers were rather massive the capitals slightly ornamented the arches plain with a drip stone terminating with a Shark's head, widely carved on the quarters of two of these arches we discovered two small Norman windows walled up six inches in width splaying inwardly towards the Nave having small shafts at the angles with ornamented capitals (one of which I have now in my possession) I considered it beautiful specimen and a moulded arch over, in taking down this wall we found several pieces of net work zigzag and other ornaments belonging to this order of which I made sketches.

On cleaning out the foundations of the old chancel the basement of an oblong projecting five feet beyond the line of wall and nine feet in length belonging to this date.

Specimens of the Early English these were very few consisting of the North wall of the Chancel having two small windows wall'd up, the wall below the East window and the rubble work of the wall for a few feet in height on the East side of the North Transept – all the other parts of the old church were of the Decorated Gothic with the exception of a few alterations of windows etc which strictly belong to no Order but to that method of repairing our Churches or rather disfiguring them which obtained since the latest date above alluded to.

The Tower and the North and South Transepts are the XIVth century the Decorated Gothic the South Transept with its large rose window it's small 2 light windows ranging on each side its high pointed stone roof supported by stone ribs and the ornamented tomb of Sir John Robert Delamere and his Lady is altogether a beautiful structure. (I have heard from good authority that) there is scarcely another roof of the kind in the kingdom, this applies to its plain simplicity as there are stone roofs almost innumerable belonging to this date and afford specimens of architectural skill (it is considered) that would compete with anything of the kind the world has ever witnessed.

The North Transept is of the same date very plain in its structure and finish, there were however a few things of interest about it an old tomb recessed in the wall of the North Gable with a stone seat containing the bones of no doubt a distinguished person and member of the church. The finish of Arch above is simply a moulding peculiar to that date in all probability terminated with a carved Finial at present it has none.

On the East side and on excavating for the floor of the New Church was taken up what was considered to have been the foundation of an Altar, on clearing the plastering from the East Wall we discovered Niches, one had been partly destroyed by the fixing of a monument the other was walled up with pieces of its beautifully carved shafts and canopy the pedestals are (for there are still those) in the form of a cross rudely worked and fixed level with the face of the wall, on these stood figures about one half the full size this was quite clear as evidenced in light and shade on the plastering at the back of the niche but we saw no fragments of the figures their destruction was undoubtedly was the work of the reformation they have been guarded by an iron fence attached to the wall as we found the holes in which it had been inserted.

I found a niche very similar to these in the gable end of the Chancel of Olveston church about nine miles from Bristol this also had a iron fence on the outside, on the inside and on clearing the plastering of a number of coats of whitewash was discovered in water colours full size figures sadly mutilated as if by spears (such was the character of the zeal of many who were professedly reformers of the Church of Christ.)

The Tower of your Church although of some humble pretensions claims our respect for the same date of the Gothic architecture situated at the junction of the Nave and the Transepts; supported by 4 massive piers having 4 arches of proportionate dimensions and a ground ceiling relieved with a few carved heads and bosses.

On freeing the masonry of these piers of the whitewash and plastering was seen Sets on all of them what (but for the walls of the Church surrounding the Tower on all sides) must have been considered sufficient to endanger its stability these were not in consequence of the foundations having given way it assumed altogether the character of a crush occasioned by the weight or pressure from above, as in all cases commenced at the Springing of the Arches and extending downwards very few cracks reaching the floor line; <u>this circumstance led to the questioning of the authenticity of the opinion entertained by the inhabitants of the town and which has been currently reported in this history of your county</u> that the Tower when built terminated with a Spire. On the discovery of these Sets and the nature of them it immediately recurred to me very probably that they took place at the time the Tower was in the course of erection and when the Tower Spire was carried to its present height if so that accounts for the present curious kind of finish and the stability of the building so much endangered at that point of its progress prudence prevented their adding the other part of the Spire the additional weight of which must have been to threatening, this supposition was strengthened as I proceeded to examine it throughout for on arriving at the battlements I could not discover those evidences which I think never fail to shew themselves where any alterations or repairs have been made in masonry as it is almost impossible to repair or make an alterations if it is almost immediate after the walls are finished so as to deceive the eye and in the quality of the mortar especially, but the finishing of your tower does not afford the slightest proof of a different date to the other parts and a close examination of its present state must I think always lead to the opinion that your Tower was never different in its situation when first finished to what it is at present.I do not profess to be Pope in this matter but I do not see how (in the absence of positive fact) any injury could award to it the merit of having terminated in a Spire while on the other hand the evidence it contains are so strong against it.

On excavating the ground at the West End of the Church to form the new approach to the entrance we found to the number of eight or ten graves of a very simple but curious description containing generally skeletons of full grown persons. These had been interred without a coffin the rock had been excavated to the depth of a few inches affording little more than room enough to receive the length and width of the corpse, undressed stones from two to three inches in thickness were fixed on edge intirely rounded sufficiently high to receive a rough flat stone covering to clear, the bones were remarkable clean the teeth in beautiful preservation. One of these graves may be found under the large entrance door, there is also a stone coffin without a lid in the immediate neighbourhood of these near the S.W corner of the S Aisle.

Your new Church W of the transept containing a Nave with a clear storey and North and South Aisles is the Perpendicular Gothic the New Chancel principally of the XIV century and although by no means rich in detail yet its architecture throughout with respect to arrangement proportion and finish has its claims for correctness simplicity and elegance equal to any of the modern built churches.'

Note Bigland writes (1792) "the Tower, which is placed in the centre, had originally a spire, which was blown down* in 1602,when it was finished with an embattled parapet.'

*MSS. Parsons and Wantner in the Bodleian Library Oxford

APPENDIX 2
WILLIAM BURGES' LETTER OF 1869

Transcription of letter from William Burges on the 1842 church with proposals for the new chancel:[366]

15 Buckingham Street
Strand. W.C.
April 28th 1869

Revd Sir

In consequence of your having expressed a desire that I should report upon the chancel of Minchin Hampton Church with a view to its improvement. I have carefully examined the edifice and now beg to submit to you the following remarks accompanied with the necessary drawings.

History of Church
Before the alterations which were made as I understand in 1841 Minchin Hampton Church must have been one of the most interesting in the County of Gloucester. From extracts of the Builders report which you have kindly communicated to me, it is evident that the Nave must have been very good Norman work perhaps rather early in date, thus we read of plain arches with a dripstone ending in a sharks head – windows apparently clerestory ones 6 inches in width with small shafts ornamented capitals and moulded archpieces of zigzag etc some Norman work is also mentioned as being discovered in connection with the foundation of the Chancel but the description is too vague to enable me to draw any inference from it.

The Early English period was represented by the "two small windows in the N. wall of the Chancel, the wall below the East Window and the rubble work of the wall for a few feet in height on the east side of the N. Transepts. All the rest of the old church was of the decorated Gothic"

From this last sentence of the builders report it would never be suspected that the South Transept is one of the most perfect and curious specimens of the Architecture of the middle of the 14th Century. There are 7 bays 6 of which on the East side are pierced with two light windows of the usual reticulated pattern, the South end is with a most magnificent composition of five lights which occupies the whole wall nearly to the apex of the roof the latter feature is very remarkable and has been frequently drawn and referred to in Architectural works. It consists of stone principals supporting a series of stone slabs, in fact it is a wooden roof executed in stone. Below the south window are two decorated canopied tombs one containing the effigy of a Knight and the other of a lady both presenting curious peculiarities of costume altogether this transept is a most beautiful piece of Architecture, then only defect being the different scale between the openings of the South and side window and we cannot be too thankful that amidst the destruction which took place some thirty years ago those who conducted the works thought fit to spare it.

The other transept presents few points of interest beyond a couple of three light reticulated windows and a canopied tomb on the North Side of the central bay between the nave, transepts & choir is vaulted and supports a truncated spire which I had not time to examine. The builders report above referred to informs us that "upon freeing the masonry of the tower piers were seen sets (cracks) in all of them these were not in consequence of the foundations having given away it assumed altogether the character of a crush occasioned from the pressure from above as in all cases it commenced at the springing of the Arches and extended downwards, very few cracks reaching the floor line."

In 1841 the nave and chancel were entirely rebuilt in a very unsatisfactory version of the perpendicular style. The only attempt at restoration being the two light decorated windows – one in the North Chancel wall and the other in the south – from careful examinations it appears that a few pieces of the ancient tracery have been reused. The plan of the Chancel is also said to have been shortened. The present East window is a comparatively small one of four lights, the North and South walls are both alike and contain the perpendicular lancets with tracery in the heads. The roof has two framed principals but no tie beam, the plaster ceiling taking the form of a 4 centred Arch.

As your instructions do not extend to the nave I have very little to say about it beyond that it is fitted with pews – the removal of which and the substitution of chairs would in my opinion effect a marked improvement even in this unsatisfactory part of the edifice.

I now propose to place before you the various suggestions that have occurred to me for the improvement of the Chancel. These may be divided into structural alterations, Ecclesiastical arrangement and Art decorations.

Structural Alterations. The present East window might be removed and another substituted more in character with the importance of the Church and the Architecture of the transepts such a window is represented in Drawing No. 6 in designing it I have endeavoured to keep to the local character of the Architecture as developed in the great window of the South Transept thus all the foliations spring out of one plane of tracery, and the circle forms a leading feature, and the minor details rather more incline to geometrical drawing than was usual at the period.

At the same time while thus copying to a certain degree the localisms of the transept windows I felt that something was required in the East window to render it more important than that in the transepts which will always have the advantage of superior size. I have endeavoured to obtain this by use of the double plane of tracery happily the present eastern wall is much thicker below the window cill than it is above and I propose taking advantage of this and by building upon it to obtain the requisite thickness demanded by the extra plane of tracery. This plan may also be expected to render the east wall less liable to damp a most important consideration if at any time it should be desired to employ decoration in this part of the Church.

The introduction of the New window will necessitate the removal of the Niche in the upper part of the Eastern gable to a somewhat higher position. A figure of the patron saint would be a great ornament in this place and a new cross gable cross would also be very desirable.

As the new East window may be expected to give so much more light than the old one I think the side wall of the Chancel we might venture to get rid of the perpendicular lancets and I should therefore propose to block them up. It may possibly be objected that the stained glass would take away any extra light but to this it may be replied that a very large quantity of richly coloured glass would be out of character with the style of Architecture, and that any window or windows may be expected to contain at least half, if not more of white glass. The middle two light decorated window would remain as at present.

Roof

The roof is of a very unfortunate construction for any improvement, the only way that suggests itself is to strip off the plaster ceiling to make a cradling of wood to board it to put on the ribs, and finally suspend it in portions, to the present principals and rafters. I have shown two ways which the ribs may be arranged Viz in Drawings No. 3 and No. 4 and also different ways of ornamenting them. I do not think it necessary to make this boarding of oak as fir if unstained and unvarnished, after a time tones down to a very charming color. The decoration might be done in black with occasional touches of red leaving the natural color of the wood for the ground where figures occur they could be done on canvass in London and fixed up in their places with copper nails and white lead.

Ecclesiastical Arrangements.
There are two ways in which the Altar and stalls may be arranged the choice will of course depend on yourself.

No. 1 arrangement see drawing No. 1
The first arrangement is to place the altar and its dossill against the eastern wall keeping it low so as not to interfere with the window. The stalls will begin at the chancel arch and run eastward. As the chancel arch extends so far into the breadth of the chancel it would hardly be possible to place the stalls against the side walls, as in that case, the priests door would be blocked up – and many of the occupants of the stalls hidden from the view of the congregation.

No. 2 arrangement see drawing No. 2
The second arrangement is to bring the stalls into the Church as far as the nave Arch of the central tower, in fact as in Westminster Abbey, an open screen would run round to define the position of the stalls from the seats of the congregation. The altar is placed in the middle of the Chancel for this there is ample authority for instance in Stone Church where the wall arcading being carried round the Eastern end clearly shows the altar must always have been disengaged.

The objections to Arrangement No. 1 are the distance of the Altar from the congregation the impossibility of those in the transept seeing the officiating Priest or reader.

On the other hand the second arrangement takes away some important sittings and prevents communication between the two transepts.

I should also suggest there is a modification of the two plans which would be obtained by bringing the west end of the stalls into the middle of the central tower.

Vestry
As regards the Vestry I presume there is no very great objection to its remaining in its present position. viz at the N. end of the N. transept but it would be quite

possible to build one on the North West side of the Chancel and thus enable you to dispense with the very unsatisfactory vestry screen concerning which I may remark that the ornamented details are all well executed in cast iron.

Fittings and Decorations

Altar
The altar should be made of hardwood either oak or chestnut to agree with the stalls. It can either be a plain table with 6 or 8 legs or an elaborately carved and moulded piece of furniture this is a point to be determined by the funds at your disposal. I may remark that £50 or £60 would cover the cost of a very fair altar.

Stalls
As in the case of the Altar any amount of money may be spent upon the stalls. They should likewise be made of hardwood as otherwise they would be apt to get dirty and look shabby above all care must be taken to make the principal parts in good solid scantlings.

The dossill.
The dossill can be made either in stone alabaster or wood. In the former case it should be entirely painted and gilded otherwise it is apt to get dirty. The Alabaster would be much dearer than stone and would only demand sufficient polychromy to get rid of the white glare, it should be applied in thin lines, and in small portions like in greek work.

The wooden dossill would consist of a frame of wood enclosing a large panel, this panel can either be occupied by a picture upon a gold ground or subdivided by a series of little panels containing ornaments, figures etc such as we see at Westminster Abbey. In the appendix will be found the other dossills but as regards this last variety of the wooden dossils I am unable to give an approximate estimate.. The subjects I should propose for the dossill would be in the centre of the "Entombment" and on either side the sacrifices of the old Testament, these I insert not as types of the "Entombment" but as types of the crucifixion in the window above. The Entombment forming the completion of the crucifixion.

Tiles.
There are various ways of covering the floors of the chancels but in this instance I think the tiles manufactured by Godwin of Lugwardine would be the most

appropriate. I should recommend that the smallest size be selected and that, at least those with patterns be glazed as all these sort of tiles owe all their richness to this process – the clay being white with an orange glazing, whereas those of Minton have a yellow clay with a transparent glaze.

Stained Glass.
The East window is so arranged that the centre of the circle would be occupied with our Lord in glory and the surrounding compartments with the Heavenly host below would be the crucifixion with scenes from the passion. The side windows might have figures of the evangelists and their respective emblems but as this part of the work is to be entrusted to Messrs Hardman I need say no more upon the subject.

Decoration of Walls & Roof.
In the accompanying drawings I have made two distinct schemes for the decoration of the Chancel and of the roof. As I before observed the roof would simply have sundry black and red ornaments stenciled or drawn upon the bare wood the figures being painted on canvass and put up afterwards.

As to the walls If they are affected with damp the plaster should be removed and Keene's cement substituted. The ornaments and figures would be executed like those of Village Churches of the 14th Century. Viz. in yellow black and red.

I have thus I hope carried out your wishes as regards my recommendations for the improvement of your chancel and there are but three pieces of church furniture which I left unmentioned these are the sedilia altar rail and pulpit. You gave no instructions that I remember respecting the first of these, the cost would greatly depend upon the richness and number of seats. The altar rail had better be made as plain as possible and can be obtained at any Ecclesiastical ironmonger in London, as to the pulpit its positi[on will] depend upon the stalls and rear[ranging] of the Nave seats. I should advise you [to obtain] a temporary portable one which you can move about until you discovered [the best] acoustic position.

I remain Revd. Sir
Your Obedient Servant
William Burges.

APPENDIX 3
THE PEWS IN 1841

The following is a partial transcription of entries made by Fenning Parke to record claimants to the existing pews, prior to the church being rebuilt: *Particulars of claims to pews and sittings in the parish church of Min.Hampton 1841.* [367] As is recorded, some sittings were disputed, some were unclaimed, several were purchased by the Committee, and the remainder were presumably allocated to the 'Allowed' claimants in the new church.

Whilst Parke listed 170 sittings in his particulars, it is not proven that the numbers relate to those marked on the plans of the pews and galleries which he also prepared in 1841, and which include 167 sittings. To complicate matters, whilst the 105 sittings on the ground floor plan were numbered in a continuous sequence, each of the first floor galleries were numbered in seven separate sequences. Unfortunately there is no concordance between the different numberings (and of course they may be unrelated) although it appears likely that the ground floor numbers do match and are listed first, followed by the galleries -numbers 151, 154 and 155 are for the 'Singing Gallery' at the west end. It is to be hoped that further documentation may come to light that allows the locations and listed names to be linked definitively.

There is no comparable record for the locations in the new church. A pair of plans of the pews dated 1870 has names annotated in pencil. The left-hand plan appears to show the existing occupants, with the right-hand plan probably showing their new allocation. The right-hand plan shows the new pulpit and lectern, with the font at the west end [368] There are no plans for the galleries. It is not clear why the plan was made -it was at the time of the Burges work in the chancel, so may be related to a wider internal reordering.

APPENDICES

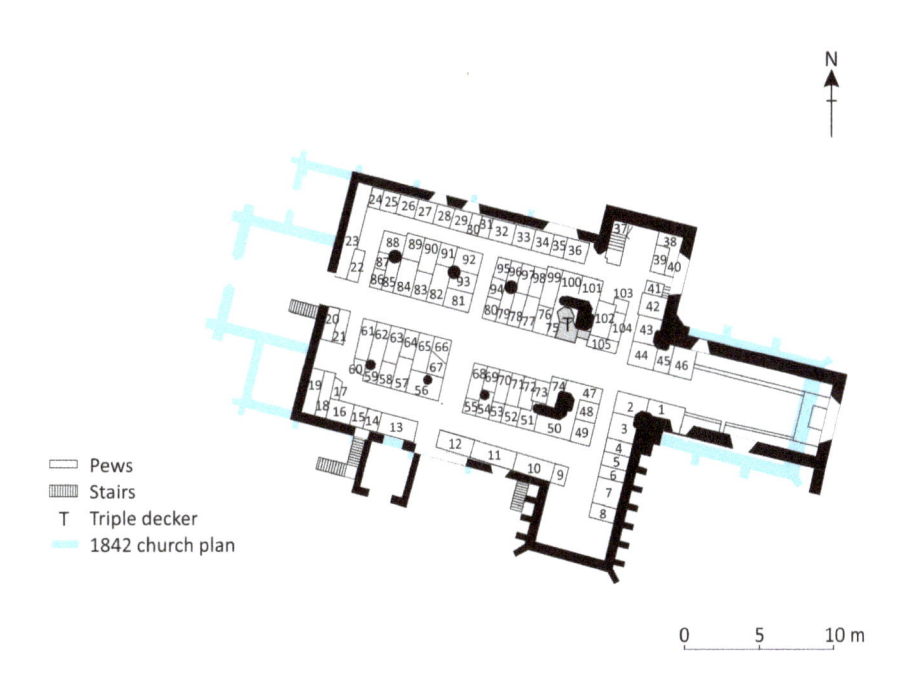

Fig. 153 Plan of the ground floor in 1841 showing the location of pews

Fig. 154 Plan of the galleries in 1841 showing the location of pews

Pew no	1841 Claimant:	No of sittings	Comments	1842 Allowed to:	No of sittings
1	Revd Charles Whateley		Rectory House. North of the pew	Revd Charles Whateley	
2	Estate of Cockin		In possession for more than 20 years. North of the pew	Estate of Cockin	
3	John Kibble		Part by purchase, part inherited	John Kibble	
4	Sarah Price			Sarah Price	2
4	Mary West (widow)			Mary West (widow)	1 or 2
				Clutterbuck	1
5	Sarah Price		claims whole pew by her father Ambrose Cosbourn	Sarah Price	
6	Hannah Rowe	3	Brimscombe	Thomas Riddler and Richard Smart	
6	Thomas Riddler		From John Watkins		
6	Richard Smart		Owner of the Nelson, Brimscombe		
7	William Lewis			William Lewis	
8	W Playne			W Playne	
9	John Fisher		Well Hill	John Fisher	
10	John Fisher			John Fisher	
11	Estate of Cockin		In possession for more than 20 years	Estate of Cockin	
12	Anne Harris		Widow of Gloucester, Gardiner's Property at Burley	Anne Harris	
12	Ann Shepphard	1		Ann Shepphard	
13	George Shachey		Purchased from Cockin	George Shachey	

14	George Shachey		Purchased from Cockin	George Shachey	
15	Edward Beale		Not yet claimed, plate claiming for Miles Beale, note to hold enquiry if related to any house	ENQUIRY	
16	Francis Chambers		Forwood Cottage	Francis Chambers	
17	Mary Taylor		Plate for Browne who has left the country	Mary Taylor	
18	Mrs Cook	1	Sprigs Well, plate	Mrs Cook	1
18	Wm Riddler	1	Given by grandfather	Wm Riddler	1
19	W F Chambers		Claims whole pew but agrees to take 4.5 sittings. Note at end of book states 'No.19 - WF Chambers expects Seat& Pews to e attached to his Houses -Granted by Committee	W F Chambers	4.5
20	Churchwardens pew		Will not be wanted in the new church'		
21	Fenning Parke	1	from Nathaniel Clarkson	Fenning Parke	1
21	Holcombe House	2	Servants	Holcombe House	2
22	Theescombe House		Theescombe House	Theescombe House	
23	William Monk	5	South end; gave up 2 sittings to Mrs Jeffries	William Monk	3
23	Mrs Jeffries		North end; sold to committee	Committee	
24	Mrs Jeffries		Claimed, sold to committee	Committee	
24	William Hill	3	Disputed Mrs Jeffries' claim	Committee	

25	George Price	3.5	Purchased from Joseph Iles	George Price	
26	Church		Erected by churchwardens	Committee	
27	Church		Erected by churchwardens	Committee	
28	Edwin Bird			Edwin Bird	
29	Walter Kirby			Walter Kirby	
30	Mrs Chalk			Mrs Chalk	4
30				Thomas Dutton	1
31	Mrs Chalk			Mrs Chalk	
32	William Ralph		Claims half	William Ralph	
32	Joseph Ralph		Claims half for White Hart	Joseph Ralph	
33	No Claimant				
34			Plate claims 2 sittings for E Lambert, and another claiming the remainder for Hannah Beale		
35	Charles Iles	2.5	Purchased 1815; purchased by committee	Committee	
36	Enoch Williams		Purchased by committee	Committee	
37	No Claimant			Committee	
38	Ann Sheppard			Ann Sheppard	
39	Ann Sheppard			Ann Sheppard	
40	George Playne		Crown Inn	George Playne	
41	Richard Horton		Bell House	Committee	
42	No Claimant				
43	Samuel Clutterbuck		St Mary's Mills	Samuel Clutterbuck?	
44	Theescombe House			Theescombe House	

APPENDICES

45	Mary Hiatt	3	White Lion Inn		
46	Rectory House				
47			The committee claim this pew for Mr Ricardo	Ricardo	
48			The committee claim this pew for Mr Ricardo	Ricardo	
49			The committee claim this pew for Mr Ricardo	Ricardo	
50	Chas Mason		claims not sold with Cowcombe estate		
50	Mrs Ireland		Cowcombe estate	Mrs Ireland	
51	Mrs Harman		Burley	Mrs Harman	
52	Estate of Cockin,		Rented to Ed. Baillett		
53	Robert George	3.5	Dispensary		
53	William Pearse			William Pearse	
54	William Nicholls and sister		From Glaziers Arms		
54	David Ricardo		Glazier arms owner, claimed for committee	Committee	
55	Samuel Davis	2		Samuel Davis	
56			Refer to 13		
57	Alexander Sinkwell		By purchase	Alexander Sinkwell	
58	Mrs Janson		By purchase by father	Mrs Janson	
59	Mrs Janson		By purchase by father	Mrs Janson	
60	Charles Ockford		Gift or exchange from Cockin	Charles Ockford	
61	Joseph Lewis	1	Brass plate	Joseph Lewis	1
61	Thomas Ridler	2	By wife, plate	Thomas Ridler	

61	John Ridler	2	By purchase, plate	John Ridler	
62	George Playne	1	The Greyhound	George Playne	
62	Lambert William T	1			
62	Samuel Jenkins' widow	2			
62	Mary Fewsters	2	By representative		
63	Estate of Cockin			Estate of Cockin	
64	Joseph Ralph	4	Purchased 3 seatings to add to own	Joseph Ralph	
65	Joseph Moody	1	From father	Joseph Moody	1
65	Joseph Hughes	1		Joseph Hughes	1
65	Samuel Davis	1		Samuel Davis	1
65	Samuel Heaven	1		Samuel Heaven	1
65	Joseph Percival	1		Joseph Percival	1
65	Robert & Samuel Dowdeswell	1		Robert & Samuel Dowdeswell	1
66	Charles Bamfield	1	Held from his wife; Purchased by F Parke	Charles Bamfield	1
66	Edmund Carrad	1	From grandmother	Edmund Carrad	1
66	James Smith	1	From Cockin	James Smith	1
67	Culver House Farm			Culver House Farm	
68	John Howard	4	New Lodge Inn, disposed to sell at £10	John Howard	4
68	Joseph Pimbury	2	Sold to committee	Committee	2
69	Philip Pearse	4	By purchase	Philip Pearse	
70	Thomas Baker	1		Thomas Baker	1
70	Francis Chambers	2		Francis Chambers	2
70	G. Guest	1		Committee	1

70	Benjamin Brooks	2		Benjamin Brooks	2	
71	No claimant					
72	William Hill	1				
72	George Scuse	1	May be crossed out			
72	Mary Clutterbuck	1	May be crossed out			
72	Mrs Harman	1	May be crossed out	Mrs Harman	1	
72	Thomas Clift	1				
72	James Smith	2		James Smith	2	
72	George Scuse	1		George Scuse	1	
72	Solomon Hill	1	Same seat as claimed by W Hill	Solomon Hill	1	
72	John Wis?/ Nephew of William Pitt	1		John Wis?/ Nephew of William Pitt	1	
73	Samuel Keene			Samuel Keene		
74	Estate of Cockin		Half the pew, Bath Farm House	Estate of Cockin		
74	Ricardo		Half the pew	Ricardo		
75	John Budd		Half the pew, exchanged with playne for 2 sittings in West Gallery	John Budd		
75	Alexander Sinkwell		Half the pew, not allowed			
75	?Mrs Shatton		Half the pew, allowed but purchased	Committee		
76	William Davis	2		William Davis	2	
76	George Playne		Claims all but 1 sitting	George Playne	2	
77	Priscilla Webber	2	Claims 2 nearest the door	Priscilla Webber		
77	Mary Stafford (widow)	2	Claims upper 2			
78	William Pearse					

78	Solomon Hill		Committee asks for more proof		
79	John Chambers		Forwood House	John Chambers	
80	George Playne		Property at Forwood	George Playne	
81	Samuel Kearsey		Half the pew	Samuel Kearsey	
81	John Neale		Half the pew	John Neale	
82	Peter Playne	5	Box estate	Peter Playne	5
83	James Pinbury's widow			James Pinbury's widow	
84	Mrs Morgan Shayler			Mrs Morgan Shayler	
85	William Haycock of Stamford				
86	James Smith	5	Disallowed		
86	Dinah Fowles		Purchased by committee	Committee	
87	James Smith	5	Disallowed	Committee	
88	Joseph Ralph and William Pearse		Disallowed		
88	Joseph Latham	1		Joseph Latham	
89	Sarah Hill				
89	Mrs Lycett			Mrs Lycett	
90	Mrs Jeffries		Half the pew, purchased by Fenning Parke	Fenning Parke	
90	William Lambert			William Lambert	
91	William Haycock			William Haycock	
92			The committee claim this pew for Mr Ricardo	Ricardo	
93	Thomas Pinbury			Hyde estate	

94	William Ralph		Bought by Elizabeth Freeman in 1791	William Ralph	
95	Joseph Hort			Joseph Hort	
96	William Hill	2		William Hill	
97	Martha Middlemore	1			
97	Fenning Parke	3		Fenning Parke	2
97	Thomas Hill	2			
97	John Cox	1		John Cox	1
97				George Playne	2
98	Joseph Ralph			Joseph Ralph	
99	Burley House			Burley House	
100	Anne Davis		Purchased by committee	Committee	
100	Richard Smith		Purchased by committee	Committee	
100	Charles Smith		Purchased by committee	Committee	
100	Mary Morgan		Purchased by committee	Committee	
100	Esther Webb		Purchased by committee	Committee	
101	William Holdman in right of his wife		This pew and 100 appears to have been constantly occupied by the Holdmans and Anne Davis and her family. Purchased by Committee	Committee	
102	Edward Wall	6.5	Attached to St Chloe School House	Edward Wall	
103	Samuel Morton		By way of his mother Deborah Morton (nee Danford)	Samuel Morton	

104			The committee claim this pew for Mr Ricardo	Ricardo	
105	William Playne			William Playne	
106	John G Ball	1	Given to the committee on condition that the gallery is taken down. 'In consideration of Mr Ball's subscription & his having given up these pews & no 114, suitable accommodation will be provided for Mr Ball's family -The Committee consider that the Pew should be attached to teh House	Committee	
107	Joseph Harman	2	from his grandfather via mother		
107	Charles Iles	2	Claimed the 2 sittings claimed by Harman as he had bought the property to which he believed they attached, 'Harman's mother attended to state that she has sat there 60 years, that her father purchased them of a person at Nailsworth. The Committee consider these sittings to belong to Harman'		
107	John Carter	1	Offered to Committee at 15 shillings	Committee	

108	John Hill of Pinfarthing	4	Bought whole pew in 1818, lets 1 sitting to S Gillman at 2/0 a year. Wishes to dispose of the seat, asks £3. If not dispued Rev Whateley will purchase at the sum named. The Committee agree to purchase this pew from Whateley at the same price	Committee	
109	Thomas Dowdeswell		For his father Joseph, left to him with other property by Dr Buckingham of St Chloe Green	Thomas Dowdeswell	
110	Jacob Scuse		Purchased from John Sims 40 years since	Jacob Scuse	
111	William Playne			William Playne	
112	William Playne			William Playne	
113	John Baker		Claimed by his representatives	John Baker	
114	John G Ball		5 sittings to be allowed to Mr Ball for this and 106	Committee	
115	Newman John	4	Inherited from his brother Darius Newman, formerly belonging to the father D Newman	Newman John	
116	Joseph Moody		From his father, William Moody who purchase it from Mrs Phipps	Joseph Moody	
117	James Poulton	4	Purchased in 1838	James Poulton	
118	Elizabeth Clark (late Ebworth)			Elizabeth Clark (late Ebworth)	
119	Joseph Rowe	2	In right of grandfather John Rowe	Joseph Rowe	2

119	Ann Jones	1		Ann Jones	1
119	Elizabeth Hathin	1		Elizabeth Hathin	1
120	William Ralph	4	In right of father George Ralph	William Ralph	4
121	William Ralph	3	In right of father George Ralph, states that John Baker has 2 and Edward Bartlett 1, and thinks that John Cosbourn's ??? Has a claim to a portion of this Pew which is 6 sittings	William Ralph	3
121	John Baker	2		John Baker	2
121	Edward Bartlett	1		Edward Bartlett	1
121	Joseph Ralph	2		Joseph Ralph	2
121	William Pearse	2		William Pearse	2
122	Joseph and Thomas Iles		And 123 in right of property at Hyde	Joseph and Thomas Iles	
123	Joseph and Thomas Iles		And 123 in right of property at Hyde	Joseph and Thomas Iles	
124	??? Sadler		In right of property at Giddynap 'This is the Facultied Pew'		
125	??? Sadler		In right of property at Giddynap 'This is the Facultied Pew'		
126	William Clutterbuck		In right of a plate	William Clutterbuck	
127	Mrs Jansen	6	Purchased by Abraham Clawel her father off Mr Cox	Mrs Jansen	
128	Hyde House			Hyde House	
129	Mrs Elizabeth Clutterbuck			Mrs Elizabeth Clutterbuck	
130	Hyde House		Servants pew	Hyde House	

APPENDICES

131	George Playne			George Playne	
132	The executors of the Rev Cockin		Disallowed?		
132	Betsy Coales		The executors of the Rev Cockin claims the east half or division of this pew in right of purchase from… The Committee are informed that Betsy ?Coales has an interest in this portion of the pew Allowed	Betsy Coales	
132	Ann Ebsworth		Wife of Richard, claims the other portion of this seat in right of gift from Francis Moyer -There is a plate Allowed. Purchased by Committee	Commottee	
133	Charles Iles	6		Charles Iles	
134			The committee believe this to belong to Mr Butt in tight of the property at Chalford (Post Office)		
135	Thomas Browning		Purchased from Samuel Gyde 1827	Thomas Browning	
136	Mrs Howell of Browne Hill		Has not yet claimed this pew - Mrs H to be asked to sell		
137	Hannah Rowe	2	In right of her husband Maurice Rowe to whom they came from R???er Watkins	Hannah Rowe	
137	Charles Iles	2	Purchased off James Cook	Charles Iles	
138	Unclaimed				

139	Joseph Percival			Joseph Percival	
140	Peter Playne			Peter Playne	
141	Peter Playne			Peter Playne	
142	Peter Playne			Peter Playne	
143	Edward Dalton	9		Edward Dalton	
144	Hyde Court			Hyde Court	
145	William Playne				
146	William Playne				
147	William Playne				
148	William Playne				
149	William Playne				
150	The executors of the Rev Cockin		In right of inheritance from Mrs Perkes		
151	Thomas Farmiloe	1	Purchased off Thomas Flower about 24 years hence		
151	William Ralph	1	Singing Gallery; formerly his father's		
151	Charles Bamfield	1	Singing Gallery; in right of his wife		
151	Solomon Hill	5	Singing Gallery; for the family		
151	Thomas Riddler	1	Singing Gallery		
151	John Clutterbuck	1	Singing Gallery		
151	Benjamn Brooks	2	Singing Gallery		
151	Samuel Davis	2	Singing Gallery		
151	Fenning Parke	1	Singing Gallery		
151	Samuel Kiene	2	Singing Gallery		

APPENDICES

151			The Committee recommend that the Owners of Sittings in this Seat should meet & consider whether they will accept an offer of Ten Shillings per Sitting -Mem. They are to be informed that the Committee are not particularly desirous of Purchasing		
151					
152	Samuel Winn	3	In right of his father	Samuel Winn	
153	William Hill	3	Admits that his father Thomas Hill let the seat - Claims it in right of his great uncle Thomas Hill		
153	Thomas Hill		In right of his father and grandfather from whom it was regularly descended to the said Thomas Hill. This pew has been sold to Mr Samuel Kearsey, May 1841 -The Committee considers that Solomon Hill has not made out his right to this pew		
154			Part of Singing Seat		
155			Part of Singing Seat		
156	Ann Sheppard			Ann Sheppard	
157	Jasper Hewer	3	Purchased off Jacob Scuse		
158			No entry		
159	Samuel Morton			Samuel Morton	

160	Philip Pease		Purchased from Mrs Mary George in 1835	Philip Pease	
161	Thomas Chandler		Given by Mrs Brokenbarrow	Thomas Chandler	
162	Churchwardens			Churchwardens	
163	Thomas Clift		Had exchanged with William Playne for sittings in West Gallery, allowed	Committee	
164	Michael Daniels		2 sittings in own right, 2 in right of late brother Jacob Daniels	Michael Daniels	
165	John G Ball		Purchased with late Thomas Browne's property. 'The Committee agree that the sitting opposite the Door of the next Pew should be equally divided between Nos 165 166		
166	Sarah Hill	4	claimed on basis of brass plate -Disallowed		
166	Richard Hill of Thrupp	2	Claims in right of his father. Solomon Hill admits is was an error to claim these 2 sittings	Richard Hill of Thrupp	2
166	Michael Daniels	1	In right of his father Samuel Daniels	Michael Daniels	1
166	Thomas Riddler	1	In right of John Watkins formerly of Brimscombe	Thomas Riddler	1
166	William Davis	2	In right of his dwelling house	William Davis	2
167	John G Ball		Purchased with late Thomas Browne's property.		

168	Charles Iles		In right of his wife to whom it came from her mother, allowed	Committee	
169	John G Ball		Claims half of 169 & 170		
170	Charles Iles	3	In right of his wife to whom it came from her mother, allowed	Committee	

APPENDIX 4
THE RECTORS OF HOLY TRINITY, MINCHINHAMPTON

From *Minchinhampton and Avening*, and the *Minchinhampton Chronicle*[869]

Rector	Date of Institution
Master Roger de Salanges	1260
Jordan de Wolverynhampton	1282
William de Prestbury	1318
Stephen Mauleon	8th May 1349
John De Houton	9th June 1349
John De Middleton	18th August 1349
Thomas De Toucestre	6th September 1360
William De Ferriby	3rd October 1360
William Potyn	
Matthew Harsfeld	4th December 1377
Alan Leverton	30th September 1390
Richard Alkerington	11th March 1393
Thomas Wysebeck	22nd February 1407
William Magot	14th June 1407
John Wodeford	18th March 1411
Robert Lover	12th February 1417
Richard Willys	13th August 1441
William Gyan LLB	1456
Richard Gyan	27th February 1489
John Reade	1507
Thomas Powell	1538 presented by Agnes, Abbess of Syon
Gilbert Bourne	1551 presented by Sir Edward Peckham
Thomas Taylor	1553 presented by William Lord Windsor
Thomas Freeman MA	1575 presented by Sir Henry Carey
George Byrch DD	1584 presented by John A Deane
Anthony Lapthorne DD	1612 presented by King James I (chaplain to King James)
Henry Fowler MA	1618 presented by Michael Halyday
William Doleman	d1649

Samuel Hieron or Hearn	1654–5
Thomas Warmestree DD	1660
John Farrer MA	1665 presented by Philip Sheppard
Ralph Willett	1717
Philip Sheppard MA	1720 presented by Samuel Sheppard
Robert Salusbury Heaton MA	1768 presented by Samuel Sheppard
John White DD	1774 presented by Edward Sheppard
Hon Harbottle Grimston MA	1778 presented by Edward Sheppard
Henry Charles Jefferies MA	1786 presented by Edward Sheppard
William Cockin MA	1806 presented by Joseph Pitt
Charles Whately MA	1841 presented by David Ricardo
Edward Colnett Oldfield MA	1865 presented by Henry David Ricardo
Frank Albert Mather MA	1885 presented by Captain Henry George Ricardo
Lonsdale Bryan MA	1896 presented by Major Henry George Ricardo
Frederick Douglas Bateman MA	1912 presented by Major Henry George Ricardo
Frederick William Sears MA	1915 presented by Lt Col Henry George Ricardo
Rex Hodson MA	1928 presented by Col Henry George Ricardo DSO DL
John Whitmore Cornwall	1959 presented by bishop of Gloucester
Michael George Peter Vooght MA	1972 presented by bishop of Gloucester
David Savage Yerburgh MA	1985 presented by bishop of Gloucester
Michael John Derek Irving B.Ed	1996 presented by bishop of Gloucester
Christopher Paul Collingwood Phd	2009 presented by bishop of Gloucester
Helen Margaret Bailey MA	2014 presented by bishop of Gloucester
Howard Neil Gilbert BA BTH	2019 presented by bishop of Gloucester

ENDNOTES

Introduction

1. Grid reference SO 87219 00814
2. Verey, D and Brooks, A 1999 *Gloucestershire I: The Cotswolds,* The Buildings of England, 478–780
3. St Ann's Gate Architects LLP, 8 Rozelle Close, Littleton, Winchester, SO22 6QP
4. Harward, C 2016 'An Archaeological Evaluation Report at Holy Trinity Church, Minchinhampton, Gloucestershire', Urban Archaeology client report; Harward, C 2017 'A Statement of Significance for Holy Trinity Church, Minchinhampton, Gloucestershire', Urban Archaeology client report
5. Harward C 2017 'A Written Scheme of Investigation for an Archaeological Watching Brief at Holy Trinity Church, Minchinhampton, Gloucestershire,' Urban Archaeology client report
6. Site code HTC16; Urban Archaeology, 2 Slad View, Gaineys Well, Stroud, Gloucestershire, GL5 1LQ; Site code HTC16
7. Nick Miles Building Contractors Ltd, 1 Wellesley Cottages, Wells Road, Bisley, Stroud, Gloucestershire, GL6 7AF
8. Centreline Architectural Sculpture Ltd, Fairfax House, Vicarage Street, Painswick, Gloucestershire, GL6 6XS
9. Site code MIN20; Harward C 2021 'Holy Trinity Church, Minchinhampton, Gloucestershire, an Archaeological Watching Brief Report,' Urban Archaeology client report
10. Account of the old church: letter from builder William Shepstone Gloucester Records Office (GA) P217 CL 2
11. Plan of 'Old Church' signed F Price P217 CW 4/9; Plan of proposed church by Foster GA P217 CW 4/9
12. Manuscript report on architecture of church by William Burges of London, 1869 GA P217 CW4/5

The Norman Church

13. Open Domesday 2020 https://opendomesday.org/place/SO8700/minchinhampton/ accessed 17/2/2020
14. The Abbey was later known as the Abbaye-des-Dames
15. St. Clair Baddeley, W 1913 *Place-names of Gloucestershire, a handbook* John Bellows, Gloucester, 109
16. Open Domesday 2020 https://opendomesday.org/place/SO8700/

minchinhampton/ accessed 17/2/2020
17 Bruce, J 1854, 'Extracts from Accounts of Churchwardens of Minchinhampton in the County of Gloucester, with Observations thereon,' *Archaeologia* **35**(2), 409–452, 411
18 GA P217 CL2
19 GA P217 CW 4/9
20 HTC16 <AF65, AF93>
21 GA P217 CW4/9
22 GA P217 CL2
23 Playne AT 1915 *Minchinhampton and Avening* 55
24 GA P217 CL2
25 Verey and Brooks 1999, 50–51
26 Verey and Brooks 1999, 50
27 Internal measurements; the measurements for Holy Trinity are based on the surviving north arcade and the 14th-century tower
28 *Reg. Regum Anglo-Norm.* ii, no. 719.
29 Carpenter RH and Ingelow B, 1889–90 'The architectural history of Avening church' *Trans. Bris. & Glos. Arch. Soc* **14**, 5–13; Baddeley, W St C, 1921 'Avening church' *Trans. Bris. & Glos. Arch. Soc* **43**, 181–90; Verey, D and Brooks, A 1999 *Gloucestershire 1: The Cotswolds, Buildings of England*, 3rd Edition 148–149
30 Baddeley, W St C, 1921 'Avening church' *Trans. Bris. & Glos. Arch. Soc* **43**, 183
31 Carpenter, RH and Ingelow, B 1889–90 'The Architectural History of Avening Church, Gloucestershire' *Trans. Bristol and Glouc. Arch. Soc.* **14**, 5–13
32 Fryer AC 1911 'Gloucestershire Fonts. Part 4' *Trans. Bristol and Glouc. Arch. Soc..* **34** 195–207

Early English

33 GA P217 CL 2
34 Verey and Brooks 1999, 53; Yates, N 2001 *Buildings, Faith, And Worship: The Liturgical Arrangement of Anglican Churches 1600-1900*, 12.
35 Watson, CE 1932 'The Minchinhampton Custumal and its place in the Story of the Manor' *Transactions of the Bristol and Gloucestershire Archaeological Society* **54**, 379
36 Glynne SR (ed), Phillimore WPW and Melland Hall J 1902 *Gloucestershire Church Notes,* 40
37 HTC16 <AF27>
38 Forrester, H 1972 *Medieval Gothic Mouldings, Phillimore,* London, 39

Decorated Gothic

39 A P Baggs, A R J Jurica and W J Sheils, 'Minchinhampton: Economic history', in *A History of the County of Gloucester:* Volume **11**, Bisley and Longtree Hundreds, ed. N M Herbert and R B Pugh (London, 1976), pp. 193-200. British History Online http://www.british-history.ac.uk/vch/glos/vol11/pp193-200 [accessed 5 May 2020].
40 Trinity Sunday is the first Sunday after Pentecost, depending on Easter it falls between late May and mid June

41	*Cal. Chart. R.* 1257–1300, 124.
42	A P Baggs, A R J Jurica and W J Sheils, 'Minchinhampton: Economic history', in *A History of the County of Gloucester:* Volume **11**, Bisley and Longtree Hundreds, ed. N M Herbert and R B Pugh (London, 1976), pp. 193-200. British History Online http://www.british-history.ac.uk/vch/glos/vol11/pp193-200 [accessed 5 May 2020].
43	GA P217 CL2
44	Bruce 1854, 411; GA P217 CW 2/1
45	Watson, CE 1932 'The Minchinhampton Custumal and its place in the Story of the Manor' *Transactions of the Bristol and Gloucestershire Archaeological Society* **54**, 383–4. St Mary Magdalene had certainly been built by 1378–80, when 'William the chaplain' is mentioned in the Clerical Roll Subsidy, and the chapel itself is mentioned in 1384 (*Reg. Wakefeld*, p. 22). In 1398 a chantry was endowed at St Mary Magdalene, with a further endowment in 1434, suggesting there was a chantry priest in place, although in 1435 the rector of Minchinhampton was still required to give service at Rodborough three times a week (Watson 384).
46	Lady Chapels were dedicated to the Virgin Mary and would have had a separate altar and officiating priest. A P Baggs, A R J Jurica and W J Sheils, 'Minchinhampton: Churches', in *A History of the County of Gloucester: Volume 11, Bisley and Longtree Hundreds,* ed. N M Herbert and R B Pugh (London, 1976), pp. 201-204. British History Online http://www.british-history.ac.uk/vch/glos/vol11/pp201-204 [accessed 5 May 2020].
47	TNA SC 6/1125/15
48	*Inq. Non.* (Rec. Com.), 407; cf. *Cal. Pat. 1345–8,* 470
49	Verey and Brooks, 1999, 54–55
50	Three Cotswold stone slates were found during the evaluation, a Minchinhampton Weatherstone ridge tile with a decorative roll moulding <AF62> would have been mortared in place along the ridge line
51	Glynne SR (ed), Phillimore WPW and Melland Hall J 1902 *Gloucestershire Church Notes, p40*
52	Habington, H 1899 'A Survey of Worcester' *Worcestershire Historical Society*
53	No 5, Playne GF 1868 p40
54	View of nave in 1901 with plaster scraped off and showing the original steeper roofline of the nave
55	GF Playne 1868 40
56	GA P217 CL 1
57	Playne, GF 1868 'On the Incised Grave-Stones and Stone Coffins of Minchinhampton Church', *Proceedings of the Cotteswold Naturalists' Field Club,* **V**, 42–3
58	Bigland, 654; Rudder 1779, 470
59	GA P217 CL 1
60	GA P217 CW 4/5
61	Verey and Brookes 1999, 54. The rose window and heavy, close-set buttresses of the south was probably an influence on Rodborough-born architect Benjamin Bucknall at Woodchester Park (Verey and Brookes 1999, 750).

NOTES TO PAGES 14–28

62 Verey and Brookes 1999, 478–80
63 Anon. 1858 'Minchinhampton Church, Gloucestershire' *The Builder*, 30th January, 75
64 Verey and Brookes 1999, 479
65 Atkyns R 1712 *The Ancient and Present State of Glostershire,* London: W. Bowyer, 453; Frith, B (ed) 1990 'Ralph Bigland Historical, Monumental and Genealogical Collections relative to the County of Gloucester, Part Two: Daglingworth–Moreton Valence,' *Glos. Record Series* **3**, 646
66 GF Playne 1868, 45
67 Playne, AT 1978 *Minchinhampton and Avening* 2nd edition Sutton, p50–52
68 Bruce 1854, 431
69 Bruce 1854, 415
70 Verey, D 1970 *Buildings of England* 316–7
71 Verey and Brooks 1999, 479
72 Watson does not give a reference for the reeves' accounts for 1330. Watson, CE 1932 'The Minchinhampton Custumal and its place in the Story of the Manor' *Transactions of the Bristol and Gloucestershire Archaeological Society* **54**, 382
73 Playne, GF 1868, 45
74 Smith 1905, 97; the mention of lions rampant and passant could be an error, or may suggest more than one design of tile was present
75 The tile is incomplete but has one complete dimension (110mm x 96mm, thickness unknown), and is in a slightly pitted dark fabric with thin white clay inlay and a black glaze. The inlay is slightly smeared and the tile appears to not be of very good quality, although the resetting and subsequent damage may contribute to this impression. The design is of an eagle displayed, facing to its left, within a diagonally set square. There is white clay in the triangular fields at two corners, but damage makes it impossible to make out the design
76 Morris, R K 1997 'European Prodigy or Regional Eccentric? The Rebuilding of St Augustine's Abbey Church, Bristol', in *Almost the Richest City': Bristol in the Middle Ages,* ed. L Keen, British Archaeological Association Conference Transactions, **19** (Leeds, 1997), 41–56; Wilson, C 'Gothic Metamorphosed: the Choir of St Augustine's Abbey in Bristol and the Renewal of European Architecture in Around 1300'; and Cannon, J 'Berkeley Patronage and the 14th-century choir', in Cannon, J and Williamson, B eds. 2011 *The Medieval Art, Architecture and History of Bristol Cathedral: An Enigma Explored,* Woodbridge, 69–147 and 148–185.
77 Harvey, J 1954 (1984 ed) 'Thomas of Witney' and 'William Joy', *English Medieval Architects: a Biographical Dictionary down to 1550,* 338–341 and 164–165.
78 Draper, P 1981 'The sequence and dating of the Decorated work at Wells', in Coldstream, N and Draper, P eds *Medieval Art and Architecture at Wells and Glastonbury, British Archaeological Association Conference Transactions,* **4**, 18–29
79 Pevsner, N 1952 *The Buildings of England: South Devon,* Penguin, 219
80 Verey, D and Brooks, A 2002 *The Buildings of England, Gloucestershire 2: The Vale and the Forest of Dean,* 408
81 For example if there are sedilia anywhere outside the chancel, they will be in the

Lady chapel, as seen in the south aisle of Portbury church, Somerset: J Cannon, *op cit, 156*

82 Cannon, J 'The Bristol Master and the Ambitions of Decorated', in John Munns ed 2017 *Decorated Revisited: English Architectural Style in Context, 1250–1400*, Turnhout, 91–112

83 Cannon 'The Bristol Master', op cit, 99–102; Pevsner, N and Cherry, B 1975 *The Buildings of England: Wiltshire*, Harmondsworth, 544

84 Cannon, 'Berkeley Patronage' op cit, 160

85 Sherwood, J and Pevsner, N 1974 *The Buildings of England: Oxfordshire*, Harmondsworth, 843–845; Pevsner and Cherry op cit, 255–256

86 Wilson, op cit, 90–93

87 Francis Woodman 1981 *The Architectural History of Canterbury Cathedral*

88 Dugdale, W 1658 *The history of St. Paul's Cathedral in London: from its foundation untill these times : extracted out of originall charters, records, leiger books, and other manuscripts : beautified with sundry prospects of the Church, figures of tombes and monuments* Tho. Warren, London, 170

89 Dugdale, W 1658 *The history of St. Paul's Cathedral in London: from its foundation untill these times : extracted out of originall charters, records, leiger books, and other manuscripts : beautified with sundry prospects of the Church, figures of tombes and monuments* Tho. Warren, London, 165

90 Cragoe, CD 'Fabric, tombs and precinct 1087–1540', in Keene, L, Burns, D, and Saint A, 2004 *St Paul's: the Cathedral Church of London 604–2004*, New Haven, 127–42

91 Cowan, P 2005 *The Rose Windows: Splendour and Symbol*, London

92 Cragoe, CD 'Fabric, tombs and precinct 1087–1540', in Keene, L, Burns, D, and Saint A, 2004 *St Paul's: the Cathedral Church of London 604–2004*, New Haven, 127–42

93 Verey, D 1980 *The Buildings of England: Gloucestershire, the Vale and the Forest of Dean*, Harmondsworth, 125–125

94 Wilson, op cit, 97–99

95 *Corpus Vitrearum Medii Aevi: Leicestershire* **X**, 180

96 Pevsner, N 1966 *The Buildings of England: Yorkshire, the North Riding*, Harmondsworth, 319–321.

97 Bony, J 1979 *The English Decorated Style: Gothic Architecture Transformed, 1250-1350*, Oxford, figs 210, 212, 215, 216; Morris op cit, 51-2; Wilson op cit, 128

98 Cannon, 'The Bristol Master', 179

99 'Chapel adjoining the Chancel of Willingham Church' engraved by Samuel Lysons (1810), in Lysons, D and Lysons S 1810 *Magna Britannia; being a concise topographical account of the several counties of Great Britain*, **2**, T Cadell and W Davies, London, 285

100 Pevsner, N 1954 *The Buildings of England: Cambridgeshire*, Harmondsworth, 400–402

101 Binski, P 2016 'An Early Miniature Copy of the Choir Vault of Wells Cathedral at Irnham, Lincolnshire' in *Journal of the British Archaeological Association*, **169** (2016), 59–70

102 Ely: Pevsner op cit. 299; Mildenhall: Pevsner, N and Radcliffe, E 1975 *The Buildings of England: Suffolk,* 364–5; Bony, op cit, fig. 316
103 Verey, D and Brooks, A 1999 *The Buildings of England: Gloucestershire I: the Cotswolds* Harmondsworth, 478–480
104 Watson, CE 1932 'The Minchinhampton Custumal and its place in the Story of the Manor' *Transactions of the Bristol and Gloucestershire Archaeological Society* **54**, 299
105 Holford, ML and Dryburgh P (eds) 2022 *Escheators' Inquisitions for Gloucestershire and Bristol, c.1260–1485,* Glouc. Records Series **37**, 105
106 Maclean, J 1883–4 'Chantry certificates, Gloucestershire' *Trans. Bristol & Glos. Arch. Soc* **8**, 275
107 WCL Reg. *Sede Vacante*
108 *Cal. Pat. 1338-40,* 32
109 *Reg. Bransford, pp. 369, 160; Worc. Episc. Reg., Reg. Carpenter, i, f. 149v*
110 Register of the Priory of Woodchester f128
111 Maclean, J 1883–4 'Chantry certificates, Gloucestershire,' *Trans. B.G.A.S.* **8**. 275
112 Verey and Brooks, 1999, 148
113 GA D7942/16
114 Holford, ML and Dryburgh P (eds) 2022 'Escheators' Inquisitions for Gloucestershire and Bristol, c.1260–1485' Glouc. *Records Series* **37**
115 P217 CL1 p18
116 Champion, M 2015 *Medieval Graffiti, The Lost Voices of England's Churches,* Ebury Press, London
117 Laurence Keen, pers. comm.
118 Playne, AT 1978, p 55
119 Harward 2017, 11–15; Pevsner 1970, 316–17
120 Habington, H 1899 'A Survey of Worcester' *Worcestershire Historical Society*
121 Pacey, A 2007 *Medieval architectural drawing,* Tempus, p71–5
122 Hislop, M 2012 *Medieval Masons. Shire* Archaeology. Oxford. pp19-20.
123 GA P217 CW 4/5

Perpendicular

124 Cal. Pat. 422-9, 205-7 and 1441-6, 272
125 Playne, AT 1978 29
126 Playne, AT 1978, 50
127 Keen, L 2015 *Gloucester Cathedral Lady Chapel. The Medieval Tile Pavement,* 6
128 The tile is in a fine, fairly hard, oxidised fabric with white quartz flecks. The full depth of the tile is 27mm, there is no keying on the surviving fragment. The decoration is crisply stamped and inlaid with pipeclay, over which the glaze is cream, appearing olive green over the tile fabric. Decoration is a segment of a circular band with two pellets, and border, with the tip of a leaf motif.
129 Eames 1980 243; Emden 1977, 38; Lewis 1999, 61–2
130 Laurence Keen *pers. comm.*

The Sixteenth Century

131   Yates, N 2001 *Buildings, Faith, And Worship: The Liturgical Arrangement of Anglican Churches 1600-1900*, 12
132   Gairdner J 1904 *English Historical Review* (January 1904), **29**, pp 98–121
133   Gairdner J 1904 *English Historical Review* (January 1904), **29**, 115
134   Maclean J 1883–4 'Chantry certificates, Gloucestershire' *Trans. Bristol & Glos. Arch. Soc* **8**, 275
135   ibid.
136   *Cal. Pat.* 1548-9, 54
137   Herbermann CG, Pace EA, Pallen, CB, Shahan, TJ and Wynne, JJ (eds) 1913 *The Old Catholic Encyclopaedia, An International Work Of Reference On The Constitution, Doctrine, Discipline, And History Of The Catholic Church;* The Encyclopaedia Press **2**
138   GDR XL Stonehouse deanery
139   GDR XX 9–10
140   Price FD 1937 'The Commission for Ecclesiastical Causes for the Dioceses of Bristol and Gloucester, 1574,' *Trans. Bristol & Glos. Arch. Soc.* **59**, 151
141   GDR XXVII, 831
142   Price FD 1937 'The Commission for Ecclesiastical Causes for the Dioceses of Bristol and Gloucester, 1574,' *Trans. Bristol & Glos. Arch. Soc.* **59**, 151–153
143   A P Baggs, A R J Jurica and W J Sheils, 'Minchinhampton: Economic history', in *A History of the County of Gloucester: Volume 11, Bisley and Longtree Hundreds*, ed. N M Herbert and R B Pugh (London, 1976), pp. 193-200. British History Online http://www.british-history.ac.uk/vch/glos/vol11/pp193-200 [accessed 5 May 2020]. The date of the second fair was changed to 29th October when the Julian calendar was changed over to the Gregorian in 1752.
144   *E.H.R.* **xix**. 115
145   Bodl. MS. Rawl. C.790, f. 9v.
146   Hockaday Abstracts. **xliv**, 1572 visit. f. 48
147   GDR **76**, 199
148   GA P 217/CW 2/1
149   Bruce, J 1854 'Extracts from Accounts of the Churchwardens of Minchinhampton, in the County of Gloucester, with Observations thereon.' *Archaeologia,* **35**, Issue 2 1854 , pp. 409-452.
150   Bruce 1854
151   GA P 217/CW 2/1; Rudge, *Hist. of Glos.* i. 343.
152   Bruce 1854, 413
153   Bruce 1854, 413
154   French, K 'Women in the Late Medieval English Parish', in M C Erler, and M Kowaleski (ed.), 2003 *Gendering the Master Narratative. Woman and Power in the Middle Ages*, Ithaca, p. 166
155   Bruce 1854, 422–3
156   Bruce 1854, 415
157   Tate, WE 1969 *The Parish Chest, a Study of the Records of Parochial Administration in England,* Cambridge University Press, 3rd Edition, 106–7; GA P217 CL1 p17

158 Yates 2001 31
159 HTC[154]
160 Dr Maureen Jurkowski pers. comm.
161 Dr James Willoughby, pers. comm.
162 Rosewell, R 2008 *Medieval Wall Paintings,* Boydell Press, Woodbridge, 211–219
163 Rosewell 2008, 30
164 Bruce 1854, 422
165 Historic England Listing text List ID 1245083; *Glouc. Rental, 1455,* sketch no. 11; *Bibliotheca Glos. ii.* 373
166 Historic England Listing text List ID 1245665; GA P154/9/CW 2/1
167 Flannel, J 2016 *Fifty English Steeples: The Finest Medieval Parish Church Towers and Spires in England.* Thames and Hudson. 179–180
168 GA P217 CL 1
169 Playne 1868, 44
170 Beeson CFC 1971 *English Church Clocks 1280–1850, History and classification,* Phillimore, 13–15
171 Beeson CFC 1971, 26
172 Beeson CFC 1971, 13
173 Beeson CFC 1971, 13; Rock, H 2008 *Church Clocks,* Shire, 14
174 Dowler G, 1984 *Gloucestershire Clock and Watchmakers* Phillimore & Co Ltd, p87
175 Derham, W 1696 *The Artificial Clockmaker, A Treatise of Watch, and Clock Work* London pp 3 & 5
176 Rock, H 2008, 21

The Seventeenth century
177 Yates 2001 34
178 Bodleian MS. Top. Glouc. c. 3, f166
179 A P Baggs, A R J Jurica and W J Sheils, 'Minchinhampton: Churches', in *A History of the County of Gloucester: Volume 11, Bisley and Longtree Hundreds,* ed. N M Herbert and R B Pugh (London, 1976), pp. 201-204. British History Online http://www.british-history.ac.uk/vch/glos/vol11/pp201-204 [accessed 16 February 2021].
180 Fullbrook-Leggatt, LEWO 1964 'The Survey of Church Livings in Gloucestershire,' 1650 *Trans. B.G.A.S.* **83**. 92
181 GA P 217/CW 2/1
182 GA P217 CW 2/1. VCH records that there was 'an abortive scheme in the late 1650s to make Rodborough a separate parish and endow the church with the rector of Minchinhampton's tithes there, and also apparently with the profits of the Rodborough lectureship: Hockaday Abs. cccxxiv.' A P Baggs. A R J Jurica. W J Sheils, 'Rodborough: Church', *A History of the County of Gloucester: Volume 11,* Bisley and Longtree Hundreds, (London, 1976), pp. 230-232. British History Online https://www.british-history.ac.uk/vch/glos/vol11/pp230-232 [accessed 14 June 2024].
183 Tate, WE 1969, 157–61

184 GA P217 CL1 p17
185 For example 'Item ij alter clothes of fflock worke' at Holy Trinity Guildford, Daniel-Tyssen JR 1869 'Inventories of the goods and ornaments of the churches in the County of Surrey in the reign of King Edward the Sixth', *Surrey Archaeological Collections* **4**, 28
186 *Churchwardens' Accounts* 19

QUEEN ANNE AND THE GEORGIANS
187 Playne, AT 1978 *Minchinhampton and Avening* 2nd edition Sutton, 41
188 GA P 272A/VE 2/1
189 Bruce 1854, 411
190 Yate 2001 36
191 Tate, WE 1969, 107–8
192 GDR 271, 166–7
193 GA P217 CW4/9
194 https://www.minchinhamptonlocalhistorygroup.org.uk/nineteenth/personalities/ accessed 31st January 2020
195 GA P217 CL1
196 Playne GF 1872 'On the Incised Grave-stones and Stone Coffins of Minchinhampton Church', *Proceedings of the Cotteswold Naturalists Field Club for 1868*, **V** 42–3
197 *Church Times*, Friday 5 May 1876, p 230
198 Harrison, J 2016 *Bells and Bellringing*, Shire Books 802, 20–21
199 Playne AT opposite p71
200 Playne, AT 1978, 70–71
201 Watson, CE 1932 'The Minchinhampton Custumal and its place in the Story of the Manor' *Transactions of the Bristol and Gloucestershire Archaeological Society* **54**, 339–341
202 Playne AT 1915 71, references *Valor Ecclesiasticus, 26 Henry VIII, 1534*
203 Bruce, 1854 422
204 Bruce, 1854 422
205 GA P217/VE/2/3 p23
206 GA P217/CL/2
207 GA P217 CL2 p8
208 Dove's Guide for Church Bell-ringers https://dove.cccbr.org.uk/tower/16728 accessed 31st January 2020
209 GA P217/2/3 p113

MINCHINHAMPTON IN 1842
210 GA P217 CL1 p42
211 GA P217/VE/2/3 16
212 Playne AT 1978 135–8; HMSO 1840 Reports from the Commission on hand loom weavers HMSO
213 Atkyns, R 1712 The Ancient and Present State of Glostershire, London
214 GA P217 CL/2

215 GA D 2052
216 Playne AT 1978 127–8
217 GA P217 CW 4/9
218 Playne AT 1978 opp.79
219 Playne AT 1978, 79
220 Playne AT 1978, 80
221 A P Baggs, A R J Jurica and W J Sheils, 'Minchinhampton: Education', in *A History of the County of Gloucester: Volume 11, Bisley and Longtree Hundreds,* ed. N M Herbert and R B Pugh (London, 1976), p. 205. British History Online http://www.british-history.ac.uk/vch/glos/vol11/p205 [accessed 31 January 2020].
222 GDR 344a, 287
223 GA P217 CL6 'Minchinhampton Church Rate' leaflet
224 GA P217 CL1 11
225 GA P217 CW 2/6
226 GA P217 CW 2/6
227 GA P217/2/3 p173
228 GA P217 CL1 p44
229 GA P217/2/3 p181 The committee comprised the Revd Whately, George Playne, John Kibble, David Ricardo, William Playne, Peter Playne and Francis Chambers
230 GA P217/2/3 p182
231 *GA* P217/2/3/184
232 GA P217/2/3 p182
233 GA P217/2/3 p186 'The Amount of Delapidations' refers to payments required under Chancel Tax, where lay rectors -owners of glebe land- are liable for repairs to the chancel, the parish being liable for the rest of the church.
234 GA P217/2/3 p186
235 GA P217 CW 2/6
236 Bruce 1854, 415. Edward Dalton was recorded as a bachelor living in St Pauls, Bristol. In 1831, aged 40, he married Elizabeth Head Lloyd of Avening, a spinster aged 35, in Avening church; they had one child, Elizabeth. The Daltons presumably moved into Dunkirk Mill after their marriage (GDR/Q2/81/entry number 275). Dalton held a pew with 9 seats at Holy Trinity in 1841 (GA P217/CW/4/2 143). There is a photograph of Dalton aged 77 in 1864 (the dates and his ages do not tally) in a photographic album by the Revd Edward Blackwell: "Clergymen who have ministered at Amberley" (GA P13/IN/4/6/2 p34/3) and of Dalton and Elizabeth in Blackwell's companion album "I. My parish and congregation" (GA P13/IN/4/6/3 p7/1-2).
237 Playne GF 1868, p44
238 It may be that this was altered in 1856–7 when A Fewster received £1.6*s.* for 'Glazing and repairs to the south window' GA P217/CL/2
239 GA P217 CL1 p45
240 GA P217 CW4/9
241 GA P217 CL1 p51
242 GA P217 CL1 p18

243 Playne AT 1978, 58
244 Playne AT 1978, 58–9
245 *Buildings of England Gloucestershire 1: The Cotswolds*, 379
246 The London Gazette 2nd February 1830, Issue 18652, p 257 https://www.thegazette.co.uk/London/issue/18652/page/257 accessed 31st January 2020
247 https://web.archive.org/web/20090810231519/http://www.leighrayment.com/commons/Scommons5.htm accessed 31st January 2020
248 A P Baggs, A R J Jurica and W J Sheils, 'Minchinhampton: Charities for the poor', in *A History of the County of Gloucester: Volume 11, Bisley and Longtree Hundreds*, ed. N M Herbert and R B Pugh (London, 1976), pp. 206-207. British History Online http://www.british-history.ac.uk/vch/glos/vol11/pp206-207 [accessed 31 January 2020].
249 A P Baggs, A R J Jurica and W J Sheils, 'Minchinhampton: Local government', in *A History of the County of Gloucester: Volume 11, Bisley and Longtree Hundreds*, ed. N M Herbert and R B Pugh (London, 1976), pp. 200-201. British History Online http://www.british-history.ac.uk/vch/glos/vol11/pp200-201 [accessed 31 January 2020].
250 A P Baggs, A R J Jurica and W J Sheils, 'Minchinhampton: Education', in *A History of the County of Gloucester: Volume 11, Bisley and Longtree Hundreds*, ed. N M Herbert and R B Pugh (London, 1976), p. 205. British History Online http://www.british-history.ac.uk/vch/glos/vol11/p205 [accessed 31 January 2020].
251 *GDR 344a, 287*
252 A P Baggs, A R J Jurica and W J Sheils, 'Minchinhampton: Local government', in *A History of the County of Gloucester: Volume 11, Bisley and Longtree Hundreds*, ed. N M Herbert and R B Pugh (London, 1976), pp. 200-201. British History Online http://www.british-history.ac.uk/vch/glos/vol11/pp200-201 [accessed 31 January 2020].
253 A P Baggs, A R J Jurica and W J Sheils, 'Minchinhampton: Churches', in *A History of the County of Gloucester: Volume 11, Bisley and Longtree Hundreds*, ed. N M Herbert and R B Pugh (London, 1976), pp. 201-204. British History Online http://www.british-history.ac.uk/vch/glos/vol11/pp201-204 [accessed 31 January 2020].

Foster's church

254 GA P217 CL1 p35
255 GA P217 CL 1
256 Colvin, H 1995 *A Biographical Dictionary of British Architects 1600-1840*, 3rd edition, New Haven and London: Yale University Press, 372–373.
257 *Buildings of England Gloucestershire 1: The Cotswolds*, 651
258 *Buildings of England Gloucestershire 1: The Cotswolds*, 197
259 *Buildings of England Gloucestershire 1: The Cotswolds*, 721
260 *Buildings of England Gloucestershire 1: The Cotswolds*, 212
261 *Buildings of England Gloucestershire 2: The Vale and The Forest of Dean*, 519
262 *Buildings of England Gloucestershire 2: The Vale and The Forest of Dean*, 624
263 *Buildings of England Gloucestershire 2: The Vale and The Forest of Dean*, 804

264 *Buildings of England Gloucestershire 1: The Cotswolds*, 572
265 GA P217 CW 4/5
266 GA P217 CL 2
267 GA P217 CW 4/5
268 GA P217 CW 4/5
269 Anon. 1858 'Minchinhampton Church, Gloucestershire' *The Builder*, 30th January, 75
270 Playne AT 1978, 57
271 See Appendix 3; GA P217/CW/4/2
272 GA P217/2/3 p185
273 GA P217/2/3 p186
274 GA P217/CW/4/4
275 GA P217 CL2
276 GA P217/CW/4/3
277 GA P217/CW/4/4
278 GA P217 CL1 p54
279 GA P217 CL2
280 The Society for Promoting Christian Knowledge was founded in 1698 by the Revd Thomas Bray and is the third oldest publishing house in England. It produced a wide range of Christian publications

1868-9 Oldfield, Burges and the new chancel
281 GA P217 CW 4/5
282 GA P217 CL 1 p48
283 Playne AT 1978, 57
284 GA P217/CW/4/4
285 Playne AT 1978, 57
286 Playne AT 1978, 57
287 GA P217 CW 4/10
288 Playne 1978, 55
289 This text is largely based on Jim Portbury's article in Minchinhampton Local History Group bulletin (Portbury, J 2007 'The History of the organ in Minchinhampton Parish Church' Minch. Local Hist. Group, **24**, 11–14)
290 GA P217 CW4/9
291 Portbury 2011, 11
292 Parish Magazine, June 1887
293 Portbury, J 2007 'The History of the organ in Minchinhampton Parish Church' *Minch. Local Hist. Group*, **24**, 11–14
294 Martin Goetze and Dominic Gwynn Ltd, 2021 'Report and quotation on the Holy Trinity organ,' dated May 28th 2021
295 Martin Crampin, University of Wales http://stainedglass.llgc.org.uk/person/38

The Twentieth century
296 *Stroud News* 18th June 1909; http://www.minchinhamptonlocalhistoryGAup.org.uk/a-z/landmarks-l/#Lych accessed 31st January 2020
297 GA P217 CW 3/6

298 GA P217 CW 3/16/2
299 Harward, C 2019 'An Archaeological Post-excavation Assessment Report: Holy Trinity Church, Minchinhampton, Gloucestershire'; Harward, C 2021, 'Holy Trinity Church, Minchinhampton, Gloucestershire, an Archaeological Watching Brief Report'
300 Cox, N 2005 'Gloucester Folk Museum and the mechanisation of the pin industry' in *Gloucestershire Society for Industrial Archaeology Journal for 2005* 4–18
301 Mills, S 1995 'The Stroud Pin Makers' in *Gloucestershire Society for Industrial Archaeology Journal for 1995*, 37–42
302 Egan, G and Pritchard, F 2002, *Medieval finds from excavations in London. 3. Dress accessories, c.1150-c.1450*, Boydell Press, Woodbridge, Suffolk, 281
303 Livings, G 2022 'Aiglets: Medieval and Post Medieval' The Society of Creative Anachronism

304 GA P217 CL 1
305 Playne, GF 1868 p40
306 After Playne 1868, plate facing p39
307 Playne, GF 1868 'On the Incised Grave-Stones and Stone Coffins of Minchinhampton Church', *Proceedings of the Cotteswold Naturalists' Field Club*, **V**, 40–41
308 Playne, GF 1868 facing p39, 40–42

Death, Burial and Memorial
309 HTC16 Sk(163)
310 MIN20 Sk(88)
311 MIN20 Sk(84)
312 Gilchrist, R and Sloane, B 2005, *Requiem: the medieval monastic cemetery in Britain*, Museum of London Archaeology Service
313 GA P217 CL2
314 GA P217/VE/2/3 87
315 e.g. Puckle 1926
316 GA P217/VE/2/3 p105
317 GA P217/2/3 p180
318 Playne, GF 1868, 58–9.
319 GDR 344a p287
320 Bruce, 1854 437
321 Bruce, 1854 451
322 Litten J 1991 *The English Way of Death: The Common Funeral Since 1450*, Robert Hale Ltd, 86
323 Litten 1991, 109; Adams et al 2006, 160; V&A E.3096-3133.1910). The excavated design is a very close match to no83 on the c.1825 'AT' catalogue; V&A E.994 to E.1022-1978
324 Litten 1991, 100–118
325 Gaimster, M 2016 'Coffin furniture and small finds' in Proctor, J, Gaimster, M and Langthorne, J Y A *Quaker Burial Ground at North Shields: Excavations at*

Coach Lane, Tyne and Wear PCA Monograph 20, 89
326 Litten 1991, 109
327 Heighway, C and Bryant, R 1999, *The Golden Minster. The Anglo-Saxon minster and later medieval priory of St Oswald at Gloucester* CBA Research Report, 117, York: Council for British Archaeology, 226, fig. 5.39
328 Litten 1991, 107
329 YCBA L 201.15 Folio B, 50
330 Reeve, J and Adams, M 1993 'The Spitalfields Project Volume 1 - The Archaeology, Across The Styx' *CBA Research Report* **85**
331 Border Archaeology *Conserving Coffin Grip Plates: History, Manufacture, Material and Conservation* https://www.borderarchaeology.com/conserving-coffin-grip-plates-history-manufactu/ [accessed 14 April 2021].
332 Boore E 1998, 'Burial vaults and Coffin furniture in the West Country' in M Cox (ed) *Grave Concerns: Death and burial in England 1700-1850*, CBA Research Report **113**, 73
333 YCBA L 201.15 Folio B, 50, detail
334 Adams J, Brickley M, Buteux S, Adams T, Cherrington R, 2006 *St Martin's Uncovered: Investigations in the Churchyard of St. Martin's-in-the-Bull-Ring, Birmingham* 2001, Oxbow Books, 110
335 Playne, GF 1868 'On the Incised Grave-Stones and Stone Coffins of Minchinhampton Church', *Proceedings of the Cotteswold Naturalists' Field Club*, **V**, opp. p38 and 39
336 GA P217 CL1, 18
337 <AF83>
338 *GA* P217 CL2
339 Playne, GF 1868 'On the Incised Grave-Stones and Stone Coffins of Minchinhampton Church', *Proceedings of the Cotteswold Naturalists' Field Club*, **V**, 42–3
340 Glynne SR (ed), Phillimore WPW and Melland Hall J 1902 *Gloucestershire Church Notes*, p40
341 Frith, B (ed) 1990 *Ralph Bigland Historical, Monumental and Genealogical Collections relative to the County of Gloucester, Part Two: Daglingworth–Moreton Valence*, Glos. Record Series **3**, 654; Rudder 1779, 470
342 Bodleian MS. Top. Glouc. c. 3, f165v
343 It is intriguing that a brass to a man from Rodborough was not in the north 'Rodborough' aisle
344 Bodleian MS. Top. Glouc. c. 3, f165v; *Bigland*, 655
345 Playne 1915 opp. p64
346 Bigland, 654
347 Frith, B (ed) 1990, 656
348 Frith, B (ed) 1990
349 *Relton, HE 1843 Sketches of churches with short descriptions, London and Oxford*
350 Landed Families of Britain and Ireland https://landedfamilies.blogspot.com/2021/08/467-baynham-and-throckmorton-of.html, accessed 1st February 2024
351 Frith, B (ed) 1990, 656–662

352 Playne 1915 opp. 67
353 Griffin, E 2018 *Diets, Hunger and Living Standards during the British Industrial Revolution. Past & Present,* **239** (1), May, 82–87
354 GB Historical GIS/University of Portsmouth, Minchinhampton SubD through time | Industry Statistics|Occupation data classified into the 24 1881 'Orders', plus sex, *A Vision of Britain through Time.* URL: https://www.visionofbritain.org.uk/unit/10552862/cube/OCC_ORDER1881 Accessed: 09/07/2021
355 Triskele Heritage, www.triskeleheritage.com
356 Price, A 2002 'Geology and building materials', in Verey, D and Brooks, A (eds) *The Buildings of England, Gloucestershire 1: The Cotswolds.* London: Yale University Press
357 Green, G W 1992 *Bristol and Gloucester Region.* British Regional Geology. London: HMSO; Historic England 2023 *Gloucestershire. Building Stones of England.* Swindon, 23
358 Pascal Mychalysin, Master Mason Gloucester Cathedral *pers. comm.*
359 Historic England 2023 *Gloucestershire. Building Stones of England.* Swindon, 19–20
360 Pascal Mychalysin *pers. comm.*
361 Harward, C 2016 'Evaluation Report at Holy Trinity Church, Minchinhampton, Gloucestershire,' Urban Archaeology client report; Historic England 2023 *Gloucestershire. Building Stones of England.* Swindon, 22

Discussion

362 Yate 2001 151–2

Appendices

363 GRO P217 CL 2
364 The architect was in fact Thomas Foster; Shepstone was the builder
365 'Mr Rickman' is the architect Thomas Rickman (1776-1841), who set out the basic chronological structure of English medieval ecclesiastical architecture in his 1817 treatise and was an early figure in the Gothic Revival: Rickman, T n.d.[1817] *Attempt to discriminate the styles of English architecture, from the conquest to the reformation: preceded by a sketch of the Grecian and Roman orders, with notices of nearly five hundred English buildings.* London : Longman, Hurst, Rees, Orme, and Brown, printed in Liverpool by J. J. Smith.
366 GRO P217 CW 4/5
367 GRO P217/CW/4/2
368 GRO P217/CW/4/4
369 Playne 1915; GRO P217 CL1

BIBLIOGRAPHY

Manuscript Sources

GA: Gloucestershire Record Office
GDR: Gloucestershire Diocesan Records
TNA: The National Archives
VCH: Victoria County History

Bodleian MS. Rawl. C.790, f. 9v.
Bodleian MS. Top. Glouc. c. 3, f165v–166
Cal. Chart. R. 1257–1300, 124.
Cal. Pat. 1338–40, 32
Cal. Pat. 1345–8, 470
Cal. Pat. 1422–9, 205-7
Cal. Pat. 1441–6, 272
Cal. Pat. 1548–9, 54
Calendar of the Register of Henry Wakefeld, Bishop of Worcester, 1375-95, 22
Calendar of the Register of Wolstan de Bransford, Bishop of Worcester 1339-49, 369, 160
Econ.Hist.Rev. xix. 115
Glouc. Rental, 1455, sketch no. 11
GDR **76**, 199
GDR XL
GDR XX 9–10
GDR XXVII, 831
GDR 271, 166–7
GDR 344a, 287
GDR /Q2/81/entry number 275
GA D2052
GA D7942/16
GA Hockaday Abs. cccxxiv
GA Hockaday Abstracts. xliv, 1572 visit. f48
GA P272A/VE 2/1
GA P13/IN/4/6/2
GA P154/9/CW 2/1
GA P217/2/3
GA P217 CL 1

GA P217 CL 2
GA P217 CL6
GA P217 CW 2/1
GA P217 CW 2/6
GA P217 CW 3/16/2
GA P217 CW 3/6
GA P217 CW 4/10
GA P217 CW 4/5
GA P217 CW 4/9
GA P217 CW4/5
GA P217/CW/4/2-4
GA P217/VE/2/3
Inq. Non. (Rec. Com.), 407
Reg. of the Priory of Woodchester f128
Reg. Regum Anglo-Norm. ii, no. 719.
Register of the Diocese of Worcester during the Vacancy of the See
TNA, SC 6/1125/15
Valor Ecclesiasticus, 26 Henry VIII, 1534
Victoria and Albert Museum E.994 to E.1022-1978
Worc. Episc. Reg. Reg. Carpenter, i, f. 149v
Yale Center for British Art, L 201.15 Folio B, 50, detail

Websites

Border Archaeology *Conserving Coffin Grip Plates: History, Manufacture, Material and Conservation* https://www.borderarchaeology.com/conserving-coffin-grip-plates-history-manufactu/ [accessed 14 April 2021].
Dove's Guide for Church Bell-ringers https://dove.cccbr.org.uk/tower/16728 [accessed 31 January 2020].
A Vision of Britain Through Time, GB Historical GIS/University of Portsmouth, Minchinhampton SubD through time | Industry Statistics|Occupation data classified into the 24 1881 'Orders', plus sex, *A Vision of Britain through Time*. A Vision of Britain Through Time https://www.visionofbritain.org.uk/unit/10552862/cube/OCC_ORDER1881 [accessed: ninth July 2021]
Landed Families of Britain and Ireland https://landedfamilies.blogspot.com/2021/08/467-baynham-and-throckmorton-of.html, [accessed 1 February 2024]
List of Stroud MPs http://www.leighrayment.com/commons/Scommons5.htm [accessed 31 January 2020]
Minchinhampton Local History Group: Fenning Parke https://www.minchinhamptonlocalhistorygroup.org.uk/nineteenth/personalities/ [accessed 3 January 2020]
Open Domesday 2020 https://opendomesday.org/place/SO8700/minchinhampton/ [accessed 17 February 2020]

Stained Glass in Wales http://stainedglass.llgc.org.uk/person/38 [accessed 6 September 2024]

Stroud News 18th June 1909; http://www.minchinhamptonlocalhistorygroup.org.uk/a-z/landmarks-l/#Lych [accessed 31 January 2020]

The London Gazette 2nd February 1830, Issue 18652, p 257 https://www.thegazette.co.uk/London/issue/18652/page/257 [accessed 31 January 2020]

VCH: A P Baggs, A R J Jurica and W J Sheils, 'Minchinhampton: Economic history', in *A History of the County of Gloucester:* Volume **11**, Bisley and Longtree Hundreds, ed. N M Herbert and R B Pugh (London, 1976), pp. 193-200. British History Online http://www.british-history.ac.uk/vch/glos/vol11/pp193-200 [accessed 5 May 2020].

VCH: A P Baggs, A R J Jurica and W J Sheils, 'Minchinhampton: Local government', in *A History of the County of Gloucester: Volume 11, Bisley and Longtree Hundreds*, ed. N M Herbert and R B Pugh (London, 1976), pp. 200-201. British History Online http://www.british-history.ac.uk/vch/glos/vol11/pp200-205 [accessed 31 January 2020].

VCH: A P Baggs, A R J Jurica and W J Sheils, 'Minchinhampton: Education', in *A History of the County of Gloucester: Volume 11, Bisley and Longtree Hundreds*, ed. N M Herbert and R B Pugh (London, 1976), p. 205. British History Online http://www.british-history.ac.uk/vch/glos/vol11/p205 [accessed 31 January 2020].

VCH: A P Baggs, A R J Jurica and W J Sheils, 'Minchinhampton: Charities for the poor', in *A History of the County of Gloucester: Volume 11, Bisley and Longtree Hundreds*, ed. N M Herbert and R B Pugh (London, 1976), pp. 206-207. British History Online http://www.british-history.ac.uk/vch/glos/vol11/pp193-207 [accessed 31 January 2020].

VCH: A P Baggs. A R J Jurica. W J Sheils, 'Rodborough: Church', *A History of the County of Gloucester: Volume 11*, Bisley and Longtree Hundreds, (London, 1976), pp. 230-232. British History Online https://www.british-history.ac.uk/vch/glos/vol11/pp230-232 [accessed 14 June 2024].

References

Adams J, Brickley M, Buteux S, Adams T, Cherrington R, 2006 *St Martin's Uncovered: Investigations in the Churchyard of St. Martin's-in-the-Bull-Ring, Birmingham 2001*, Oxbow Books

Anon. 1858 'Minchinhampton Church, Gloucestershire' *The Builder*, 30th January, 75

Atkyns, R 1712 *The Ancient and Present State of Glostershire,* London: W. Bowyer

Baddeley, W St C, 1921 'Avening church' *Trans. Bris. & Glos. Arch. Soc* **43**, 181–90

Beeson, CFC 1971 *English Church Clocks 1280–1850, History and classification,* Phillimore

Washbourn, J 1823 *Bibliotheca Gloucestrensis: A collection of scarce and curious tracts relating to the County and City of Gloucester; illustrative of, and published during the Civil War Part the Second*, Washbourn & Son, Gloucester

Binski, P 2016 'An Early Miniature Copy of the Choir Vault of Wells Cathedral at

Irnham, Lincolnshire' in *Journal of the British Archaeological Association*, **169** (2016), 59–70

Bony, J 1979 *The English Decorated Style: Gothic Architecture Transformed, 1250–1350*, Oxford

Boore, E 1998, 'Burial vaults and Coffin furniture in the West Country' in M Cox (ed) *Grave Concerns: Death and burial in England 1700-1850*, CBA Research Report **113**

Bruce, J 1854 'Extracts from Accounts of the Churchwardens of Minchinhampton, in the County of Gloucester, with Observations thereon.' *Archaeologia*, **35**, Issue 2 1854, 409–452

Cannon, J 'Berkeley Patronage and the 14th-century choir', in Cannon, J and Williamson, B eds. 2011 *The Medieval Art, Architecture and History of Bristol Cathedral: An Enigma Explored*, Woodbridge

Cannon, J 'The Bristol Master and the Ambitions of Decorated', in John Munns ed 2017 *Decorated Revisited: English Architectural Style in Context, 1250–1400*, Turnhout, 91–112

Carpenter, RH and Ingelow, B 1889–90 'The Architectural History of Avening Church, Gloucestershire' *Trans. Bristol & Glos. Arch. Soc.* **14**, 5–13

Champion, M 2015 *Medieval Graffiti, The Lost Voices of England's Churches*, Ebury Press, London

Church Times, Friday 5 May 1876, 230

Colvin, H 1995 *A Biographical Dictionary of British Architects 1600-1840*, 3rd edition, New Haven and London: Yale University Press

Corpus Vitrearum Medii Aevi: Leicestershire **X**, 180

Cowan, P 2005 *The Rose Windows: Splendour and Symbol*, London

Cox, N 2005 'Gloucester Folk Museum and the mechanisation of the pin industry' in *Gloucestershire Society for Industrial Archaeology Journal for 2005* 4–18

Cragoe, CD 'Fabric, tombs and precinct 1087–1540', in Keene, L, Burns, D, and Saint A, 2004 *St Paul's: the Cathedral Church of London 604–2004*, New Haven, 127–42

Daniel-Tyssen, JR 1869 'Inventories of the goods and ornaments of the churches in the County of Surrey in the reign of King Edward the Sixth', *Surrey Archaeological Collections* **4**, 28

Derham, W 1696 *The Artificial Clockmaker, A Treatise of Watch, and Clock Work London*

Dowler, G 1984 *Gloucestershire Clock and Watchmakers* Phillimore & Co Ltd

Draper, P 1981 'The sequence and dating of the Decorated work at Wells', in Coldstream, N and Draper, P eds *Medieval Art and Architecture at Wells and Glastonbury, British Archaeological Association Conference Transactions*, **4**, 18–29

Dugdale, W 1658 *The history of St. Paul's Cathedral in London: from its foundation untill these times : extracted out of originall charters, records, leiger books, and other manuscripts : beautified with sundry prospects of the Church, figures of tombes and monuments* Tho. Warren, London

Eames. E 1980 *Catalogue of Medieval Lead-Glazed Tiles in the Department of Medieval and Later Antiquities in the British Museum*, British Museum Publications, London

Egan, G and Pritchard, F 2002 *Medieval finds from excavations in London. 3, Dress accessories, c.1150-c.1450* Boydell Press, Woodbridge, Suffolk

Emden, AB 1977 *Medieval Decorated Tiles in Dorset,* Phillimore & Co. Ltd

Flannel, J 2016 *Fifty English Steeples: The Finest Medieval Parish Church Towers and Spires in England. Thames and Hudson*

Forrester, H 1972 *Medieval Gothic Mouldings, Phillimore,* London

French, K 'Women in the Late Medieval English Parish', in M C Erler, and M Kowaleski (ed.), 2003 *Gendering the Master Narratative. Woman and Power in the Middle Ages,* Ithaca

Frith, B (ed) 1990 Ralph Bigland Historical, Monumental and Genealogical Collections relative to the County of Gloucester, Part Two: Daglingworth–Moreton Valence, *Glos. Record Series* **3**

Fryer, AC 1911 'Gloucestershire Fonts. Part 4' *Trans. Bristol & Glos. Arch. Soc.* **34**, 195–207

Fullbrook-Leggatt, LEWO 1964 'The Survey of Church Livings in Gloucestershire, 1650' *Trans. Bristol & Glos. Arch. Soc.* **83**, 92

Gaimster, M 2016 'Coffin furniture and small finds' in Proctor, J, Gaimster, M and Langthorne, J Y *A Quaker Burial Ground at North Shields: Excavations at Coach Lane, Tyne and Wear* PCA Monograph **20**

Gairdner, J 1904 *English Historical Review* (January 1904), **29**, 98–121

Gilchrist, R and Sloane, B 2005, *Requiem: the medieval monastic cemetery in Britain,* Museum of London Archaeology Service

Glynne, SR (ed), Phillimore, WPW and Melland Hall, J 1902 *Gloucestershire Church Notes*

Green, G W 1992 *Bristol and Gloucester Region.* British Regional Geology. London: HMSO

Griffin, E 2018 *Diets, Hunger and Living Standards during the British Industrial Revolution. Past & Present,* **239** (1)

Habington, H 1899 'A Survey of Worcester' *Worcestershire Historical Society*

Harrison, J 2016 *Bells and Bellringing,* Shire Books

Harvey, J 1954 (1984 ed) 'Thomas of Witney' and 'William Joy', *English Medieval Architects: a Biographical Dictionary down to 1550*

Harward, C 2016 'An Archaeological Evaluation Report at Holy Trinity Church, Minchinhampton, Gloucestershire', Urban Archaeology client report

Harward, C 2017a 'A Statement of Significance for Holy Trinity Church, Minchinhampton, Gloucestershire', Urban Archaeology client report

Harward, C 2017b 'A Written Scheme of Investigation for an Archaeological Watching Brief at Holy Trinity Church, Minchinhampton, Gloucestershire,' Urban Archaeology client report

Harward, C 2019 'An Archaeological Post-excavation Assessment Report: Holy Trinity Church, Minchinhampton, Gloucestershire'; Harward, C 2021, 'Holy Trinity Church, Minchinhampton, Gloucestershire, an Archaeological Watching Brief Report,' Urban Archaeology client report

Harward, C 2021 'Holy Trinity Church, Minchinhampton, Gloucestershire, an Archaeological Watching Brief Report,' Urban Archaeology client report

Heighway, C and Bryant, R 1999, 'The Golden Minster. The Anglo-Saxon minster and later medieval priory of St Oswald at Gloucester' *CBA Research Report,* **117**, York: Council for British Archaeology

Herbermann CG, Pace EA, Pallen, CB, Shahan, TJ and Wynne, JJ (eds) 1913 The Old Catholic Encyclopaedia, An International Work Of Reference On The Constitution, Doctrine, Discipline, And History Of The Catholic Church' The Encyclopaedia Press **2**

Hislop, M 2012 *Medieval Masons*. Shire Archaeology. Oxford

Historic England 2023 *Gloucestershire. Building Stones of England.* Swindon

Historic England Listing text List ID 1245083

Historic England Listing text List ID 1245665

HMSO 1840 *Reports from the Commission on hand loom weavers,* HMSO

Holford, ML and Dryburgh, P (eds) 2022 'Escheators' Inquisitions for Gloucestershire and Bristol, c.1260–1485' *Glouc. Records Series* **37**

Keen, L 2015 'Gloucester Cathedral Lady Chapel. The Medieval Tile Pavement'

Lewis, JM 1999 *Medieval Tiles of Wales: Census of Medieval Tiles in Britain*, Llyfrau Amgueddfa Cymru/ National Museum Wales Books

Litten, J 1991 *The English Way of Death: The Common Funeral Since 1450*, Robert Hale Ltd

Livings, G 2022 'Aiglets: Medieval and Post Medieval' The Society of Creative Anachronism

Lysons, D and Lysons S 1810 *Magna Britannia; being a concise topographical account of the several counties of Great Britain*, **2**, T Cadell and W Davies, London

Maclean, J 1883–4 'Chantry certificates, Gloucestershire' *Trans. Bristol & Glos. Arch. Soc.* **8**

Martin Goetze and Dominic Gwynn Ltd, 2021 'Report and quotation on the Holy Trinity organ,' dated May 28th 2021

Mills, S 1995 'The Stroud Pin Makers' in *Gloucestershire Society for Industrial Archaeology Journal for 1995,* 37–42

Morris, R K 1997 'European Prodigy or Regional Eccentric? The Rebuilding of St Augustine's Abbey Church, Bristol', in *Almost the Richest City': Bristol in the Middle Ages,* ed. L Keen, British Archaeological Association Conference Transactions, **19** (Leeds, 1997), 41–56

Pacey, A 2007 *Medieval architectural drawing,* Tempus

Minchinhampton Parish Magazine, June 1887

Pevsner, N 1952 *The Buildings of England: South Devon*, Penguin

Pevsner, N 1954 *The Buildings of England: Cambridgeshire,* Harmondsworth

Pevsner, N 1966 *The Buildings of England: Yorkshire, the North Riding,* Harmondsworth

Pevsner, N and Cherry, B 1975 *The Buildings of England: Wiltshire* Harmondsworth

Pevsner, N and Radcliffe, E 1975 *The Buildings of England: Suffolk* Harmondsworth

Playne, AT 1978 *Minchinhampton and Avening* 2nd edition Sutton

Playne, GF 1868 'On the Incised Grave-Stones and Stone Coffins of Minchinhampton Church', *Proceedings of the Cotteswold Naturalists' Field Club*, **V**, 39–46

Portbury, J 2007 'The History of the organ in Minchinhampton Parish Church' Minch. Local Hist. Group, **24**, 11–14

Price, A 2002 'Geology and building materials', in Verey, D and Brooks, A (eds) 1999 *The Buildings of England, Gloucestershire 1: The Cotswolds* London: Yale University Press

Price, FD 1937 'The Commission for Ecclesiastical Causes for the Dioceses of Bristol and Gloucester, 1574,' *Trans. Bristol & Glos. Arch. Soc.* **59**, 151–153

Puckle, BS 1926 *Funeral Customs: Their Origin and Development*, TW Laurie Ltd, London

Reeve, J and Adams, M 1993 'The Spitalfields Project Volume 1 - The Archaeology, Across The Styx' *CBA Research Report* **85**

Relton, HE 1843 *Sketches of churches with short descriptions*, London and Oxford

Rickman, T n.d.[1817] *Attempt to discriminate the styles of English architecture, from the conquest to the reformation: preceded by a sketch of the Grecian and Roman orders, with notices of nearly five hundred English buildings*. London: Longman, Hurst, Rees, Orme, and Brown, printed in Liverpool by J J Smith.

Rock, H 2008 *Church Clocks,* Shire

Rosewell, R 2008 *Medieval Wall Paintings,* Boydell Press, Woodbridge

Rudder, S 1779 *A New History of Gloucestershire*

Rudge, T 1811 *The History and Antiquities of Gloucester,* i

Sherwood, J and Pevsner, N 1974 *The Buildings of England: Oxfordshire*, Harmondsworth, 843–845

St. Clair Baddeley, W 1913 *Place-names of Gloucestershire, a handbook* John Bellows, Gloucester, 109

Tate, WE 1946 *The Parish Chest, a Study of the Records of Parochial Administration in England,* Cambridge University Press, 3rd Edition

Verey, D 1970 *Buildings of England: Gloucestershire 1: The Cotswolds, Buildings of England*

Verey, D 1980 *The Buildings of England: Gloucestershire, the Vale and the Forest of Dean*

Verey, D and Brooks, A 1999 *The Buildings of England: Gloucestershire 1: The Cotswolds*, 3rd Edition

Verey, D and Brooks, A 2002 *The Buildings of England: Gloucestershire 2: The Vale and the Forest of Dean,*

Watson, CE 1932 'The Minchinhampton Custumal and its place in the Story of the Manor' *Trans. Bristol & Glos. Arch. Soc.* **54**

Wilson, C 'Gothic Metamorphosed: the Choir of St Augustine's Abbey in Bristol and the Renewal of European Architecture in Around 1300' in Cannon, J and Williamson, B eds. 2011 *The Medieval Art, Architecture and History of Bristol Cathedral: An Enigma Explored,* Woodbridge, 69–147 and 148–185.

Yates, N 2001 *Buildings, Faith, And Worship: The Liturgical Arrangement of Anglican Churches 1600-1900*, Oxford University Press

INDEX

This index includes most personal and place names, and selective subjects. Minor places are in or near Minchinhampton; most other places are in Gloucestershire unless stated otherwise.

Abbaye-aux-Dames, Caen (France) 16, 36, 46
Abbaye de la Sainte-Trinite, Caen (France) 6
Acton Court, Bristol 47
Adams, – 93
aglet 144
Agnes, abbess of Syon 49
'Ainsloe' 25–6
aisles (principal references) 2–4, 36–41, 103–5, 109–17, 146–9
alabaster 126
Allen, Charles 128
altars 18, 20–1, 26, 34–6, 39–41, 49, 51, 55, 60, 62, 64, 68, 96, 124, 127, 133–4, 136, 183, 185–6, 192
Amberley 97, 106–7, 111, 117
Anderlays, Androse, *see* Ansleyes
Ansley (Ansloe), John and Lucy 16, 25–6, 28, 180, 181
Ansleyes (Androse) chapel 26, 36, 67–8
Ansloe, *see* Ansley
apse 9, 30
arcades 7, 8, 10–11, 15, 19–20, 32, 39, 84, 110–11, 113, 119, 147–8
Arlingham 164
arms, coats of 25–6, 75–7, 112, 163; *see also* escutcheons
Arndell, Edward 149
Arome, Philip 34
ashlar masonry 17, 37, 110; *see also* freestone
Ashwell, Peter de 34
Atkyns, Robert 25
aumbry 41, 136
Australia 92
Avening 6, 9–11, 34–6, 46, 79

Avening, Peter of 34
Avery, Thomas 75

Baldwin, Samuel 163
Banwell (Som) 103
Baptists 66, 92, 106
Barcelona Farm 117
Barnfield, Samuel 82
Barnfield, William 74
Barratt, A, & Co. 142
Bath 143
Bath and Wells, bishop 51
Bayly, Richard 75
Baynham, Alice, Anne and Joseph 162–4
Bedwyn, Great (Wilts) 30
belfry 86, 88, 99
bellfounders 88, 89
bells 36, 37, 49, 51, 65, 76–7, 86–91, 93, 99, 121, 133, 142, 153, 164, 180
Berkeley, Thomas, Lord, and family 29
Beverston 76, 89
Bigland, Ralph 22, 25, 66, 161–3, 165–6, 187
Birmingham 129, 143, 154–5, 158
Bisley 66, 164
Black Death 16, 34, 42
black letter text 59, 62–4
Blore, Edward 125
boiler 113, 121
books 53–4, 56–8, 60, 61, 64, 72, 75–6, 81, 99, 116, 121, 153–4, 158; *see also* library
Bourne, Gilbert 50–2, 61
Bradford (W Yorks) 92
Bradley, James 152, 167
brass, brasses 22, 81, 87, 89, 116, 134, 144,

& 160–2, 164, 167, 180
Brigad, W 176
Brimscombe 97, 99, 103, 106–9, 111, 117
Bristol 1, 2, 23, 27, 29–30, 32–3, 47, 66, 89, 101, 108–9, 129, 143, 157
Brooks, Alan 33
Bruce, John 26, 53–5, 180
Bryan, John 66
Bryans, Herbert W 127, 130
Bubblewell Farm 117
Buck, Jeremy 74, 81, 128
Burges, William 2, 4, 6, 22, 32, 45–6, 109–10, 123–5, 127, 129, 140–1, 183, 188–93
Burgh, Maud de 16
burials 6, 29, 41, 92–3, 104–5, 144, 146–55, 158, 161, 167–73, 181
Bute, Marquis of 125
buttons 143–4, 151
buttresses 22, 28–9, 94–5, 97, 99, 111, 124

Caen (France) 6, 9–10, 12, 16, 36, 46, 180
Cambridge 103, 109
Cambridge, Samuel 89
candlesticks 76
Canterbury 27, 30
Canynges, William 47
Cardiff Castle 125
Carpenter, – 149
Carrad, Edmund 99
Cerney, North 51
Cerney, South 52
Chalford 34, 109, 174
chalices 41, 76, 160
chancel (principal references) 8–12, 15–19, 36–41, 103–5, 109–12, 123–5, 144–6, 181–3, 189
Chandler, R 117
chantries 16, 22, 26, 29–30, 33–4, 36, 40, 41, 47–52, 87–8, 160, 168, 181
Chartres (France) 31
Cheltenham 32
Cherington 97
chest 57–60, 171
Chester, St Werburgh's (Cathedral) 28
chevron decoration 7, 8, 11
Chichester Cathedral 64
church-house 54
churchwardens 53–4, 57, 59, 61, 71, 80, 82, 84, 89–90, 98–9, 104, 119–21, 139

churchwardens' accounts 4, 26, 52–3, 56, 64, 74, 80–1, 84, 87–8, 128, 149, 152–3, 179–82
churchyard 2, 6, 36, 59, 68, 74, 93–4, 110, 122, 132, 134, 141, 143–7, 149–53, 155–8, 162, 165–9, 170, 181
Cirencester 71–3
clepsydra 69
clerestory 2, 8, 39, 46, 74, 94, 111–12
clocks 69–70, 76, 87, 101, 121
cloth hangings 64
cloth industry 14, 92, 161
cloths, altar and pulpit, etc 41, 72, 75, 76, 168
Clutterbuck, Daniel, and family 82, 99, 164
coats of arms 25–6, 75–7, 112, 163; *see also* escutcheons
Cockin, William 85, 96–7, 99, 101, 103, 182
coffins 21, 22, 144, 146, 149, 151–60, 168
Coldruppe, William 62
Colsburne, – 69
Comley, – 132
Common Prayer, Book of 57–8, 60–1, 64, 72, 75, 76, 99, 121
communion 41, 50–1, 54, 57, 61, 64, 72, 75, 87, 121
communion table 51, 64, 75, 76, 124
Conway, EP 133, 178
Cooper, Tuesby and 154, 157–8
Cornwall, John 138
Cosbourne, Roger 68–69
Coulson, John 129
Crackstone Farm 117
Crauden, Prior 33
Croft, John 34
Cromwell, Oliver 75, 145
Cromwell, Thomas 49
crossing 3, 15, 23, 37–9, 80, 117, 124–6, 136, 140, 146, 182
cross-slabs 19, 23, 105, 144, 145, 158–61, 180
crypts 157, 167

Dalton, Edward 101, 181
David's, St, cathedral 32, 47
Dean, Forest of 175
Deane, Elizabeth 162
Deane, John a 66,
Deane, Richard 72
Decorated period 14–45, 96, 109, 111, 181,

185
De La Mare (Delamere) family 25–7, 185
Derby 70
desks, clerk's and reading 68, 71–2, 74, 76, 80, 117, 121
diseases 169–73
Domesday Book 4, 6
doors, doorways 8, 10–1, 19, 28, 38–9, 41, 57, 65, 68, 74–5, 81–2, 84, 94–5, 99, 101, 103, 109, 111–12, 121, 124, 126, 146, 151, 153, 174
Dorbye, Nicholas 73
dossill 192
Dunkirk Manor 101
Dursley 60

eagle 25–7
East Smithfield (London) 84
Eden, FC 2, 123, 134, 136–7, 141, 183
Edwards, John 50
effigies 24–27, 160, 162–3, 180
Eisame, – 152–3
Ely Cathedral 33
encaustic tiles 26, 124, 136
Erasmus, Paraphrases of 59–60
escutcheons 154–6; *see also* coats of arms
Eton College (Bucks) 103
Eton, Violet Hylda 136
Exeter Cathedral 27, 30

faculties 3, 80, 102–3, 136, 140
fairs 14, 52
Falconer, Peter 136–8
Falconer, Toby 138
Feilder, Edward 69–70
Feltham-King, Antony 2, 138
Filder *see* Fielder
Fletcher, Joan 81, 181
floors 2, 3, 9, 21, 26–7, 40, 48, 67, 82–3, 111–13, 115–21, 125–6, 140–1, 143, 146–7, 149–50, 158–9, 162; *see also* pavements
Flowar, John 69
font 11, 16, 20, 55, 59, 68, 75, 81, 115, 117, 124, 134
Forest of Dean 175
Forwood 34
Foster, Thomas 2, 4–5, 101–3, 108–10, 115, 117, 119–20, 123–4, 139, 182
Foster, William 58

Fowler, Henry 74, 81, 128
Fowler, John 82
Framlingham (Suffolk) 38
Francis, St 111–12
Franklin, – 101
Freame, Anne and Robert 163–4
Freeman, Thomas 61
freestone 17, 162, 174; *see also* ashlar masonry

Galicia (Spain) 121
galleries 72, 76–7, 80, 82–5, 92–8, 111, 115–19, 125–8, 174, 182, 183
Gatcombe Park and House 79, 105, 116, 120, 170
Gee, Mrs 116
Gibson, John 84
Gilman, Daniel 81
Glanville's Wootton (Dorset) 47
glass, glazing 30–2, 39–41, 47–8, 51, 67–9, 73, 121, 124–5, 127, 129–30, 138, 141, 143, 193; *see also* windows; tracery
Goda, Countess 6
Godwin, William 124–5
Goetze, Martin 129
Gravener, Richard 51
graves, gravestones 59, 93, 104, 112–13, 144, 146–53, 167–8, 187
graveyard 1, 6, 16, 66, 68, 96, 135, 146, 150–1, 154, 167
Great Bedwyn (Wilts) 30
Guiting, Temple 9
Gwynn, Dominic 129

Halesowen Abbey (Worcs) 47
Hampton (Hamton), Alys, John and fasmily 22, 36, 86–8, 161, 163–4, 180
Hancockes, – 149
Hanham 109
Hardenhuish (Wilts) 106
Hardman, John, and company 124–5, 127, 129–30
Harman, William 132
Harris, Jonathan 76
hatpegs 84
hats 85
heating 2, 3, 85, 113, 119, 121, 131, 139–41, 147
Helder, Richard 74
Heytesbury House (Wilts) 47

INDEX

Hickman, Thomas 79
Hill, George 72
Hill, Norman and Beard 129
Hiron, Samuel 75
Hodson, Rex and Mollie, 149–50
Hodson, Thomas 136
Hollar, Wenceslaus 31
Hooper, Bishop 50, 52
Horsley 89
hourglass 69, 71, 75, 80, 85
Hugyens, Christian 70
Humphries, Dan 129
Hurstpierpoint (Sussex) 85
Hyde Court (House) 53, 121
Hyde, Laurence 51

income 14, 34, 51, 53–4, 75, 170
Ingelow, Carpenter and 10
Ingeram, John 65
Irnham (Lincs) 33

Jenkins, Samuel 181
Johnson, Robert 134
Jones, Charles 117
Joy, William 27, 29

Keen, Laurence 39
Keene, Antony 81
Keene, Samuel 53
Kempe, CE and company 130, 132, 134–5
keys 65, 68, 75, 146
Kibble, J 116
King's Stanley 84
Kip, Johannes 66, 70, 78–9, 93, 95

Lady Chapel 2– 3, 16, 21, 22, 26–30, 33–4, 36, 46, 51, 131, 133–4, 141, 150, 177, 180–1, 183
Lamers, The Lammas 26, 97
Laon (France) 31
Lapthorne, Anthony 74
Laurance, chaplain 13
leadwork 17, 40, 46, 64–6, 68, 73–6, 95, 99
lectern 124
ledgers 113, 144, 149, 162
Leo, Pope 49
library 72, 179; *see also* books
Lincoln Cathedral 32
Loe, St 26
London 31, 84, 109, 157–8

Longfords House 87, 124
Lord, Nicholson and, Messrs 129
lychgate 105, 132–3
Lypiatt (Lypeat), Nether 163–4

Mallard, Marget 152
Malmesbury (Wilts) 65
Malvern (Worcs) 47
Manning, Francis and John 81
Marcle, Much (Herefs) 13
Mare, De La 25–7
market, market house 1, 14, 42, 52, 81, 84, 87, 92, 121, 132, 176, 181
Masasi, Diocese (Tanzania) 138
masons 16, 27, 32–3, 37, 39, 42–5, 66, 68, 73, 99, 163, 181
mass dial 69
masses 12, 21, 29–30, 33–4, 36, 41, 49, 60, 146, 158
Mauleon, Stephen 42
Mayo, John 61
Mears, T 90
Melcombe Regis (Dorset) 42
memorials 16, 22, 26, 34, 41, 64, 73–4, 87, 93–7, 103, 111, 115, 124, 126, 132, 134–36, 144, 146–7, 149–50, 152, 158, 161–7, 180–2
merchants 15, 16, 47, 84, 87, 92, 144, 161
Middleton, John de 34
Mildenhall (Suffolk) 33
Miles, Nick 3
Millward, William 149
Minety (Wilts, formerly Glos) 143
monuments 20, 25, 64, 73, 84, 94, 106, 158, 162–5, 168
Mortimer, Lady Margaret, and family 29
mouldings 8, 13, 39, 46, 73, 113, 175
Much Marcle (Herefs) 13

Nailsworth 101, 174
nave (principal references) 2–4, 7–10, 18–20, 38–41, 80–2, 103–5, 109–17, 189
Newman, John 65, 88
New Zealand 92
niches 20–1, 24–5, 36, 41, 61, 111, 160, 186
Nicholls, William and sister 181
Nicholson and Lord, Messrs 129
Norman period 1, 6–10, 12, 15–17, 19–20, 37, 46, 84, 86, 96, 105, 158, 177, 181, 185, 188

239

Nickolls, William 82
North Cerney 51
Northamptonshire 23

Ockepool, – 66
Ogden, Elizabeth 84
Okely, William Ignatius 109
Oldfield, EC 123–4, 126
Old St Paul's Cathedral (London) 31, 109
Olveston 109
organs 55, 82, 97–8, 115, 117, 121, 126, 128–9, 141, 162
Ottery St Mary 27
Oxford Movement 109, 123, 182

Painswick 17, 42–3, 55, 65–6, 71, 110, 174–5
paintwork 9, 10, 37–41, 49, 62–4, 69, 70, 72, 74–5, 77, 121, 130, 134, 136–7
Parke, Fenning 22, 53, 82–4, 89–90, 95, 104–5, 128, 166, 179–80, 182, 184
Parker, James 90
Paschal candle 55
Passelowe, Wyllam 88
Paul's, Old St, Cathedral (London) 31, 109
pavements 26–7, 39, 47–8, 68, 124, 143, 149; *see also* floors
Payne, Edward 130, 149
Perks, Nathaniel 90
Perpendicular style 17, 30, 46–7, 108, 110, 124, 182
Perrie, William 149
pest control 59
pews 2, 7, 9, 41–2, 64, 72, 80–2, 84–5, 96, 99, 101, 113–17, 119–20, 126, 136, 139, 141–3, 147, 164, 173, 181–2, 194–211; *see also* seats, seating
Pimbury, Cosburn 166
pins 55, 143, 151, 153
pipes, organ 128–9
pipes, tobacco 142–3
piscina 41
plaster, plastering 8, 21, 38, 40, 46, 49, 60, 62–4, 66, 68, 76, 110, 115, 121, 165
Playne, AT 8, 25–6, 46, 86, 96, 97, 105
Playne, Edward 132
Playne, GF 21, 35, 84, 130, 145, 161
Playne, George 90
Playne, William and Mary 124
Playne family 120

plumbers 65, 68, 73, 75, 99
Pokmore, – 56
population 6, 42, 51, 80, 92, 97, 146, 168, 170, 172–3
porch 2, 15, 23, 39, 41, 62, 65, 68–9, 74, 81, 93–5, 99, 137–8, 152
Portbury, Jim 128
Powell, John Hardman 124, 129
Powell, Thomas 49
Prayer, Book of Common 57–8, 60–1, 64, 72, 75–6, 99, 121
Prestbury, William of 16, 21–2, 33–4, 36, 42, 180
Pugin, AWN 125, 129
pulpit 50, 68, 71–2, 74, 76, 80, 84, 94, 96, 115, 117, 121, 123–4, 126, 138, 182
Purdey, Roger 89

Quakers 92, 105, 155
quarries 17, 40, 105, 174–5

Randwick 109
Ralph, G 90
rectors 212–13
Redcliffe, St Mary (Bristol) 33, 66
Reformation 21, 49–50, 52–4, 63, 86–7, 97, 168, 177, 179, 182
Relton, HE 14, 20, 23, 28, 31, 46, 70, 84, 95, 99, 162–3
reredos 41
Ricardo, David, senior 79, 84, 105–7
Ricardo, David, junior 92, 97, 99, 101, 103, 105–9, 112, 116–17, 123, 139, 152, 182
Ricardo, Henry David 123
Rimar (Rimer), William 73
Rodborough 16, 54, 75, 106, 109, 111, 161
Rodborough aisle 6, 15, 80
rood loft and screen 2, 38, 40, 49, 51, 55, 57, 61, 134, 136–7, 140–1, 182–3
roofs 8, 15, 17, 19, 22–3, 29, 32, 45–6, 64–6, 68, 73–6, 96, 104, 110, 112–13, 122, 124, 141, 170, 175, 190–1; *see also* vaults
Rowden, John 90
Rowe, George 95
Rudge, John 152
Rudhall, Abraham, Abel and John 89–90
Russell, John, Lord 98

St David's cathedral 32, 47
St Francis 111–12

INDEX

St Loe 26
St Mary Redcliffe (Bristol) 33, 66
St Paul's, Old, Cathedral (London) 31, 109
Sainte–Trinité, Caen 6
Salange, Roger 13
Saxon period 6, 144
Scarborough (N Yorks) 23, 32
Schire, Walter 33–4
schools and schoolmasters 52–3, 82, 84, 97, 104, 106, 117, 125, 179–80
Scuse, Jacon 90
seats, seating 9, 50, 68, 72, 75–6, 80–84, 92, 101, 111, 115, 117, 119–21, 128, 139, 181; *see also* pews
Sebrok (Sebroke), Abbot 38–9
Sewelle, Rychard 149
sheep 14, 42, 54, 92
Sheppard, Edward 105
Sheppard (Shephard), Philip, Samuel and family 79, 105, 170
Shepstone, William 4, 6–10, 12, 15, 19–20, 22, 66–7, 101, 105, 108–9, 123, 145–6, 151, 180, 184–7
shrouds 143, 151–4
Simmons, Alfred 70
Simpkins, George 117
Sion, *see* Syon
Slye, Thomas 65–6
Smith, A 95
Smith, Campbell 136
Smith, Daniel 105
Smith, John and Sons 70
Smith, Thomas 75
Smith, WH 120
Smithfield, East (London) 84
South Cerney 52
Southwell Minster (Notts) 32
Spennel, – 55
Spenner (Spynner), Edward 57–8
Spileman, Adam 33
spire 15–17, 37, 64–7, 186–7
Spitalfields (London) 157–8
Spreadbury, H Vernon 130
Spynner *see* Spenner
stairs 38, 77, 82, 84–5, 93, 95–7, 99, 111, 121, 126
Stanford-on-Avon (Leics) 32
Stanley, King's 84
Stonehouse 71, 145
Strasbourg Cathedral 31

Stroud 1, 71, 73, 95, 106, 108–9, 121, 132–3, 143, 163–4, 176, 180
Suffolk, Earl of 46
sundial 69, 95
Swaine, Goody 152
Syon Abbey (Middlesex) 46, 49, 87

Tanzania 137–8
Taylor, John 90
Taylor, Thomas 51, 52, 89
Temple Guiting 9
Tetbury 69–71
Tetbury Street (Minchinhampton) 84, 92, 106, 172
Tewkesbury Abbey 30
Thistlethwayte, HJ 53
Thomas of Witney 27
Thynne, John 51
tiles, encaustic 26, 124, 136, 192–3
Todenham 17
tombs 8, 13, 15, 18–19, 21, 24–5, 28–30, 36, 39, 41, 64, 93, 96, 104, 146–9, 160, 165–7
tower 2, 4, 8, 10, 15–16, 18–19, 29, 37, 38, 46, 51, 65–7, 69, 73–4, 82, 86, 88–9, 99, 101, 103–4, 110, 174, 178–9, 182, 185–7
Townsend, A 90
tracery 15–18, 23, 30–2, 37, 39–40, 42–5, 103, 109–10, 113, 124; *see also* glass; windows
transept, north 12–13, 15–16, 20–2, 33, 36, 38, 61, 68, 82, 84, 104, 112, 115, 117, 128, 146, 160–2, 164, 181, 185–6, 189
transept, south 3, 13, 15–16, 19–20, 22–33, 35–40, 45, 67, 74, 82, 84, 86, 93, 95–6, 99, 101–2, 111–12, 115, 120, 124–9, 131, 133–4, 145, 149, 160–1, 178, 181, 183, 185–6, 189
Trevis, Edward 75
Tuesby and Cooper 154, 157–8
Turner, – 117
typhus 105, 153, 170

Ulster, Maud, Countess of 16
Unnan, Edward 88
Urchfont (Wilts) 29

vaults 23, 29, 32–3, 37, 66, 147–8, 160, 162; *see also* roofs

Verey, David 22, 33
Vgnolles, – 80

Wales 47
Walsall 129
Wantner, Abel 161
Warmestree, Thomas 75
Watson, CE 26
weathercock, vane 65–7, 73, 75
Webb, Geoffrey 127, 133–4
Webb, William and Nathaniel 68, 162
Wells Cathedral 27, 29–30, 33
Westbury on Severn 163–4
West Indies 75
Weymouth 42, 103
Whateley, Charles 99, 101, 103, 105, 107–8, 123, 139
Whitehead, William 79
Whiteshill 109
Whitfield, George 93
Whitminster 109
Wilby (Norfolk) 71

Wilkinson, Priscilla Anne 105
Willingham (Cambs) 32–3
Wilson, Christopher 32
Wiltshire Almshouses 106
Wimbolt, John 130
Winchester Cathedral 30
windows (principal references) 18–23, 28–33, 44–6, 67–9, 110–13, 123–5, 190; *see also* glass; tracery
Windsor, Andrew, baron of 49, 61
Windsor, Edward 52, 66, 68
Windsor, Thomas, Lord's 79, 89
Witney (Oxon) 30
Witney, Thomas of 27
Woodruff, Robert 75
Woollcombe-Boyce, Harold Courtenay 134
Woollcombe-Boyce, Sarah Louisa 136
wool trade 14–17, 42, 79, 87, 92, 151, 153, 173
Worcester, Bishop of 18
Wright, James 174

York Minster 28

www.ingramcontent.com/pod-product-compliance
Ingram Content Group UK Ltd.
Pitfield, Milton Keynes, MK11 3LW, UK
UKHW051956130425
457314UK00003B/8